THE LIFE OF SIR JOHN MOORE

by the same author

Decline to Glory

A Reassessment of the Life and Times of Lady Hester Stanhope

University of Salzburg, 1997

The Life of Sir John Moore

Not a Drum was Heard

by

ROGER WILLIAM DAY

LEO COOPER

First published in Great Britain in 2001 by
LEO COOPER
an imprint of Pen & Sword Books
47 Church Street, Barnsley, South Yorkshire, S70 2AS

Copyright © 2001 by Roger William Day

ISBN 0 85052 801 1

Typeset in 13/14.75PT Sabon
by Phoenix Typesetting, Ilkley, West Yorkshire

Printed in England by
CPI UK

DEDICATION

To the memory of Stanley Balaam, fighter-pilot, artist, philosopher and Bible scholar; a latter-day example of the 'complete man' of the renaissance.

"The man to his just purpose true
No howling mob's foul-tempered scream and cry,
No tyrant's frown, brow-beating, eye to eye,
Shall move, what his strong mind holds wrong to do"

"The man who lives by right and makes no ill
Is armed of Olympus; no heathen dart he needs
To brandish, neither bursting quiver fill
With venomed reeds."

Quintus Horatius Flaccus

Contents

Acknowledgments

I am grateful for the assistance of: Mr Stanley Balaam; The British Library Department of Prints and Drawings; The Association of The Friends of Sir John Moore, Corunna; Mr B. Kaye, 'K' Rare Books and Prints; The House of Commons Information Service; The House of Lords Information Service; The Military Museum Library, Corunna; The Military Museum Library, Minorca; The Public Record Office; The Royal Green Jackets Association, Corunna; The St Lucia National Archives and Ms Victoria Huxley, Windrush Press.

Foreword

When I was writing the reassessment of the life of Lady Hester Stanhope, I came across frequent mention of the name of General Sir John Moore, the man she claimed to have loved for all of her extraordinary life. The fact that she chose the box with his blood-stained gauntlet from the battle before Corunna instead of a casket containing her jewellery when taking to a lifeboat in a shipwreck proved this love to me and I became curious to know more of this man who could have won the heart of a woman of such formidable intellectual power and overwhelming personality, the niece and hostess of Pitt the Younger.

I found that all references to him in encyclopedias were concerned only with the last three months of his life, covering his expedition into Spain from Portugal, and in particular his retreat to Corunna, where he turned and fought the pursuing French. Moreover, even the most educated of my friends, when asked what they knew of Sir John, merely mumbled, "Ah, yes! the retreat to Corunna: 'Not a drum was heard, dee-dem, dee-dum!'" My book search agency supplied me with, first, some popular histories from the 1970s' 'nostalgia for lost Empire' period, which, as with works concerning Lady Hester, did not do justice to the subject, for they left out most of the qualifying backdrop of the historical context in which events evolved. These works were written without source references in the text, always a cause for suspicion. I then obtained the nineteenth century works upon which these dramatized versions had been based, General Moore's journal and collected letters, together with an 1834 biography written by his brother James, Napier's *Peninsular War* of 1828

xi

and so on. The sins of omission, and condemnation by faint praise, in the modern works were revealed. This prompted me to collect more detailed archive material, from St Lucia to Minorca, and to begin a reassessment of the complete life and times of Sir John, in the same manner as the by then published *Decline to Glory* concerning Lady Hester Stanhope.

The work was written from the onset only with a view to discovering the objective truth about Sir John's life. It is thus an attempt to rekindle the memory of this man of unassailable integrity and courage, and as a reminder that, in a world of corrupt and intriguing politicians, a man could, and still can, rise from humble beginnings to the top of his profession without compromising either his integrity or his humanity.

Roger William Day.

CHAPTER ONE

Moore's Formation

John Moore was born in the Trongate district in the centre of old Glasgow on 17 November 1761, in the first year of the reign of King George the Third. The country was still in a state of patriotic fervour brought about by the continuous victories of its military forces over those of the autocratic regime of Louis XV. The triumphs of Rossbach, Minden, Plassey and Montreal had broken the ambitions of the French tyrant both as Europe's leading land power and as a colonial sea power, while Britain had gained two whole subcontinents upon which to build a world-wide trading empire. Democracy had been seen to have triumphed over the claim of the divine rule of kings.

The reality of this democracy was, however, that the patriotic masses who had filled the streets to cheer Kings George II and III, together with their First Minister William Pitt, had no part to play in the selection of government, which was in reality an extended oligarchy, whose privileged members alone could vote and hold office.

The parliament of the day had three main groupings, which at that time were not political parties as we know them today, but loose associations of men of similar political views. They were known as 'Whigs',[1] 'Tories'[2] and 'Independents', but did not in any way subscribe to an electorial system of universal suffrage. Rather, the Whigs believed in the right of the aristocracy to rule the country, with the King reduced to as much of a mere figure-head as they could make him, while the Tories adhered to the right of the King to govern through the parliament, retaining the right of veto through the Royal Prerogative. The so-called Independent members were usually the nominees of some large landowner who 'owned' the seat by virtue of owning all the property on which the voters lived in such 'pocket boroughs'. They would, therefore, mostly vote according to local and not national interests as their masters dictated.

Moore was born into the genteel or middling class, the son of a Reverend-cum-physician who was married to the daughter of a renowned mathematics professor at the city's university. Virtually the only way in which such a boy might hope to rise socially beyond the position in life of his parents was to find favour with the nobility and hope to serve them well enough to be rewarded by their assisting him in his chosen career. Here lay the true power of the aristocracy, for only by this mutually understood system of patronage might the doors be opened to the higher levels of the professions, which were normally reserved for their own class's non-inheriting sons.

John attended the High School of his native Glasgow and grew into a good-looking youth, tall and graceful with regular pleasant features, brown hair and hazel eyes.[3] His parents had, however, found it necessary to apply constant attention to make him control his high-spirited nature, teaching him to gain mastery over himself. Such exercises obviously succeeded, for he later became known as a well-disciplined youth with a gentle and generous nature, combined with a high sense of duty.

Meanwhile his father, the Reverend Dr Charles Moore, had gained the patronage of no less a figure than the Duke of Argyll's heir, Colonel Campbell of Mamore, whilst serving with him as a military surgeon on the field of Maastricht. He also held some fame locally as a writer on morality and was considered to be a man of a high cultural level. He had also served as physician to the Dowager Duchess of Hamilton's children and now seemed to her the obvious choice for the post of tutor to her sixteen-year-old son Douglas, 8th Duke of Hamilton and premier Duke of

Scotland, whilst he finished his education by taking a grand tour of Europe. The Duchess's concern was both for her son's health and his virtue, for his late father had been known as a heavy drinker and womanizer. Moreover, consumption was rife in her family and had recently claimed the life of Douglas's elder brother George, the 7th Duke, whilst he himself was frail, slightly built and over-tall for his age, which had further sapped his strength.

The Dowager Duchess then married Colonel Campbell, becoming the Duchess of Argyll, as he had succeeded to his father's title. Dr Moore's position was now greatly enhanced for he was held in high regard by the two most powerful families in Scotland. The post was formally offered to him and he gratefully accepted, with the then enormous allowance of five hundred pounds a year in expenses, plus an annuity of a further one hundred pounds. In addition, the well-mannered and intelligent son of Dr Moore was invited to accompany the Duke as a companion who could not possibly encourage him to go astray.[4]

The first city to be visited was Paris. Soon after their arrival two incidents occurred which would cause John to seek further to suppress his inclination for spontaneous and irresponsible actions whose consequences had not been thought out.

The first came about by his having been left alone in a room in which had been left a travelling box containing a brace of heavy-gauge pistols. He could not resist the urge to open it and experience the sensation of handling an instrument capable of snuffing out a man's life. Holding the weapon at arm's length, he aligned the sights and let his finger caress the trigger. Never imagining that the pistol would have been left primed and loaded after the journey, he squeezed just a little, intending to say "bang!". There was no need, however, for at that moment he was thrown backwards across the room as it filled with the acrid grey mist of burnt powder and plaster dust. From a fist-sized hole in the lath-and-plaster dividing wall came a woman's screams, while the near deafened John dropped the weapon in horror.

Fortunately, his father was in a nearby room and rushed to the woman's aid. By sheer luck the .50 calibre round had merely grazed the arm of a servant girl who was making up a bed. Dr Moore soon had the girl's arm salved and bandaged, while a few guineas made her feel more than compensated for her near brush with death.[5]

Soon after it was John's turn to experience the deadly reality of playing with another weapon, but this time the lesson was to be received in his own flesh. The Duke was five years older than John, but at sixteen was not yet too old to be beyond enjoying rough horseplay to enlighten a dull afternoon. It was the fashion of the time for even young boys to wear swords and to be instructed in their use for protection against street robbery. Naturally, the fencing classes were with blunt foils, further protected by felt tips. The Duke, being bored, suddenly drew his weapon and, calling "en garde" at John, he began to fence with his small companion, who not only had the disadvantage of a far shorter reach, but also held a smaller sword, scaled down to match his height. The trusts and parries became harder and faster, and the laughter changed to grim determination as the Duke found what he had assumed to be a lap dog attacking him with the grim determination of a terrier. Finally the inevitable occurred and John was unable to sidestep one of the Duke's long thrusts, which ran through the side of his waistcoat, causing blood to flow copiously.

Moore's only reaction was to exclaim "Ha!" and to look the Duke fixedly in the eyes. Douglas turned pale with fright at what he had done and, dropping his sword, ran calling for the Doctor's assistance. It was found that the wound was a long gash down the rib cage, for, as the Duke was so much taller, he had thrust downwards and the blade had run over the inclined rib bones rather than entering between them, with possibly fatal consequences.

The gash was soon sown up and bound by Dr Moore and the end result of the painful incident was favourable to John, for, after making his apology, the remorseful Duke felt able to drop the remaining stiffness in which his rank trapped him. In this way he opened up his true self to John as if to a brother, and so began a warm friendship that would last for the rest of Moore's life.[6] Regardless of this new relationship, John always travelled in the second coach with the stiffly correct Mr Andrew Templeton, the Duke's valet.

After these near escapes experimenting with weaponry the physical courage of young John was unexpectedly put to the test by a group of French youths while he was walking in the Tuileries palace gardens with his father. Dr Moore was engrossed in the study of a group of statues, John became bored and wandered away along the path, where he encountered a group of young Parisian nobles. At that time the children of the French nobility were dressed as miniature versions of their parents. Silk and lace adorned their brocaded jackets and waistcoats, whilst above rouged faces their powdered hair was piled high in frizzled curls forming two cones, with bangs hanging down to the rear.

The plain broadcloth of John's suit, with its military-style cuffs and lapels, caused titters of derisive laughter among the group of exquisites, followed by disdainful remarks, which, while not understood as yet by John, were clear enough in their meaning by the tone of voice. John's reaction was to advance straight towards this group of painted fops and knock them to the ground one by one with his fists. The education of these Parisian boys had not included such crude means of self-defence as boxing, while John had received lessons from the Glaswegian pugilists; thus, by the time that his father was aware of the commotion, the whole group of dainty French youths lay in a heap like so many logs.

The doctor picked them up and applied salve to cut lips and eyebrows and wiped the worst of the blood from their silk lapels. Unfortunately, he only succeeded in making more of a mess of their make-up and they reeled away cursing, before they too became the subject of ridicule. John was severely reprimanded by his father and led straight back to spend the rest of the day in his room at the hotel. No doubt, however, the father was secretly pleased to see his son defend his honour against such odds and with such devastating results.[7]

The Duke's party stayed in Paris for only a short time, as the moralistic Dr Moore saw nothing but a hotbed of vice and depravity among members of the society in which his young charge's rank obliged him to move. Once the Duke began to show an interest in some of the courtesans who offered their favours to Europe's most eligible bachelor, Dr Moore organized the move to the other extreme of austere, Calvinistic Geneva. An offer of accommodation from a fellow clergyman was accepted by the Duke and his tutor, while John was placed in a boarding school to catch up with his formal education.

Even before the age of twelve, John had expressed an interest in an army career and both parents viewed this as an ideal outlet for his fiery disposition. His education was, therefore, already inclined towards the subjects most useful to an army officer. The majority of his time was spent studying geometry, mathematics and engineering; as secondary subjects he worked at Latin, geography and history. Meanwhile his father guided him in an appreciation of poetry and the works of the current prose writers of the highest level.

In a letter to his wife of September 1774 Dr Moore also mentions that their son, now nearly thirteen, "draws well and now writes and speaks excellent French".[8] His life was not all serious study, however, for his father goes on to praise his abilities as a dancer, fencer and superb horseman. He had also impressed his father by drawing up a plan for a hypothetical attack upon Geneva, with all the weak points in the defences pinpointed, together with proposed troop dispositions and artillery emplacements shown and their positioning explained.

When autumn came the party began their planned visits to the German states, hoping to arrive before the winter snows made the Alpine roads impassable.

It is from this point that it is possible to say that Moore's military training began. In a letter to his brother James, dated Hanover, 2 May, 1775, he mentions that "At Brunswick the Duke got a Sergeant who came every day and taught us the Prussian (musketry) exercise. We are both pretty alert, and could charge and fire five times in a minute. We fired thirty times each, the last day of the exercise."[9]

Towards the end of May they arrived at the Prussian capital of Berlin and were personally greeted by Frederick II, now generally referred to as Frederick the Great. The Prussian army was personally organized by that great tactician and was considered to be the best in Europe. The Duke's party were soon invited to observe a three-day period of manoeuvres on a grand scale, involving 40,000 infantry, cavalry and artillery, pitched against each other in mock battle.

If this were not stimulus enough to young John's military enthusiasm, he was also introduced to George Keith, the old Earl Marischal of Scotland, who had finally accepted the impossibility of the Stewart cause succeeding and taken service with the Prussian King. He had initially been introduced formally to pay his respects to the premier Duke of Scotland, but, upon finding in John Moore an already well-studied apprentice in the theory of the career to which he had dedicated his life, the old veteran spent many hours instructing John in the reality of warfare that was not to be found in books. Indeed, so much did the old warrior come to like the enthusiastic youngster that when they parted he presented him with a fine pair of Prussian pistols and a pocket-sized edition of Horace. Moore would carry these with him for the rest of his life and after his death they became treasured heirlooms of the family.

The Duke's party reluctantly left Berlin and travelled on to Vienna, where his rank gave him an immediate audience with the Emperor, Joseph II. While the protocol for the meeting was being arranged, John accompanied his father on a visit to the Emperor's first Minister, Prince Kaunitz, who was so taken with his charm and intelligence that he took the unprecedented step of insisting that the young commoner be included in the audience. This was the more extraordinary as not even the young sons of high nobility were tolerated in the court. When presented, the Emperor was not disappointed by his Minister's insistence and, after questioning John on military matters like a jovial uncle, he was so impressed that he offered him an immediate commission in the Austro-Hungarian army, with the promise of accelerated promotion under his own Imperial patronage. The young Moore did not hesitate in politely declining, for his patriotism for his native land was intense, and the enemy that he would fight was already clearly defined in his mind, as he stated in a letter to his brother Graham, who was about to enter the navy.

21 October 1775, Vienna: "I hope that in some years after this you and I will thrash the 'monsieurs' both by land and by sea; but I hope we won't make war on the Spaniards, for the Spanish Ambassador is the best and kindest man I ever saw."[10]

This letter, which was written at the age of fourteen, when his desire for an army career had finally been established as his life's objective, could be seen almost as a precognition of the form that fate would dictate his path to take.

From Vienna they returned in leisurely fashion to Geneva. During his time in the Germanic states John had studied the language intensively as an aid to his military career, for, with the arrival of the Hanoverian Kings, British and German regiments frequently fought side by side.

Upon their return to Geneva Dr Moore wrote to his wife that "Jack quitted Geneva a boy and returned a man", adding that "even though he had been caressed by the high and mighty his manner is manly and noble, yet it is simple and he assumes no airs; he is a charming youth."[11]

To complete the grand tour, Italy had been kept until last and would only be visited briefly, for the Reverend Moore was concerned lest the Duchess's fear of its reputation for a universally dissipated lifestyle should prove true, to the detriment of his charge's morals. Venice, Rome and Naples were all visited between July and August of 1775, the longest stay being at Rome, where the Duke remained for a period sufficient for a group portrait of himself and the Moores to be executed by Gavin Hamilton, a Scottish artist resident in the city. In the background are the ruins of Rome's splendour, which had so moved Dr Moore; of more interest is the clear way in which the poses demonstrate the social relationship between the three travellers.[12]

At Naples John's dangerous lack of a sense of fear for his personal safety gave him an early baptism by fire when he climbed Mount Vesuvius while it was in a state of minor eruption. Just as he had peered into the crater and was about to begin the descent a deep rumble warned him to throw himself into a glissade down the ash slope, followed by a rain of burning rocks and stones. He was partially enveloped in this fiery avalanche and suffered minor burns to many parts of his body, but was out of bed within a week, looking as if he was the survivor of a siege, as Dr Moore put it.

In mid-August the three travellers split up, with the Duke and John returning to London, while Dr Moore went on to Paris to observe the social upheavals there at first hand for a book that he planned. Before leaving Naples John had received the most marvellous news possible for a boy with his ambitions. A letter arrived stating that, as a favour to his friend and patron Douglas, his stepfather the Duke of Argyll had obtained for him an ensigncy in the 51st Regiment, currently assigned to garrison duty in the fortifications of the port of Mahon, Minorca.

John, however, had first to reach his fifteenth birthday in November, for being in his sixteenth year was the minimum age for a commission. He was accepted, but placed on leave of absence while returning home to make his farewells to his family. He travelled overland with the Duke and crossed the Channel to spend some time lodging with him at the home of Lady Derby. From there he wrote to his father in Paris on 16 September 1776, stating "that Lady has been doing all she could to turn him [the Duke] into a fop, but that do as they choose they will never make him like coxcomb dress, for no one is more sensible of the ridiculousness of this than himself."[13]

The rest of his leave was spent with his mother and the family at their Glasgow home, until in the early weeks of 1777 he travelled via Marseilles to join the 51st under the command of Colonel Pringle. The overall command of military forces on the island was in the firm hands of General Murray, who had led the left wing of Wolfe's army on the Plains of Abraham and had later been Governor of Quebec.

CHAPTER TWO

First Battle

General Murray had the reputation of being a strict disciplinarian with a fierce temper, who would permit no drinking or gambling in the harbour forts under his command. Ensign Moore was, however, so precise in the attention which he gave to all of his duties that he soon won the approval of even this demanding taskmaster.

Socially, he had no trouble being accepted by his peers among the junior officers, as may be seen from a letter written to his mother several months after his arrival: "I am very intimate with two or three officers and I am upon a bad footing with none of them".[1]

Once the excitement of his new life had become mere routine, Moore began to hanker for the excitement of the active duty for which he had enlisted. He expressed this wish in a letter to his father and was astonished and elated by the contents of the reply. The Duke of Hamilton had been taken up by the military fervour which was sweeping the country as a result of the rebellion of the American colonies. The point of view of the British ruling class was simple: they had been forced to expend vast sums to defeat the French attempt to take over the British settlements and had now not only succeeded in reversing the situation by driving them from their Canadian strongholds, but had also completely expelled them from the northern part of the sub-continent. That the American colonists should be so ungrateful as to refuse to pay back the cost of their salvation via taxation and now, moreover, begin an armed uprising, would not be tolerated. The Duke, therefore, felt it his duty to apply to the King and his government for permission to be allowed the honour of raising his own regiment to be sent to fight the rebels, bearing all of the costs of outfitting it from his own pocket.[2]

Six companies were quickly raised and trained by General MacLean, a well-regarded officer who had held high rank in the Portuguese forces. The Duke wisely admitted his lack of military experience by appointing himself a mere Captain. The one vital officer, from the Duke's viewpoint, was the Quartermaster, for, as he was paying all costs, he had to have an officer in whom he could put complete trust to keep honest accounts and he immediately thought of his young friend Ensign Moor. The Duke, therefore, used his influence with the Prime Minister, Lord North, who approved of his patriotic actions, to request the transfer of Moore to his own regiment to fill the post of Quartermaster, with immediate promotion to Lieutenant.

Not only was Moore, at the tender age of seventeen, to be trained in the vital aspects of regimental accounting and the functioning of the commissariat but his promotion had been by merit, so saving his family the expense of purchasing his Lieutenancy at some point in the next five years.

When the Regiment was considered to be fully trained by their commander, it was ordered to embark for Halifax in Nova Scotia to be integrated into the British Army, with its headquarters in New York. Unfortunately, the Duke's sudden passion for soldiering had been superseded by his love for a lady and His Grace now saw his duty to lie in marriage and the creation of an heir to the Dukedom. Much to Moore's disappointment, he resigned his commission and left his new regiment to sail off to do battle without him.

As soon as the transports had successfully made the crossing, the Regiment was ordered to join Sir Henry Clinton, Commander-in-Chief of the British Army, to build a fort by the

Penobscot River from which to blockade the main rebel supply port of Boston.

In June 1779 the men landed on a deserted, woody coast and an excellent spot was selected for the construction of the fort. After some argument between the General, with his practical experience, and the theorists of the army engineers, a plan was agreed upon and all hands set about the felling of trees and the raising of embankments. The woodland, that would finally be felled to provide a clear field of fire, was for the time being left standing to provide camouflage for the building.

The sounds made by such a huge building project in the silent woods carried for miles, however, and very quickly the Bostonians were alarmed to hear of the attempt being made to cut off their lifeline of commerce and war material. Fear made them all work together rapidly to build a fleet with which to land a force to oust the British before the fortifications were completed, with a blockading fleet operating from beneath the covering fire of heavy batteries.

In only six weeks six large frigates and thirteen armed privateers, together with twenty-four transports, were equipped and 3,000 troops kitted out and ready to board, together with all the artillery and stores needed to lay siege to the unfinished British fort. On 24 July this fleet appeared in the mouth of the Penobscot and was seen by British scouts.

MacLean immediately consolidated his work force to raise a small section of the walls of the fort to a defensible height and sent out pickets to cover the only possible landing site on the river bank. All attempts at a landing were repelled for three days by these pickets concealed in the trees. On the third day this vital picket duty was given to the untried men of the Hamilton Regiment, commanded by a Captain, and Lieutenant Moore was posted to the left side of the small beach, with twenty men under his command.

That morning the Bostonians brought up three frigates at first light, which began to fire broadsides into the woods, using both single- and double-headed round shot. Trees and branches were shattered and crashed down upon the heads of the inexperienced troops, combining with the roar of the heavy naval guns at close range to completely destroy their morale. The equally inexperienced Captain ordered his men not to fire into the packed boats, which now began to row to shore under the barrage, but to wait until they were close enough to be picked off individually as they clambered ashore. The Bostonian troops in the lead boats leapt ashore from the front of the boats with such speed, covered by their comrades in the boats to the rear, that the raw troops under the Captain fired only one volley before they were outnumbered and the Captain ordered them to retreat to the fort.

Lieutenant Moore, however, rallied his company by crying out, "Will the Hamilton men leave me? Come back and behave like soldiers."[3] His men returned and began to fire rapidly into the Americans assembling on the beach, forcing them to break for cover and advance no farther inland.

When the panicked Captain arrived at the fort he gasped out to General MacLean that the Bostonians had landed in overwhelming force and, unable to contain them, he had retired to protect the fort. The General asked, if that was the case, where was Moore and why could he hear British muskets still firing? The wretched Captain could only mumble that he supposed Moore to be cut off. Fortunately, the General sent out an experienced officer with a detachment comprising sufficient men to rescue Moore's company and, if possible, drive the Americans off the shore. When he arrived he found that Moore's troops still had the rebels pinned down on the beach, but at a cost of seven dead among the original twenty.

The reinforced men under Moore's command continued to prevent the American force from moving inland, but, when they found courage to crawl to either end of the beach to outflank the defenders, the Captain ordered an organized retreat to the fort, which was executed with no further casualties among the British.

In a letter to his father Moore modestly mentioned the incident: "I got some little credit, by chance, for my behaviour during the engagement . . . not for anything that deserved it but because I was the only officer who did not leave his post too soon."[4]

Moore's calmness under this introduction to the reality of warfare earned him the respect of his commander and his responsibilities were increased to commanding the fort's reserve company. Fifty men were selected by General MacLean to be ready to rush out from a sallyport to the rear of the fortification; should the enemy show signs of success in storming the frontal defences, they would then be attacked by Moore's men in the wide trench from both sides simultaneously and be put to the bayonet.

However, while Moore had already established his lack of fear under fire, for which he would become famous, it was only known to his family that he was lacking in the basic business of an infantry soldier, namely killing the enemy. He relates that at one point he had the commander of the landing forces so squarely in his sights, as he stood waving his sword to encourage his men forward, that he had only to touch the trigger to have killed him. Instead of doing so, and possibly throwing the whole advance up the beach into confusion, Moore uncocked his piece and replaced it on his shoulder.[5] No motive is given for this action, but it must be assumed that, while he had no personal fear of death, the moralistic upbringing that he had received prevented him from actually killing a man other than as an act of self-preservation. Indeed, nowhere can mention be found in his meticulous diaries, kept to the very eve of the final battle at Corruna, of his actually killing a man by his own hand: a fascinating paradox, that, while his genetic make-up had failed to provide him with a normal sense of self-preservation, allowing him to gallop about numerous battlefields to rally men from the front at the points where his presence was most needed, he may never have directly taken another's life.

The American Commander, having been spared by Moore, did not think fit immediately to rush the half-prepared fortification of the British. Rather, he followed the text-book formula of establishing a defensive circle about his beachhead and then calmly to unload the artillery and stores required for a prolonged seige. This proved to be his great mistake, for the defenders were given time to regain their composure and to strengthen the wood- and stone-filled ramparts, whilst the Bostonian force meticulously dug in its siege batteries out of range of the fort's cannon.

General MacLean had, naturally, sent off a number of gallopers by various routes asking for assistance once the rebels had landed in overwhelming numbers. Therefore, after only some three weeks of the American siege, the latter were forced to flee to their boats when they sighted a British fleet entering the river's mouth, having as its centre an awesome line-of-battle ship carrying three tiers of heavy cannon on each side. The American fleet fled up river, hoping that the British would carry too much draught to follow. Unfortunately for them, several fast frigates were capable of this, which put the Bostonian sailors into a panic, whereby they tangled up in each others' rigging and ran aground.

Some of the grounded vessels were captured intact, while the others were put to the torch by their crews before they fled into the woods. However, their flight was not to be to safety, for a battle then began between the soldiers and the sailors, with each band accusing the other of cowardice. The resulting madness left the majority of the force dead or wounded at the hands of their supposed comrades and only a few hundred made the return through the woods to Boston alive.

Moore's calmness and competence were now recognized by his being promoted in the field to Captain. His reaction to this was to apply for reassignment from the relatively quiet garrison duties of Nova Scotia to a front-line fighting regiment. He was therefore despatched to the British Headquarters in New York to await reassignment.

On arrival he went to sit quietly in the first coffee shop that he came across. No sooner had he been served than, to his intense surprise, his brother James, an army medical officer, walked in the door, having also arrived for reassignment from the army of Virginia. James was able to calm John's fears for their brother Graham, for he had had word that he had survived his own first battle, as a midshipman in Admiral Byron's fleet, which had just defeated the Count D'Estaing off the Canadian coast.

The two brothers were able to live together in a Dutch farmhouse, which they rented on Long Island, while awaiting orders. Unfortunately, instead of new assignments a messenger arrived to tell them that Lord Cornwallis's army had been surprised and surrounded at Yorktown, by both an American and a large French Army, and so forced to surrender, putting an humiliating end to the conflict.

When the British paraded for the ceremony of surrender, their band played a non-military popular tune of the day entitled 'The World Turned Upside Down', which amused the French expeditionary force, whose strength and knowledge of the fortifications had carried the day. Its irony was seen later to be strangely reversed, for the heavy increase in taxes levied by King Louis XVI to pay for this revenge upon the British would be the cause of the final revolt of his subjects to autocratic rule, spurred on by the populist American constitution, which he had decisively helped to establish.

The British forces were allowed to evacuate their forces that winter and the two brothers sailed home together on a large military transport, surviving a hurricane in the West Indies and cunningly beating off the attack of a smaller French privateer in the approaches to the English Channel. The Captain achieved this by hiding hundreds of troops with muskets under the gunnels. The French frigate pulled alongside to claim the supposedly unarmed cargo vessel without wasting cannon fire, only to have most of its crew shot to pieces as the open decks were raked by a hail of balls from the unexpected mass volley.

The Moores landed fit and well at Falmouth, from whence they lost no time in taking a carriage to London, where the family now lived, Dr Moore having established himself as a nationally successful writer. A joyous reunion took place with all the family present, except for Graham, who was still on active service in the Western Ocean. All the sons had served and survived to return whole and healthy, a near miracle in the brutal warfare and unhealthy troop facilities of that time.

CHAPTER THREE

Moore the Politician

Peace was finally signed between Britain and the newly recognized nation of America and her European allies in 1783. The effect upon Moore's career was that The Duke of Hamilton's Regiment was disbanded, but he was retained by the government as a Captain on half-pay.

He then entered London society while living with his family, but soon tired of such an artificial existence. Ironically, he had generally been well thought of in that world of distorted mirrors. Within his small circle of friends he was respected as direct, open and cheerful, but in crowded gatherings filled with strangers he was always seen as formal and reserved.

In the autumn of that year he was invited to return to Scotland as a guest of his patron, the Duke of Hamilton. The Duke soon realized, however, that his friend was restless, doing no more with his free time than study books concerning military tactics and dreaming of action; he therefore made the point to Moore that, as all were aware that a man succeeded to the command of armies more by dint of such political influence as he had than by his abilities as a soldier, it would be a useful move at this stage in his career to enter parliament.

The Scottish boroughs of Lanark, Lithgow, Peebles and Selkirk comprised a seat that was, in effect, the Duke's to dispose of, as a majority would automatically vote for the candidate whom he proposed. Moore agreed with the Duke's suggestion and agreed to take the seat as an independent, but only on the strict understanding that he would indeed be truly independent to vote as he saw fit and not on the Duke's instructions. Moore's sincere principle of only accepting a course of action if he saw it as correct and honourable, both in civil and military matters, was the facet of his character which similarly minded persons found so appealing, and the Duke immediately agreed to give him a free rein in all his parliamentary activities. Moore, therefore, entered parliament in March 1784, when Pitt went to the country to break the self-serving coalition that Fox and North had mounted against his patriot politics.

Moore had only to observe the young Pitt for a short period to become convinced that he was sincere in his crusade to have the house pass measures for the good of the country as a whole, rather than engage in horse trading with the self-interested cabals of the time. This was reason enough for him to cast his vote consistently for the 'Pittites'. However, apart from this manifestation of anti-Whig sentiments, he could not find the enthusiasm to be fired up by political matters. Nevertheless, Burke, who sat with the opposition, complimented Dr Moore on the fine quality of his son's speeches.

Apart from allying himself with Pitt, the other important contact he made that would affect his later military career was to win the confidence of the Duke of York, who would soon be made Commander-in-Chief of all British military forces.

In spite of his always voting with the Tory Pittites, he was ever after regarded as a Whig in conflict with a Tory government, owing to the patronage of the Duke of Hamilton. The personal diary which he kept reveals, however, that his true beliefs were those of natural justice for the common people, be they low-ranking soldiers, Caribbean slaves or Irish peasants. Nevertheless, these personal beliefs were of no hindrance to him in obeying his orders to repress rebellion, even among those very people whom he saw as unjustly and unwisely suppressed to benefit the interests of the privileged classes. To Moore orders were to be obeyed and their morality to be discussed later, the alternative being chaos.

Once known and respected by the political society of London, he made it his main aim to look for openings that would return him to active duty in the army. During 1787 he heard of two new battalions which were being recruited to strengthen the 60th Regiment in Europe, with the inducement of seven guineas a head.[1] The knowledge of French and German that he had acquired made him perfectly suited for command as the training officer of these men and his newly acquired influence saw to it that his name was placed at the head of the list. He was duly appointed with promotion to Major at Chatham training camp, where he earned a reputation as a kindly but strict commander, who was equal in his treatment of all his officers, and, more unusually, also of the 'common soldiery'.

After a period of six months the regiment which he had trained was reviewed by the inspecting General and certified as excellent in all respects. Major Moore's reward was to be transferred back to his initial regiment, the 51st, now garrisoned at Cork.

CHAPTER FOUR

Ireland and Gibraltar

Upon his arrival Moore was dismayed to find the degree to which the Regiment had deteriorated in all respects from the time that he had known it as an Ensign in Minorca, under the strict command of General Murray.

The Regiment was now under the command of a Lieutenant Colonel Jaques, who was a mere time-server. He refused to implement any of Major Moore's suggestions for improvements, jealous of Moore's newly won reputation as an exceptional training officer, whom he suspected had been sent to rectify his own deficiencies.

Moore had arrived with no such instructions, and, indeed, throughout his career he was never known to conspire by word or deed against a superior, always carrying out the orders that he was given, even if he disagreed with them. Nevertheless, when on active service he would make his opinion known face to face with his commander in private, in the hope that his reasoning would prevail before disaster occurred. Events almost always proved Moore to have been right in his assessments, which did not endear him to superiors of lesser ability, either military or political.

In this instance, as garrison duty only was involved, he made his feelings concerning the command known only in his private diary. He complains of "a Commander proud of his own ignorance"[1] and thereafter did his best to put himself on good terms with his fellow officers without public discussion of the Commander's deficiencies.

22

Just as he was settling into the routine of garrison duty and the pleasant social life of the Irish gentry in and around Cork, the Regiment was told to prepare itself for war with Spain in Central America and the Caribbean. Mr Pitt had decided to let the Spanish and their allies know that he was truly his father's son before they became too bold and aggressive. During 1789 they had decided to probe his resolve by attacking and occupying a British fur-trading settlement on the Pacific coast of Canada, so renewing their claim to the whole Pacific coast from Cape Horn to Alaska.

The attack on this settlement at Nootka Sound, on a bleak coast near to Vancouver island, was met by Pitt with an immediate ultimatum to withdraw or face British retaliation by the seizure of either Cuba or Venezuela.

All the Regiment were excited at the possibility of action, with the one exception of their Commander. Faced with the prospect of actually fighting, he used the excuse of his young family's welfare to retire from the service. Major Moore immediately applied to purchase the man's commission and was granted the Lieutenant Colonelcy, with the command of his boyhood Regiment included.

The state into which the once crack 51st had fallen since its ignominious expulsion from Minorca by the surprise French-Spanish attack[2] of 1782 is best described in Moore's own words, in a letter to his father upon taking command: "Every department of the staff was more or less deficient, particularly the commissariat and medical branches. The regimental officers are, as well as the men, hard drinkers; and the latter, under a loose discipline, were much addicted to maeaudering (sic) and acts of licentious violence, which made them detested by the people of the country . . . But the most crying infamy was that which resulted from the employment of 'crimps' on a large scale. Our government made contracts with scoundrels (bearing the King's commission) to furnish so many hundred men for sums of money."[3] This was the army equivalent of the Navy's 'press gangs', but the resultant reluctant victims were far more difficult to manage than in the controlled environment of a warship.

Confirming Moore's opinion, Sir Charles Banbury described the army at the beginning of the Napoleonic Wars in 1793 as being "lax in its discipline, entirely without system, and very weak in numbers. Each Colonel of a regiment managed it altogether. There was no uniformity of drill or movement, professional pride was rare, professional knowledge still more so."[4]

This statement underlines the value of Moore, who was one of those dedicated few who tried by their own studies to become truly professional soldiers. All his free time was devoted to the study of books on fortifications, training and the tactics of the great Roman generals in the original Latin texts.

He immediately began turning the drunken rabble that he had inherited back into the polished military machine that he had been proud to join in his youth. Writing to his father from Cork on 17 February 1792, he stated that he had been forced to have two soldiers and a corporal flogged for drunkenness while on duty, only to find that two days later a lieutenant had left his post for a drunken riot round the town.

To prove that in his Regiment there was not one set of rules for the men and another for the officers, he had the "blackguard" arrested and locked in his quarters. He then gave him the option of selling out his commission to the next Ensign in line for promotion or sending a report to the Commander-in-Chief with the recommendation that he be expelled from the army; he wisely took the money and resigned.[5]

The other officers congratulated their new Commander on his wise handling of the matter, which gave him the opportunity to rid the Regiment of several other grossly incompetent officers. It was not, however, until 30 September 1793 that he felt able to inform his father that he had restored his Regiment "to good working order, and I now wish it to be used".[6]

The Spaniards backed down and finally evacuated their force from Nootka Sound, so, instead of sailing for Central America, the 51st embarked from Cork on 8 March 1792, destined for more garrison duty at Gibraltar. Here Colonel Moore continued to instill in them the discipline required for combat, which was soon to come, for Revolutionary France declared war on Great Britain in 1793.

At the start of hostilities a French Royalist force had taken over the vital naval port of Toulon and invited the British to take over the walled city together with the huge Mediterranean fleet moored in its harbour. This was swiftly achieved by a British fleet, commanded by Admiral Hood, entering the port and manning the walls with its marines.

Meanwhile, the liberation movement in Corsica had the French shut up in their forts and asked the British to evict them, then to garrison and assist in the rule of the island as a strategic replacement for Minorca.

After much bureaucratic delay, the 51st embarked to reinforce the 74-year-old Admiral Hood and his marines in Toulon, now besieged by a republican rabble of an army, but still complacent, for the General given command by the people's committee had been an artist in civilian life, with no military experience whatsoever. The overall plan was to defensively garrison Toulon and, with the French fleet manned by Royalists, sail on to take control of Corsica.

CHAPTER FIVE

Toulon and Corsica

The Governor and the military commander of Gibraltar had argued concerning the latter's right to despatch, unrequested, infantry and field artillery to reinforce Admiral Hood in Toulon, with the result that all was referred to London. Meanwhile, a new factor had been added to the balance of forces at the besieged port. A young Captain of artillery, previously in hiding for his support of the independence movement in his native Corsica, had been pardoned by the Revolutionary Committee and sent to assist the siege; his name was Napoleon Bonaparte, which meant nothing as yet to the British.

The defenders had meanwhile decided to sally out and drive off their incompetent, but annoying, besiegers. General O'Hara marched out with the majority of the marines and the Royalist Vendée forces, only to have his swiftly advancing troops decimated by a perfectly placed crossfire of artillery shells from the newly constructed emplacements of the relief artillery commander. Only now did the stubbornly arrogant Admiral Hood make the official application for assistance from the army based in Gibraltar. This untied the bureaucratic tangle and the 50th and 51st Regiments were ordered to set sail immediately in the already provisioned transports, but against an untimely north wind. It was during this ten days of tacks that a bored Colonel Moore found an old army issue note book, bound in strong brown leather, and began to keep a journal.

The belief that his abilities as a land commander were equal to those well proven at sea was Hood's undoing at Toulon and, unfortunately, by the time that the relief force was off the coast a frigate met them with the information that Toulon had been evacuated and that they should rendezvous with the Naval force at Hyeres Bay. The Revolutionary troops had taken the fortifications so rapidly, once breached by Captain Bonaparte's artillery, that there had been no time to ready the theoretically captured French Mediterranean fleet for sea, apart from a few vessels. The remainder, some thirty assorted warships, were put to the torch, but so hurriedly that many were saved to form the rump of a new battle fleet, which equalled the British in number once the Spanish allied their forces to those of France in 1795.

The fiasco of Toulon's occupation was the more frustrating to Colonel Moore and the 51st as the frigate containing all of their personal effects and equipment had become separated from the main force in fog, then lured into Toulon by the raising of a British flag and captured. Moore's enthusiasm for his overall commander, Admiral Hood, was further dampened when interviewed by him in the safety of Hyeres Bay, aboard his flagship *Victory*. Hood abruptly acknowledged him, accused him of arriving too late to be of assistance and curtly dismissed him.

The fleet spent twelve days waiting while consultations took place on how to proceed with driving the French from the strongholds in which the Corsican partisans had them trapped. The overall commander of all operations was to remain Admiral Hood, whilst General Dundas was to be subordinate to him as commander of army forces. The first action decided upon was to send Colonel Moore, together with Sir Gilbert Elliot, King's commissioner with authority over the whole of the Mediterranean, and Major Koehler of the Royal Artillery, who was also Chief Quartermaster of Admiral Hood's command, to meet up with the partisan leader, General Paoli, on Corsica to assess the best way to cooperate in the removal of the French from the island prior to it becoming a British strategic base. The frigate *Lowestoffe* took them to the island and on the afternoon of 14 January 1794 a small boat rowed them the three miles to shore at the remote Isola Rossa off the north-western coast of Corsica.

They were met by General Paoli's nephew, Signor Leonate, who assured the British group that the whole of the countryside was in the hands of his men, with only some 2,600 French troops bottled up in their fortifications at Fiorenza, Bastia and Calvi, the majority being inside Bastia. Plans were made accordingly and it was only after surrender that the French were found in fact to number 7,000. A disaster would have occurred to the inferior British force sent against them had it not been for an equal overestimation on the part of the French concerning the fighting abilities of the partisans. Thus their threefold numbers only served to starve them out of their strongholds more quickly than otherwise believed possible, saving many British lives.

The British negotiating party was now taken inland, travelling for three days over mule tracks to the mountain village of Murato, half-way to Bastia, where General Paoli had his headquarters. Sir Gilbert's concerns over a protracted negotiation concerning Britain's role in governing the island were obviated by the aged General stating that he was tired of politicians and treaties. He claimed that he spoke for the Corsican Council when he said that their wish was to be placed permanently under British protection, or even direct government, asking no more than the civil liberties given to subjects of such other British overseas possessions. However, elections must be held for an assembly to represent Corsican interests in internal government once the French were driven out.

The British interest in the island and its large safe ports was as a base with which to threaten the French and Spanish coasts. This was vital, as they had been ejected from Minorca in 1781 by a surprise attack of combined Spanish and French forces, regardless of the Treaty of Paris in 1763, which conceded the island to the British in perpetuity.[1]

The political aspects having been so quickly resolved, Sir Gilbert returned to the fleet to be taken on to Elba, while Moore and Koehler remained for several days to explore and map the coast around the fortified towns of Fiorenza and Calvi, with regard to landing places and vantage points for artillery emplacements.[2]

On 25 January 1794 the whole British fleet, including twenty-one ships of line-of-battle, each with an average of 100 cannon, showed itself off the coast to give courage to the partisans and take off the two reconnoitring British officers. The fleet then sailed on to Elba to unload refugees from Toulon and make ready the equipment judged necessary for the landing on Corsica.

While the British concentrated on naval supremacy in the Mediterranean, the Revolutionary Convention in Paris sought for a leader to put order into its rabble of an army, which lacked experienced officers, owing to the fact that so many had been executed as aristocratic Royalist supporters, the fact having just been underlined by their total defeat by the British, who had driven them from the Netherlands. Citizen Barras put forward the name of a previously unknown young officer of artillery who was being hailed as the 'hero of Toulon'. Napoleon Bonaparte was now promoted to Brigadier-General and quickly transformed 30,000 squabbling ruffians into the basis of the best army that Europe had known since the fall of Rome.

Meanwhile, in Elba Admiral Hood had loaded every piece

of ordnance and provisions thought necessary for the taking of Corsica and by 7 February a squadron led by *Victory* transported Lieutenant-Colonel Moore, who now commanded The Royal Scots as well as the 50th and 51st regiments, into the Gulf of Fiorenza, landing the invaders near to the unique round gun platform on Mortello Point.[3] In all some 650 soldiers, accompanied by 150 seamen, came ashore, totally unopposed by the French. Moore was naturally suspicious and ordered a slow advance, whilst scouting ahead to see what surprise the French had in readiness for them. He was not to be disappointed, for the French had taken full advantage of the delay in launching the far from secret invasion to bring up artillery to fortify the approach to the Mortello tower and placed heavier pieces in the existing fortification and tower of Fornoli, capable of providing additional covering fire had the British marched blindly on to attempt to seize the Mortello gun tower. The tower was known by both sides to be the necessary first objective, which had to be taken to allow ships to anchor freely in the bay. Moore, therefore, took the heights overlooking the French positions and dug in, before reporting back to General Dundas on board the *Victory* as to the changed situation.

There followed a fortnight of stalemate, with the 6-metre-thick walls of the round tower deflecting even full broadsides from the *Victory*, while its defenders succeeded in using red hot shot to set fire to a line-of-battle ship the *Fortitude* and killing sixty men aboard the frigate *Juno* by raking it with grapeshot. The turning point came when Major Koehler found the perfect spot to bombard the French in safety. A sheer mountain cliff that the French had deemed unsurmountable by artillery was quickly scaled by the seamen, who used their knowledge of ropes and pulleys to haul up two 18 pounders and an eight-inch siege mortar.

The next day this battery opened fire on the artillery defences of the Mortello tower and succeeded in dismounting many of its guns. The fortification was then surprised and taken that night by moonlight, using a silent bayonet charge. Soon after, a red-hot shot from the *Victory* succeeded in entering one of the tower's embrasures and set it on fire, so forcing the occupants to surrender. So surprised were the French at the ease with which the British had captured the Mortello fortification that they abandoned its twin at Fornoli without firing another shot and pulled their entire force into the massive fort of Bastia on the other side of the mountainous peninsula of Cape Corse. That they were able to escape was due to the fact that the partisans disobeyed their orders to cut off this line of retreat, in favour of robbing the dead and wounded of both sides after the siege of Mortello.[4]

The advice of General Dundas was that Bastia could only be blockaded and starved into surrender or bombarded into submission from the heights now occupied by the well-entrenched French. Admiral Hood, however, claiming that his overall command of all forces at Toulon still pertained on land, overruled him and ordered a certain Captain Nelson to take heavy guns ashore and set up a battery on a low hill near the port, protected by 600 marines.[4]

Bastia was believed to contain some 3,500 battle-hardened and disciplined ex-Royalist troops, so that even if Nelson had succeeded in breaching the walls from such a distance the 1,200 British troops under Dundas' command could not have succeeded in taking the citadel. Hood had a reputation for casting aside all reason and winning victories at sea against superior odds by sheer courage; thus at first it was supposed he was applying the same doctrine of "act first, think afterwards" to the vastly slower land actions. Soon the realization came to Dundas that the unnecessary siege was for political consumption at home to cover his failure at Toulon. Merely blockading the port to starve the enemy into submission did not have the same ring of glorious victory with the British public as heavy bombardment and bayonet charges. Dundas refused to be a part of the decimation of three regiments to restore Hood's prestige and resigned his command to register his protest.

It is now known that Nelson had intercepted French despatches stating that in fact 6,000 men held Bastia, but, as this might have swayed even the intransigent Hood and spoiled Nelson's first chance of personal recognition for his bombardment, he kept this information to himself.[5] The vast amount of powder and ball used in the two-week bombardment was such that it left the fleet severely depleted, with the result that it was later temporarily driven from the Mediterranean.

Just as Moore and Dundas had predicted, after two weeks the French Commander, General Gentile, surrendered. He told Moore that, while he had always been in a position to sally out and destroy the battery, this would not have given food to his men, for most of the British provisions were aboard the fleet.[6]

A short time before the surrender of this, the main French stronghold, 600 reinforcements arrived from Gibraltar with General Charles Stuart, who was known for his efficiency. General D'Aubant gratefully handed over his command of the army to Stuart, along with the problem of controlling the valiant, but unreasoning, Admiral Hood.[7]

A further 800 men arrived under General Trigge to garrison Bastia[8] and the next objective, the last serious French point of resistance, was Calvi, once more on the opposite side of the mountainous peninsula. The 40 miles of near impassable terrain, especially for artillery, made a seaborne landing again the only logical option.

CHAPTER SIX

Victory and Disgrace

The force which sailed to take Calvi was consolidated into a body of 2,000 men named simply The Reserve, with Lieutenant-Colonel Moore in command. The landing took place on 29 June 1794 in a port already held ready by Paoli's partisans, and so was without incident, apart from two days of torrential rain causing delays.

On first seeing the town and its twin fortifications, Moore knew that the landing was to be the only easy part of the assault. The certainty of blockade, and an inevitable surrender by dint of starvation, was no longer assured. The *Agamemnon*, under Captain Nelson, was now his only heavily armed support vessel and was moored in Porto Agro, where the landing had occurred. The rest of the fleet had suddenly left to chase the seven line-of-battle ships which the French had energetically repaired and sent out of the unblockaded Toulon to link up with frigates sailing from Brest. To the French in Calvi, therefore, there was some hope of relief, which had been totally absent previously.

Moore's orders were to take the town's forts by battery and assault of the walls, not to begin a prolonged siege, but the sight which greeted him from the heights was not at all encouraging for such an action. To the front of the town was a strong stone fort named Mozello, whose flank was covered by a second fort placed on a rocky promontory at the coast known as Mollinochesco. The whole of this defence system was covered by two outlying batteries in redoubts and surrounded by an earthwork. Worse still, in front of it was a mosquito-infested swamp that must reduce any besieging force by fever within a few days.[1]

The decision was made, therefore, swiftly to breach and reduce by bayonet charges both forts at once from one fixed heavy battery. On this occasion the French were not content merely to observe with resignation while the implements of their destruction were set up. Rather, they sallied out from the coastal fort, but were halted by the partisans until British light infantry, reinforced by field guns, drove them back inside the walls.[2] Against all military theory, the defenders of this expertly designed fortification system were equal in number to the attackers; all the odds were therefore heavily in their favour, apart from time.

On 5 July a diversionary night attack was made on the coastal fort and, while the French vigorously defended their rear wall, a combined company of soldiers and sailors dragged up heavy guns unnoticed. That same night and on the one following they worked furiously to establish a hidden forward breaching battery. A second emplacement was built at the rear to act as a decoy, until all was in position for a breach and assault. The French wasted much of their irreplaceable munitions on this decoy, firing at it for all of the first day.

The ruse worked perfectly and the main heavy battery went quite undetected until it roared into action. Despite the element of surprise, the French quickly repositioned guns to fire into the British emplacement, as a result of which several men were killed or wounded and two guns dismounted during the first day's battering. The British gunners accepted the risk, however, and merely fired more rapidly, to finish the work before the enemy finished them.

The result was to intimidate the French into evacuating the coastal fort and redoubt under cover of darkness the next night. The movement did not go undetected, however, and both Moore and General Stuart personally supervised the traversing of the battery to bear on the main fort and the throwing up of strong traverses for its protection.[3] The next day concentrated fire silenced the enemy's guns one by one, until it became possible to build a naturally protected battery out of range of the remaining redoubt only 500 yards from the walls, making their fall inevitable. The French were extremely ingenious at this point and began to fire their guns at the outcrops of rock around the British battery *'en ricochet'*. At such close range they not only bounced balls into the position, but also a hail of rock shards. One of these struck down Moore's batman, while another struck Captain Nelson in the eye, half-destroying it, which thereafter caused him to wear the eye-patch that became emblematic of his image. Nelson valiantly bandaged the torn eye and continued to command the naval contingent.

After this incident Moore tried to persuade his General to retire to a safer position, but Sir Charles stated that he could only assess the right moment to send in the infantry to carry the breach from close up. The argument he gave was that it was better that one man should die than hundreds under his command, were the breach assaulted when impracticable. Moore recorded that this noble reply was to be his inspiration to lead from the front for the rest of his life.[4]

On 18 July the breach was considered sufficient, and the next day a second breach was finished, to be attacked together with the redoubt as a diversion to split the defenders. Colonel Moore and Captain McDonald of the Royals now calmly led their men forward through a hail of cannon and musket fire, carrying sand-bags from which to cover the artificers who would hack down the spiked palisades placed to fill the gap. Moore, however, noticed that a cannon ball had cut a path through already and he instantly led his men single-file through the wall. While they assembled in the breach, not only musket fire and grenades rained down upon them, but also two shells with short fuses. In this maelstrom of exploding metal Moore was knocked unconscious by a shell fragment grazing his head. However, he quickly regained consciousness and climbed the ramp with the Grenadiers, who were now streaming through and cheering. The reason soon became apparent and General Stuart found Moore, blackened with powder and streaked with the blood from his head wound, standing on a pile of rubble surrounded by his men cheering as they saw the French running for the cover of the town. The General "clasped Moore to him like a son and offered him his most profound congratulations."[5]

Only thirty British casualties occurred in the taking of the fort, despite the quantity of explosives and ball thrown at them; indeed far more died of fever in the field hospital.

The town was now bombarded and set on fire in several places, but, as no return fire was given, the French commander was offered the incentive of the same generous terms of repatriation upon surrender as at the fall of Bastia. However, he asked for a period of truce for twenty-five days, as he could not honourably surrender when naval assistance might be on its way. General Stuart offered him twelve, after which he could surrender under the same conditions, and this offer was accepted.

While it may seem beyond all logic to give such a period of grace to an enemy who was completely surrounded and without artillery when a force far superior to the besieger's might appear at any moment, a key fact was left out of all contemporary accounts. The hospital reports show that two-thirds of the British force was incapable of fighting, for they were in the grip of endemic fever, malaria. The real fear was that the British would not be able to keep up the appearance of a ring of steel round the town before the French surrendered, much less attack them. Moore, uncharacteristically, does not give a hint of the reality of the situation in his diary, leaving the world to marvel at the chivalrous gallantry of the British towards a beaten foe.

The twelfth day came with no help having arrived and, honour bound by the articles of war, the French duly marched out in formation to lay down their weapons before General Stuart. This was on 2 August and by the 11th Moore was able to write to his mother to tell her that the plaster had fallen off his head wound and that it was found to be healing well. The 51st Regiment had also been the least affected by malaria, owing to the strict regulations which he had enforced as the son of a military surgeon. In addition he had medicines and orderlies to administer to the sick which he had accumulated over the last three years and which no other regiment in the British army possessed to such an extent.

Soon after their victory Lieutenant-Colonel Moore and his General, together with three accompanying officers, made a tour of the island. The purpose was to see for themselves if the attitude of the population in general was as pro-British as General Paoli had stated. The peasants cheered them from the fields and they were given a reception by the nobility of Ajaccio. Well pleased, they returned to Bastia to find that Sir Gilbert Elliot had arrived in the role of Viceroy. Paoli had wished full union with Britain as a guarantee of continuity, and so the powers of the Viceroy were basically those of a Lord Lieutenant of Ireland.

Paoli had said that once this was achieved he would leave the island and retire to spend his old age in England.[6] The country was well known to him, for he had spent 23 years in exile there, after his failed uprising against the French in 1769. Unfortunately for the Viceroy, he now delayed his departure until he could see a parliament functioning and his volatile countrymen content under British rule. Sir Gilbert was determined that Paoli should not be allowed to form a second focus of power. Accordingly, he left the old General out of his circle of local advisers, the chief among whom was a man of no consequence in island politics or society by the name of Pozzo de Borgo. Previously he had been known only as a lawyer in the mountain villages, with a bad reputation in money matters. He had volunteered to run the Corsican commissariat, supplied with necessities by the British, and was thus in a position to put himself forward on the arrival of the Viceroy. The people were infuriated that their hero had been snubbed by the British representative, while a cunning rogue was instead at his right hand to parcel out official funds and positions to those who could offer the best bribes.

Not only did Sir Gilbert almost immediately alienate the native populace but he set about interfering in military matters, which his formal position as their political master did not allow him to do, much less with his total ignorance of army affairs.[7] After various confrontations, with London failing to clarify the scope of the chain of command, General Stuart resigned in protest. After a defiant triumphal tour of the island, he left the disappointed citizens of Corsica on 7 February 1795. The Viceroy appointed General Trigge in his place, who was totally lacking in experience and who did not even know the geography of the island, but this was offset in Sir Gilbert's already paranoid mind by the fact that the mild-mannered Trigge would never question his authority and would follow his orders explicitly, no matter how militarily disastrous or politically foolish. Moore was now made Trigge's Adjutant-General and tried his best to maintain both army efficiency and good relations with the populace which he had helped free. The Viceroy, for his part, neglected to maintain the defences and still held all Corsicans in the contempt that he had expressed on his first reconnaissance of the island.[8]

He now decreed that the island's parliament was to assemble, but not in the centrally placed Corte, as was the custom. Rather, it must meet in Bastia for his convenience and under his observation. Regardless of this exercise of Viceregal power, the assembly voted that General Paoli should be its President, although he was neither a candidate nor even present. The astute old General thanked his countrymen for this honour, but declined to accept, citing age and infirmity.[9] The real motive was to avoid further undermining the British representative's authority, though personally disliking the man and his despotic ways. Rather, he urged Sir Gilbert to work with, and not against, the parliament, while ridding himself of the detested Pozzo de Borgo. When Sir Gilbert stated that he would rather die than set aside his friend, the old General retired to his native village, but still sought to keep his aggressive partisans in a submissive state while waiting for conditions to change for the better, preferably by Sir Gilbert being replaced.

Moore believed it to be part of his duty to be informed of the position and opinions of the old patriot. To this end he paid a visit to Paoli at home. The arrangements were far from secret and he was accompanied not only by a British and a Corsican Regiment Colonel but also by Lord Huntly, who had recently arrived with heavy naval and army reinforcements.[10]

On his return to Bastia an emissary came from Sir Gilbert to inform Moore that unless he undertook to break off all further contact with General Paoli's faction he could not be allowed to remain in Corsica. He stated that he had knowledge that Paoli was plotting against him locally and had even engaged in a secret correspondence with London to undermine him.[11] Moore was highly indignant at such accusations and in an interview with the Viceroy told him bluntly that, unless he was to be openly accused of active conspiracy, he would continue to express his opinion on Sir Gilbert's or any other government, taking this as his right as a free man. In reply to these democratic sentiments the Viceroy informed him that he had already complained of Moore's conduct to both the King and his Ministers and that he had orders to send Moore back to London as and when he saw fit. These orders would now be executed in the light of Moore's attitude and as of 2 October he had 48 hours to leave the island.[12]

Concerning this conversation, Moore recorded in his diary that "my feelings were so strong and my indignation such as at times to bring tears to my eyes, and for a moment to stop my speech".[13]

No doubt Sir Gilbert drew great satisfaction from the effect which his manipulations had produced upon the man who had so recently calmly walked first into the breach at Calvi.

The orders were indeed delivered within a few hours and he sailed for Italy on 24 November. Before his departure he had the pleasure of receiving affectionate ceremonies of farewell from not

39

only his own 51st Regiment but also the Corsican Regiment and the Corsican Supreme Council.

General Paoli also left some days later, after receiving a personal letter from King George III. Moore's prophecy that the only man who could have controlled his feisty countrymen had been purposely alienated by the Viceroy was soon to be proved true. The hatred of Sir Gilbert's despotism, once his mind had been turned by near complete power, became greater among the Corsicans than their fear of re-invasion by the French. In 1797, a year to the day after Paoli's departure, the partisans rebelled and drove the British from their island, which was swiftly reoccupied by the French who remain, uneasily, until the present day.

British strategy in the Western Mediterranean was now temporarily confined to what could be achieved from Gibraltar. One man's actions had undone what so many brave men had given their lives to achieve. However, with the destruction, by the then Admiral Nelson, of the French Fleet at the Battle of the Nile, the island of Minorca was retaken in 1798. The magnificent harbour of Mahon, together with the acquiescent population, were seen by all as vastly superior for a base, compared to its temporary and troublesome substitute. The possession and defence of both would, doubtless, have consumed more manpower than their close proximity warranted.

Moore returned to England overland and the vagaries of the wind caused him to spend some days in Cuxhaven in conversation with General Paoli, who had caught up with him. In fact the General went first to England and, almost certainly, his respected opinion softened the way for Colonel Moore, as in Cuxhaven he had referred to Sir Gilbert as "the meanest spirited of men".[14]

The change in the character of Elliot, previously known in Ministerial circles as an affable man, had, therefore, provided yet another important witness to add to the growing list of well-thought-of men expelled by the Viceroy prior to Moore making his protests. Mr Pitt received him coldly and he was sent on to the Colonial Secretary, the Duke of Portland, who was more forthcoming. An explanation was given as to the government's awareness of the problems being made by their new Viceroy, but, once having appointed him, they could only be seen to be backing his decisions in what were deemed as minor matters. Moore replied, quite courageously, that it was one thing to inform him verbally that his army career would not be affected by this mere clash of personalities, but until he was given vindication before his peers by a prompt and appropriate reassignment he would consider himself grievously injured.

On leaving, Moore was called to one side by Secretary Dundas[15], Mr Pitt's greatest personal friend, and surprised to be told unofficially that such a public demonstration of Pitt's confidence in him would soon be forthcoming. Moore, while pleasantly surprised, by now had little faith in mere words from Ministers and continued to consider his career ruined without so much as a trial.

In his despondency he had forgotten the friendship which he had enjoyed with the Duke of York, who now sent for all of Sir Gilbert's despatches and analysed them one by one with a secretary taking notes. Armed with sufficient evidence that the Viceroy had acted towards Moore out of jealousy and personal malice rather than the national interest in time of war, he quietly presented Moore's situation to his father, King George. Unaware of this high intervention, Moore was delighted to read in the official despatches that he had been promoted to Brigadier-General on merit and assigned to a force bound for action in the West Indies.

Without officially pronouncing one word of criticism against Sir Gilbert, the King and his Ministers had completely vindicated Moore in the eyes of the military and political establishment. Significantly, when Sir Gilbert's autobiography was written, no mention was made of his wild accusations against Moore.

After spending some days in Bath enjoying the company of the Duke of Hamilton, Moore travelled on to the Isle of Wight to attach himself to a foreign corps that was assembling at Cowes.

On 28 February 1796 this force of 100 ships set sail for Santo Domingo, under the command of General Abercromby. The objective was to seize and restore order in the French islands, where the garrisons had gone over to the revolutionary cause, freed the slaves and unleashed a murderous chaos.

CHAPTER SEVEN

The West Indian Expedition

Moore's first impression of the assembly of British, Royalist French, Dutch and German troops is best left in the words of his journal entry for the day prior to his sailing:

> "The confusion of this place is beyond anything that could be believed; everything is in disorder, and the expedition will sail in as sad a state as ever expedition did sail from this country."[1]

In fact he was astonished to be informed the following morning that he would not even meet the foreign corps that he had been promoted to command. The men had been confined aboard transports for three months and were now seen as so weak that they must be taken ashore to be exercised back to fitness. However, General Sir Ralph Abercromby had personally been advised not to leave so valuable an officer as Moore behind. The commissioners of transport had, therefore, assigned him a transport ship, but where it was anchored was unknown and he spent five hours being rowed around in the mist in the vast anchorage before it was found.

Moore wisely confined his displeasure to his diary, for, after the treatment that he had received in Corsica, he did not wish to add to his undeserved reputation as a troublesome subordinate.

The welcome that he received from the jovial Captain Lecky of the *John and James* transport somewhat alleviated his depression, however, for he ended a letter to his mother from the ship, stating that he had been invited to join the Captain's mess for the voyage and that he was about to do justice to the roast beef about to be served. In this same letter Moore asks his family to intervene to make sure that the rest of his luggage be sent after him, for he had received his changed orders at such short notice that he had nothing but his travelling portmanteau with him, and this he complained held only seven changes of shirts and underwear. To remedy this state of affairs he had purchased fifteen more in Southampton.[2] Here is proof indeed that the then strange Swiss Calvinist concept of bodily hygiene, which he had acquired during his studies there, was as rigorously applied to himself as it was imposed by him upon the men whom he commanded.

The ship sailed well, for it was freshly copper-bottomed and was also clean and well provisioned. The six weeks of sailing to the fleet rendezvous off Barbados was, therefore, a pleasant enough experience. The transport arrived on 15 April 1796 and was placed under the command of Admiral Sir Hugh Christian.

Initially, in the confusion, Moore was given command of a cavalry regiment destined for Santo Domingo, but, after the intervention of Sir Ralph, he was placed where his talent as an infantry commander could best be put to use. Sir Ralph made him second in command to General Alexander Campbell's division, which was to soon sail to take control of the French Antilles, or the Windward Islands as the British called them. Sir Ralph would be the overall commander of a force of some five thousand troops, with the first objective being St Lucia, followed by St Vincent and Grenada. All this information he dutifully reported to his father in a letter of 17 April 1796.[3]

Moore, it would appear, had some doubt as to the ultimate ability of the expedition to restore order in the West Indies, for he wrote in this same letter to his father, a week before sailing into action, advising all their friends who owned property in the islands to sell immediately. His reasoning was that, as the French had freed and armed the slaves, the British would inevitably be forced to do the same to take the islands, owing to lack of experienced British troops. The result would be, he stated, that the slaves, once taught to be soldiers, must logically turn on their oppressors and drive both the French and English plantation owners from the islands. Such private opinions are typical of Moore, who would nevertheless fight to the last to do his duty, even if he saw the overall political situation as dubious or socially unjust.

On 25 May he entered in his journal that he embarked for St Lucia with 5,000 troops and 100 artillerymen. The remaining troops were split; some sailed for Dominica, while others served as a reserve at Barbados, joined by the foreign corps from England. The War Office list of the numbers and regiments which took part is given in the appendix, but the most significant figure is that 3,100, or 25% of the whole force at Barbados, was made up of blacks from the new West Indian Regiment and the Pioneer Corps. The black soldiers were to prove the best fighters of all during the campaign. The fact that they were acclimatized and mostly immune to tropical diseases was one obvious advantage. Secondly, their service was until retirement and freedom, with a terrible fate if captured by the French black troops whom they fought, a sound motive to fight like true warriors. In comparison the sickly British soldiers, mostly rounded up in slum districts or tricked when drunk at market, fought only to survive against the slim chance of returning home. The black troops were dispersed, with 100 attached to each British regiment. While still informal rangers, they dressed in appropriate clothing for the climate, whereas the British troops fought in their thick serge uniforms intended for European use.

A boost to Moore's morale was given when he found his old friend Captain Paul Anderson of the 51st Regiment unassigned and was able to take him as his Brigade Major, so giving him perhaps his only confidant among an officer corps that he would later grow to despise.

The only military objective of significance at St Lucia was the

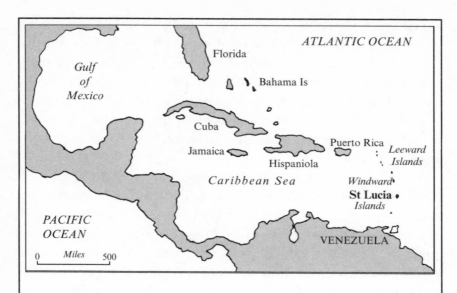

ATLANTIC OCEAN

Florida

Gulf
of
Mexico

Bahama Is

Cuba

Puerto Rica

Jamaica

Hispaniola

Leeward
Islands

Caribbean Sea

Windward

St Lucia

Islands

PACIFIC
OCEAN

VENEZUELA

0   Miles   500

St Lucia

Pointe du Cap

Ance le Cap

Choc Bay

Vigle Point

Castries

Cul de Sac Inlet

△ Morne Fortuné

Caribbean

Sea

ATLANTIC

OCEAN

Ance de la Soufrière

Soufrière

Soufrière
Hills

Fort Vieux

Cap Moule à Chaque

0   Miles   5

magnificently built French Fortress of Morne Fortuné and the only safe anchorage to launch an attack upon it was at Choc Bay in the extreme north of the island. The pre-revolutionary French government had sent expert engineers to fortify this anchorage. Colonel Hope and General Moore were sent ashore, with several good brigades, to silence these guns and allow a full-scale landing. Moore was sent ashore first, landing to the north on a beach which he called Ance le Cap, but which appears on a contemporary French map as Ance Becune (*ance* means bay and *morne* heights in Creole French). The landing was made without problems, apart from the firing of a cannon at extreme range, but, once spotted, the advance company of the Jagers of Lowestein was soon engaged with the enemy at Longueville House on Cap Plantation.

Here Moore received a message to re-embark his men, as various accidents to the vessels due to land Hope to the south of the anchorage fortifications meant that he could not arrive until evening. Moore, at the risk of seeming insubordinate, sent a reply to Sir Ralph stating that it would not only be disgraceful to follow this order, but also dangerous when engaged with the enemy skirmishers. The suggestion which he offered in his reply was to hold his position during the day, and then move immediately by moonlight to the rear of the enemy fortifications that were the objective. To achieve this aim he intended to use the two fine brigades of the 42nd Highlanders, which made up the core of his reliable force.[4] Sir Ralph replied confirming this initiative. Hope and his men landed at dusk and, in a pincer movement, closed behind the coastal gun emplacements, meeting Moore at dawn, only to find that the defenders had fled during the night, this being 29 April.[5]

General Campbell now became so ill that he handed the command of the invasion to Moore, who saw it as the chance to prove himself with his first independent combat command. The anchorage was now safe and the fleet was able to anchor behind Ance du Gros Islet and put the rest of the troops ashore. Sir Ralph immediately rode inland with Moore to ascertain how best they might advance on the main fort on Morne Fortuné, which lay in the centre of a plain south of a range of hills separating it from their landing place. The decision was made that an attack across these jungle-clad hills was the least expected route, but would only meet with success were Moore to attack immediately, despite having passed 60 hours without sleep. Accordingly, he set out with 1,200 men, in two groups, marching behind Royalist French guides along jungle tracks in single file, with the intention of taking the 500 French picketed on the highest hill, Morne Chabot, by means of a silent bayonet charge under the full moon.

Unfortunately Moore's advance company ran into an enemy picket and were fired upon, losing the element of surprise. They were next halted by a strong wooden fence overgrown with bushes and thus unseen by scouting parties. The order was given to the troops to combine their strength and push it over, but the intertwined tropical vegetation was stronger than the fence. Next Moore gave the order to leap over the barrier, but the troops held back, stating it to be impossible, and that, even if not, a fusillade of fire surely awaited them on the other side, where the main road ran, bordered by a hedge. Imagining his career ended by these half-trained cowards, Moore himself leapt over the fence and was met only by the sound of the tree frogs. The men then found the will to vault the obstacle, being literally led from the front by their Commander.

However, as they crossed the road and advanced up the heights they were met by heavy and accurate volleys of fire from the black French defenders. The British were ordered to charge and rush the hill with the bayonet, while the defenders reloaded and sought to hit running targets, but they panicked and began to return the fire uphill, making perfect targets as they stopped to reload. The rear ranks also began to fire uphill, shooting into their forward comrades from the back. Moore ran about berating the men to charge before they were all shot down and at last one group swept up to the crest. The screams of the bayonetted defenders urged on the rest of the British, sheltering below, to follow like a pack of hounds. In minutes the hill was taken and all who had not run back to the fort were ruthlessly put to the bayonet. Moore damned his men as worthless soldiers and claimed that they would have been massacred by veteran troops. As it was, seventy British lay dead or dying as the penalty for not obeying orders.[6]

A drum signalled Hope's men from the lower ground and in the light of the breaking dawn another hilltop was revealed, Morne Chasseur, which was far closer to the fortress, being further south, but a three-mile struggle parallel to it through the jungle to the west was necessary. Leaving 500 men to guard the high ground just taken, the rest of the force struggled on to the closer hill before the enemy saw their plan and occupied it. The manoeuvre worked to perfection and Moore established a skirmishing line only 600 yards from the enemy's outer earthwork defences. Field guns were dragged to the heights and opened fire at 1200 yards, not capable of damaging the fort, but driving the defenders from their outer defences to the safety of the walls.

Sir Ralph now ordered a chain of posts to be set up to cut off the fortresses from the landward side, preventing supplies which still arrived from Guadeloupe from coming to the aid of the defenders or their escape to the jungle. So began a month of stalemate.

During this period two attacks of the British on outposts of the fort failed. The first was on three gun emplacements at the base of the hill on which stood the fortress. These contained heavy guns which menaced the all-weather anchorage of Cul de Sac Inlet. Three groups from different regiments set out simultaneously for their objective. The left- and right-hand advances carried the emplacements, driving out the defenders, but, unfortunately, the centre group, the Foreign Corps led by General Perryn, stopped to rest before crossing the river, "as the men were exhausted". The guns of this central battery were then brought round to fire on the captured emplacements to either side and, while Perryn's men rested, his momentarily victorious comrades were massacred. Such a gross error of judgement could not go unpunished and Perryn was sent back to England in disgrace.

The second attempt was to seize the battery on Vigie Point at the mouth of the inlet. Regrettably, however, the naval bombardment was inaccurate, but did succeed in setting fire to the Castries township behind the objective. Two thousand women and children rushed to the fortress for shelter and were let in, so halving the ability of the 2,000 black French defenders to hold out on the supplies they had.

Moore realized that the same situation now pertained as at Calvi in Corsica, namely that the guns on the heights could not breach the walls, but that, with control of the enemy's outer earthworks, a heavy siege battery must be brought up to make a breach at close range. Sir Ralph had wanted Moore to be brought along for his imaginative tactics and luckily was not a commander who resented his subordinate's genius. Orders were therefore given to cut a road and bring up 18-pounders, followed by 24-pounders, using sailors from the ships-of-the-line.

However, the black French soldiers were fighting for greater aims than their White Revolutionary counterparts in Corsica. As soon as the first set of heavy guns were in place and began to fire on a flèche, or arrow-shaped, defence outwork, the defenders swarmed out to spike and dismount the howitzers and mortars firing at them. Moore observed the movement and galloped down from the height to rally his men to drive back the French by a full bayonet charge, which succeeded. The date was 24 May and the rainy season had begun, so the road intended for the 24-pounders was rendered unusable. The defenders again sallied out to destroy the existing guns, only to meet the same line of charging bayonets, and were saved from total massacre by the cover of their own guns firing grape shot from the walls as they retired.

The flèche was now taken and its guns reversed to fire into the main citadel of the fortress. Such were the number of casualties from this bombardment and the failed charges that the next day the fort's Commander, General Cottin, previously a saddler from Guadeloupe, sued for terms of surrender. On being informed that his men would be treated as French prisoners of war, he accepted and they filed out to be taken off the island by waiting transports. Upon surrendering, he declared that they would have fought on hoping for relief from other French-held islands, but the civilian refugees had consumed the food and water and he was down to his last barrel of powder in the magazine.

On 1 June General Moore led his men into the fortress and raised the Union Flag. A ceremony then followed, whereby General Sir Ralph Abercromby proclaimed Brigadier-General Moore as Governor and Commandant of the island. Moore had tried every excuse to escape this appointment in order to follow the action to the other islands to be taken, for he loved fighting but loathed administrative paperwork and garrison duty. Sir Ralph would hear none of this, however, and declared Moore to be the only man at his disposal capable of subduing the remaining guerilla bands in the hinterland and administering the island at the same time.[7]

Again, his desire not to cause problems forced him to accept and he was left with a garrison of 5,000 men to subdue the whole island. The expenses allowed for his addition duties as Governor were 30 shillings and 6 pence a day. Luckily for Moore he had no family, for this and his army pay would be all he had with which to keep up appearances. However, as events turned out, he would spend almost all of his time there on military matters and not entertaining visiting dignitaries. In this manner he actually accumulated sufficient to pay all his debts, with funds left over.

CHAPTER EIGHT

Governor Moore

At this point some facts which have been left out of every previous biography of Moore must be made clear. Imperial security, doubtless, dictated that the one fact never made clear was that the defenders were 99% black ex-slaves, made French citizens, and not predominantly white French soldiers who had turned Republican. The fact that 2,000 black men had defied the world's then supreme power for a month of seige, outnumbered three to one, with 7,000 British in reserve, plus sailors and marines, was a fact to be kept from other subject races around the world. From an historian's viewpoint it was little enough to ask of his patriotism that he refer always to the 'French' defenders without further explanation. A real betrayal of the calling is, however, that they conveniently forget to include any mention of the fact that the British had previously reached this point of holding the fortress in 1794, only to be defeated in a massed battle in the southern hills by the then less trained ex-slave army; they were also driven out of Fort Charlotte, as they had renamed it, but allowed to sail away, instead of being massacred.

Luckily for the truth, Fortescue, in his *History of the British Army*[1], mentions this defeat, but his 7-volume 1915–20 work was hardly for the masses of the Empire. The facts are that, after the departure of the Royalist Governor in 1793, the population was composed of 18,500 black slaves, 2,200 white settlers and 1700 free mulatos. Discontent rumbled like the dormant volcano under the Soufrière Hills until the black population was unleashed in a wave of terror after the proclamation of the abolition of slavery in all colonies by the Assembly in Paris in February of 1794.

All whites who had not joined the revolutionary faction or fled were brutally massacred, along with their families, as they paid the price of 150 years of cruel slavery. Taking advantage of the confusion, the British sailed in three months later, under Admiral Jervis, and took over the main Morne Fortuné fortress and the capital of Castries, which they renamed Charlotteville. The commander of the British army expedition was none other than HRH Prince Edward, destined to become the grandfather of Queen Victoria. When it became clear, after several defeats, that, rather than holding the island from the fortress, the British were shut up inside it for protection, an expedition under Colonel Stuart landed directly at Ance de la Soufrière, close to the Republican army and their main base to the south of the island in the Soufrière Hills. After marching swiftly inland on the wide track, supposedly to rout the French Black Army in their stronghold of the Fort Vieux fortifications, the British army was amazed to find itself outmanoeuvred and finally routed at the massed battle of Rabot. Those who returned through the series of ambushes on the main road to the northern Fort Charlotte found the defenders dying of yellow fever; they thus fled directly to ships in Tapion Bay and away. Fort Charlotte was forced to ask for terms from the Republican Army. The force was organized by a mysterious General Victor Hughes from Guadeloupe, who, to save face, was made out to be white, but whose portrait clearly shows a man of mixed blood.[2] The French Governor Goyrand, magnanimous in victory, wisely allowed the few hundred remaining sick British, with their wives and children, to file unmolested from the fort to waiting transports. The organized and victorious defence shown by these freed slaves, contradicting the official history of only their initial brutality, was enough to keep these events out of British published accounts of the island's history and Moore biographies, even during the 1960s and 1970s, these being the decades of cries for full independence by the Caribbean island nations from a then swiftly failing Britain.

These facts were, of course, well known to Moore, but with the bulk of the trained black French army transported off the island, he imagined that his task would be less difficult than that given to his royal predecessor. The real decisive factor in the fighting for the islands was Yellow Fever, or 'Yellow Jack', and it will be worthwhile to understand the reasons for the selective nature of the virus before following Moore's attempt to subdue the rest of St Lucia and *L'Armée Francaise dans les Bois*.

Yellow Fever had always been endemic among the rodents and mammals of West Africa, being transmitted by the 'Egyptian' mosquito. With the first shipments of slaves came the virus, quickly followed by the mosquitoes riding with the ships. Over millennia the negroes of West Africa had developed a certain immunity to this liver-destroying virus; they could become sick, but mostly recovered. However, to the whites it was as deadly as the chickenpox virus proved to be when suddenly introduced to the aborigines of Australia. The infection of the liver cells produced the same yellowing of the skin as jaundice, hence the name Yellow Fever. In the jungle the infection was more virulent than in the towns, as it came, not somewhat attenuated by the immune system of other humans, but direct from mice or monkeys.[3]

On 3 June the fleet sailed off and Governor Moore, considering the troops that he had been left to command, wrote in his journal that "it is hard to say whether the officers or the men are worse".[4] Also "They had fought badly against half-trained men and must have been massacred by regular troops."[5] The only troops who had fought in a valiant and disciplined way had been the British blacks of the West Indian Regiment, admittedly acclimatized and immune to the jungle fevers. Indeed their founder and commander, Colonel Malcolm, had been killed leading his men in the last charge which drove back the enemy before the surrender of Fort Morne Fortuné.

Moore certainly felt betrayed by the bulk of the fleet disappearing without consulting him, merely informing him and hauling anchor. While the island was well enough protected by two ships-of-the-line and various frigates, it was the removal of the reserves of troops that caused him frustration. Confiding in his diary, he wrote that "The General and the Admiral have cleared themselves of all responsibility by running away from it . . . large detachments under proper officers ought to have been despatched to disarm the blacks [in the jungle]. A week, or ten days, would have probably done this . . . As it is the island is in a most precarious state."[6]

Moore posted companies of soldiers at strategic points all over the island and continually made surprise visits to them to maintain discipline and vigilance. He regretted that regulations entitled the men to half a pint of 'new rum' a day "for their health". The black population were, he found, not surprisingly, totally committed to the Republican cause and "no information could be obtained from them either by bribes, threats or even hangings".[7]

To add to his sense of injustice, on 8 July he heard that Admiral Christian and General Abercromby had been temporarily relieved and sent home to rest. He, on the contrary, who had made their victory possible, had been left with a seemingly impossible task as his reward.[8]

From the day that the fleet sailed it had rained heavily and incessantly. Fort Charlotte had no barracks and the men were placed in wigwam (sic) tents close to the marshy flats where the river discharged into Cul de Sac Inlet. Making no connection between the concentrations of mosquitoes and Yellow Fever, they naturally began to fall sick in large numbers. There was no hospital in which to isolate or tend the sick, for a hospital ship that had served for the invasion had sailed with the fleet, leaving nothing for Moore's troops.

Moore was appalled at the death rate among the men under his command, but, even so, he was contemptuous of them as soldiers.

He wrote in his diary that "The men are so infamous that they had to be forced to charge a party of brigands who were already half-beaten . . . The composition of the officers is horrid . . . I may lose my life and reputation without a possibility of doing good."[9]

He sent Sir Ralph an extremely frank letter to follow him to England, complaining that he had left him with an impossible task by sailing away as he had. Initially, Sir Ralph was annoyed by the letter and replied tartly to his protégé, stating that Moore "must be more patient, and that it was his duty to struggle with these difficulties, of which he wished to hear no more".[9]

However, within days he must have reflected on the harshness of this attitude, for he sent Moore reinforcements of 300 black troops of Druault's Corps to add to those of O'Mearer's Rangers.[10] A "kindly letter" was also received at the same time, so restoring Moore's flagging morale sufficiently for him to write a more optimistic appraisal of his position to his father. In his letter of 20 August 1796 he wrote that "Despite the general sickness being perfectly alarming, I have not had even a headache . . . I have not only the brigands to pursue, but the west coast to guard from succours which might be thrown in to them from small boats from Guadeloupe . . . The brigands have at least been humbled; many have returned to the plantations and above 300 have been killed. Whether I shall be able to establish tranquillity I know not . . . It is not this climate alone that kills troops, but bad management. A Roman legion would have undertaken constant exercises with sea and river bathing, and been healthy. I AM SURE THAT I AM RIGHT!"[11]

Moore continued in his thankless task, attempting to instil military zeal into officers content to let their men die from neglect as a means of being sent back to England and 'pressed' men who were content to surrender.[12]

Meanwhile, when attacked in one camp, the brigands mostly slipped away to another part of the island to plunder and burn, often awakened by an 'accidental' musket shot as the British troops closed in.[13]

Again he mentions that only the black corps fought like soldiers of the British army! The black corps were, therefore, sent to hunt down the brigands in the woods and the reluctant troops out from Britain used to guard the coast and plantations. In this way the numbers being carried off by Yellow Fever rapidly diminished, for they were away from the mosquitoes. The brick-built sugar processing buildings had remained undestroyed by fire and now served as barracks on every plantation.

Seeing the island so well covered by British troops, the plantation owners began to return and then to ill-treat the pacified slaves. However, they were swiftly reprimanded by Governor Moore, who held the island under martial law, making clear that the black population had equal protection under his rule, even if now returned to slave status. Had he not threatened the planters in this way, many slaves would have again been off to the woods to help the brigands. However, the fields were still mostly being worked by females and children. Moore grew to dislike the slave owners, who were the cause of the insurrection being particularly fierce on St Lucia. Conversely he began to have a soldier's respect for the tenacity of the brigands to fight on for freedom.

St Vincent had now been completely subdued, with the surrendering armed slaves being well treated. Hearing this, the brigand leader of St Lucia, La Croix, wrote to Moore to ask what terms he might expect if he too gave up his arms. The Governor replied that he and his men would be treated as any other captured French prisoners of war. La Croix stated that he needed eight days to confer and would then give his decision, but no word ever came and the skirmishes continued.[14]

In November Moore collapsed from fatigue and was taken off to the cooler air of the Soufrière Hills to rest, but in a few weeks he was fully recovered, except for a hyper-sensitivity to sunlight.

On 18 January he wrote to his father to tell of a day which he had spent with General Sir Ralph Abercromby, who had returned to Martinique. A sloop had been sent to pick him up, to allow him to report directly to his Commander on the state of affairs in

St Lucia. Moore tells his father that, during this interview, Sir Ralph had stated that "It was just to relieve me after so long a spell in St Lucia but he was at a loss, if I left it, as to who to send in my place . . . Regardless, he offered to try to give me the Governorship of Grenada . . . or that an new post, permanent even in peacetime, of Quartermaster General of the West Indies Army, was his to offer at once . . . I declined, stating that I had no wish to remain in the West Indies . . . My wish was to be employed in actions and I would stay employed in St Lucia if, on the occasion of his being sent into action, he would promise to take me with him . . . He said he certainly should employ me and was much obliged by my offering to return to St Lucia . . . He also stated that he had spoken of me often to the Duke of York in favourable terms."

The letter continued by mentioning that of the original 5,000 British troops 3,000 were dead of Yellow Fever and only the black corps could fight the brigands in the woods. Moore ended on this pessimistic note: "Be prepared to hear that the island is wrested from us. I wish I was quit of it."[15]

Moore wrote again on 12 February 1797 to complain to his father that Sir Ralph had indeed sailed off to new action against the Spanish in Trinidad, but "had left him regretfully behind as he was irreplaceable". Moore felt deceived and depressed by this turn of events.[16] He continued, regardless, to hunt the brigands as before, in a war of relentless attrition.

In May of that year he wrote to tell his father that his health had broken, that he was down with some form of fever, but not Yellow Jack, and a huge abscess was forming on his right hip. In fact he was in much worse condition than he confessed to in this letter and a frigate was sent to evacuate him immediately to Martinique on the direct orders of Sir Ralph. His life was doubtless saved by this act, for he was so moribund after the lancing of the abscess that he was carried on board on a stretcher. A ship was quickly found to return him to England via St Kitts and during the voyage the cool, invigorating sea air, combined with his own superb physical condition and treatment with Peruvian bark, or quinine (suggesting malaria), saw him completely restored to health. On 9 July he arrived at Falmouth accompanied by his friend Major Anderson and by the 14th was reunited with his family in London.

Unfortunately, as soon as he stepped on to home soil he lost his brevet rank of Brigadier General and reverted to his previous peacetime rank of Colonel.

One more service was required of him in reference to St Lucia. The Duke of York asked for a frank private appraisal from the forthright Scotsman as to the true viability of continuing to hold the island, now that so many others were under British control. Moore stated that he would recommend the continuance of controlling it for the one reason that it had the only hurricane-proof harbour in all the Windward Islands, in the form of Cul de Sac Inlet, where an entire fleet could be safe.

Meanwhile, in St Lucia Colonel Drummond of the 43rd had taken command, continuing with Moore's tactics unchanged. In November the guerilla bands under La Croix surrendered, on the condition that they were not returned to slavery, but rather sent to Africa. Unfortunately, they knew nothing of how to survive in that continent. Thus, in one of the great ironies of history, their fighting skills were recognized by an offer to indeed go to West Africa, but only by volunteering to join the same West Indian Regiment which had hunted them down, which was now fighting there. In this way the problem of what to do with them was solved, with the honour of both sides satisfied. The island settled down to rebuilding its agricultural economy, but with the aid of a black population of only 10,000 as opposed to the 18,000 before the start of the French Revolution.[17]

CHAPTER NINE

Ireland

At the time of the court martial of Wolfe Tone Moore expressed himself at a loss to understand the true motives behind an Irishman's political thinking. The reason was that Tone was the founder of the United Irishmen, who had fomented the rebellion that Moore was there to suppress, while its members were both Catholic Irish and members of the fanatically Protestant Orange Order. Though hating each other, they appeared to resent even more the British Government which stood between them.

Before examining the actions in which Moore was involved while trying to carry out his instructions to restore order and fight off a French invasion, it will be well to examine the broader issues of Irish and Anglo-Saxon historical interaction.[1]

From the time of the Celtic expansion during the 3rd century BC to the Christian conversion of the 3rd century AD the Irish had developed their own culture, unspoilt by Roman invasion. The only foreigners who had managed to get a foothold were the Vikings, but not before the 9th century AD.

The Irish Christian Church had, therefore, developed on its own and did not concede authority to the Pope. To redress this anomaly, Pope Adrian IV issued a Bull in 1155 giving Ireland to the English King Henry II as an inheritance on the condition that he conquered the island and established Papal orthodoxy and authority. Once this could be achieved, the Irish Earls and Bishops would hold title to their lands from the Pope, under English civil and ecclesiastical administration.

No national administration existed in Ireland, where the great Earls ruled their lands independently, while acknowledging one among them as High King. Centuries of civil war had taken place between the Kings of Ulster and those of Connaught as to whom should hold this title, the rivalry between that province and the rest of the island being well established before the coming of the English.

After a struggle of 150 years the Earls finally tired of constant warfare against English invasions and in 1310 called a parliament which accepted the English monarch as their King and their church dogma as that of Rome. As a result they retained their lands and titles, but under Norman Feudal law. The parliament so assembled continued until 1800. However, at each attempt at insurrection, the Irish nobles involved had their lands confiscated by the English King and placed in the hands of Englishmen whom he wished to reward.

Revolt and reclamation were always followed by English expeditions, which retook the lands, and more, as punishment. Always the English held on to their stronghold of Dublin and its hinterland, which was known as the Pale. The Irish parliament was called in 1541 and again voted to make lasting peace by giving the right of kingship to Henry VIII, as he had broken with Rome and their land would thus no longer be a Papal vassal. The Earls and the Irish Catholic Church were left alone to run the country by Henry so long as they paid their taxes and sent him soldiers when he needed them.

The problems caused by the Spanish claim to the English throne, backed by the excommunication of Queen Elizabeth, changed such religious leniency. After a revolt backed by a Spanish invasion of Ireland, the Queen ruthlessly crushed both, with a vast seizure of estates. Moreover, she introduced the Supremacy Laws, whereby all Catholics were barred from public office.

Under James I the Puritan English parliament began to agitate for a sole Protestant Church of Ireland and the remaining Gaelic

61

Catholic Earls once more rebelled. Their defeat resulted in their fleeing the land in 1607, and again their lands reverted to the crown. These lands were settled as plantations by Scottish Protestants and Dissenters, predominantly in Ulster. However, elsewhere the Irish could also rent land from the King, but, whilst they remained Catholic, at twice the rent of the settlers. A review of the law in 1609 then found that no Irishman could own land freehold, but as tenants at will, for all the country was the King's property from the Papal inheritance of 1155. Even the smallest farmers had, therefore, to pay rent. Moreover, Catholics could not set up denominational schools. However, the persistence of the Druidic oral tradition for the passing on of the ancient sagas and lists of historic injustices kept the illiterate peasantry vastly more aware of their identity than their British counterparts.

To add to the total deprivation of rights of the Catholic Irish, both native or from earlier English immigration, the parliamentary borough boundaries were changed to assure a Protestant majority in the Irish parliament. At every opportunity the Crown continued to give Irish titles and land to Englishmen.

Charles I, with his Catholic tendencies, raised men and money for his war with Cromwell by giving religious concessions to the Irish Catholics. A civil war thus broke out in Ireland, but for different causes to that in England. Cromwell retook the country and punished the rebel Catholics by taking ten counties to give as farms to reward his army. He was also far more ruthless than in his English battles. Were a town not to surrender, he killed all the rebel population upon taking it; in Wexford and Drogheda alone he slaughtered 10,000 people.

The restoration saw some redress for those who had helped the father of King Charles II. After this process, however, the Irish held only one third of the land, and that mostly mountainous.

James II restored some Catholic interests, but for that he was sent into exile in 1688 and William of Orange became King. The Irish rebellion which followed was defeated once more and all that

James had given was rescinded by parliament, together with the seizure of 750,000 more acres from the Catholic aristocracy who fled to France. Now only 13% of the country was in Irish hands.

The cautionary lesson that repression cannot work for ever was taught to the British by the loss of America, and to calm Ireland the most repressive laws against Catholics were rescinded. In 1782 internal independence was given to the Irish Parliament. However, as all Ministers were appointed by the King, who had also the veto of all acts passed, it was only a gesture; the overwhelming majority of members were still Protestant.

In 1793 Mr Pitt, the British First Minister, passed an act giving the vote to all eligible Catholics. Amazingly, the King's Lord Lieutenant, or Viceroy, refused to implement it. The United Society of Irishmen was, therefore, forced into being with Tone as its leader. The Viceroy had, in effect, usurped power and they saw it as their right to seek the aid of France to restore civil government by the forming of an Irish Republic.

Into this cauldron of simmering ancient injustice, disobedience, and incipient civil war, coupled with threat of invasion, Colonel John Moore was sent. He landed at Dublin on 2 November 1797.

The War Office figures show 76,000 troops at its disposal at that time in Ireland, of which 20,000 were cavalry.[2] The militia regiments were considered to be of dubious loyalty, for the men were all Catholic, whilst their officers were Protestant; the dislike was mutual. The result was that the army was in a complete state of unreadiness and corruption.[3]

Moore recorded in his journal that he intensely disliked the brutal repression that descended upon the population at the merest hint of any uprising. Calm might be seen on the surface afterwards, but the disaffection of the subjugated people greatly increased. He wrote that he could only see a solution to the corruption, intrigue and manipulation at all levels by the appointment of a temporary dictator, brought from the outside for objectivity.

The Irish peasantry were, in his view, treated more harshly than the slaves whom he had returned to their owners in St Lucia. There his marshal law upheld the rights of both slave and master, and tranquillity had returned. In Ireland the peasants were subject to arbitrary justice by landowners and conniving magistrates, being deported or hung for sedition on the merest hint of evidence. A firm line was seen to be drawn between the application of the law for the 800,000 Protestants of the ruling class and the 3,000,0000 Irish whom they controlled.[4]

In response to Tone's promise of a vast insurrection, the first French invasion attempt was made on 10 December 1796, when a fleet left Brest transporting 15,000 veteran French troops and arms for the rebels. Had it arrived it would have posed a formidable threat once the rebels were armed. Unfortunately, the concept of sailing past the British scout frigates in the foul weather of midwinter worked only too well, but with the consequence that the French fleet was dispersed in a storm. Of the eighteen ships-of-line and thirteen frigates, only a few reached their destination of Bantry Bay at the southern tip of Ireland. Only the commander of the expeditionary force, Hoche, knew the secret orders after disembarkation. Therefore, after waiting several days, and being repulsed on the beach by the militia, the ships sailed back to Brest. Had the full landing been successful, as planned, only 6,000 troops could have been sent against it, for they were dispersed about the country maintaining order.[5]

The main effect of this failed invasion was to show the Irish rebel factions that the French were serious in their promise to send aid. The same realization shook the British government into an attempt to be prepared, should they come again.

The next attempt, however, came from French-controlled Holland, in October 1797, when a Dutch fleet set out from Texel. Admiral Duncan immediately set out and intercepted them at Camperdown, shattering half their number and capturing the rest as prizes.[6]

Moore was now assigned the important command of the forts

protecting Cork Harbour, Kinsale and Middleton under the Commander of the Southern Section, Lieutenant General James Stewart.[7]

Once he had put these defences into order, Moore was given the district of Bandon to command, which lay inland to the west of Cork. Here he first put the question of his men's loyalty to him in order by investigating one regiment's complaint that their pay was, in part, being kept by their Colonel. Moore investigated the matter according to King's Regulations and, when it was proved beyond all doubt to be so, he had that officer arrested for court martial. The Colonel happened to be Lord Westmeath, who imagined himself beyond investigation, but Moore added to his list of enemies in high places by this action.

To the men he was now a hero and they complied with his desire for lenient treatment of the people of the coast whom he was sent to disarm. A simple method was used: the villages which gave up guns and pikes in believable quantities were paid for the soldiers' rations, those who denied possessing weapons had the soldiers quartered in their houses until the weapons were found. In this just fashion 400 firearms and 800 pikes were collected without violence. When he arrived he had been informed that the Catholic troops would likely join the population and fight with the French, but by such fair but strict treatment at all levels he was now confident that both were on his side, except at Westmeath.[8]

Sir Ralph Abercromby now toured the country as the new Commander-in-Chief and drew up a report for the Minister. In this he stated that the army was subject to every abuse and licentiousness, also that they were subversive of all discipline, which rendered them formidable to all but the enemy.[9]

He sent corrective orders to the Colonels of the deliquent regiments, which, as they were all members of the aristocracy, they took as a collective insult to the army and used their influence to form a cabal for Sir Ralph's removal. The rebellious elements rejoiced, claiming that the reason for the unrest was the abuses laid upon them by the army, as they had always claimed. When the newspapers took up the issue, Sir Ralph resigned in protest at his treatment for merely telling the truth. The Viceroy did, however, issue a decree that civilians could no longer be court martialled, but must be tried before magistrates. Summary executions at the will of the landowners were thus reduced as a result of Sir Ralph's report.

Despite being warned by Sir Ralph against such a move for the sake of his career, Moore also sent in a letter of resignation to London. The reason given was that his lenient nature would not allow him to participate in the brutal repressions now being planned, nor could he fight off an invasion when no plans existed to do so.

Whether his letter arrived is not known, for the country around Dublin suddenly exploded in an insurrection, cutting the post. The insurgents had been accumulating muskets and pikes from France and overwhelmed the small garrisons, but not the city itself. The countryside was ravaged, with all the great houses of their oppressors burnt and entire families murdered, even young children. Ten days were required for the army to regain control of the area, and then mostly because the rebels, accompanied by several captured field guns, marched on to take New Ross, up river from Waterford Harbour.[10]

Here they were repulsed, with the loss of 2,000 men, but then attacked Arklow with no better result. The harbour and town of Wexford were not heavily garrisoned, as they were considered loyal, and the rebels took the town, harbour and nearby Enniscorthy, controlling all the country between. Here they took up a defensive position and set up a training camp on Vinegar Hill, hoping for help to come quickly from France.[11] The force was a maximum of 6,000 men, with a good number of muskets, and all armed with long pikes to counter cavalry. The strongpoint upon which they intended to make a stand was Carrickburn Mountain.

Additional revolts broke out in various other places and Moore's Corps of 1,000 men was given no less than three orders of march until the final one put them on the road to Taghmon, 7 miles from Wexford. The troops had been marching for seven days and now were suddenly confronted by a huge mass of rebels, between 5 to 6 thousand men, all armed with a firearm or a pike. The bulk of Moore's militia had never been in battle before and should have been joined earlier by two regiments of patriotic English volunteers, who appeared after the battle.

The battle was a short, sharp business and victory over the rebel mass was only achieved by Moore and Anderson constantly exposing themselves by riding from one weak spot to another, so maintaining their men in disciplined formations. The two field guns decided the day and Moore admitted that, outnumbered as they were, it was discipline, and the fact that they had more powder and ball than the rebels, that saved them from annihilation.

Moore was now approached by a rebel delegation from Wexford, where the rebels held important hostages who they claimed would be spared if the army would withdraw. Moore, quite rightly, replied that he had no authority to make any treaties with the rebels, but immediately abandoned his orders to march to Taghmon and sped to the relief of Wexford.[12]

With the advance of his now enlarged column towards the town, rebels were seen running out of the place that they had terrorized for twenty-two days. Smoke began to appear from several houses and Moore sent in 200 men to free the hostages and quench the fires. In this they were successful, but regrettably almost 100 hostages had been killed on the bridge and thrown naked into the river. Hundreds more were, however, freed in a state of euphoria, for they had been told they would all be dead by the evening. Moore was cheered through the streets as the "saviour of Wexford".[13]

Meanwhile the main body of the army, under General Lake, had swept through the rebel camp on Vinegar Hill. They left behind them a carpet of dead, whilst the survivors dispersed into the hills. The army now assembled at Wexford, the leaders of the insurgents were court-martialled and hung from the same bridge as their hostage victims. The principal men to be executed were 'General Roche', a Catholic priest and the 'Governor of free Wexford', Keogh. Among the general mass of rebels, those who handed in their arms were given a written free pardon and sent home. Unfortunately, many were nevertheless hung or shot by their landlords' men, despite Moore proclaiming that he would retaliate against them by legal process, for they were and always had been the cause of unrest.[14] The remainder dispersed to reassemble in the Wicklow Mountains, 50 miles to the north, still hoping for French assistance to arrive.

On 7 July Moore wrote to his father to tell him that he had been promoted to Major General and been given the hard task of closing the passes and then to flush out the rebel bands. Marquess Cornwallis had now been made both Viceroy and Commander-in-Chief, the beneficent, incorruptible temporary dictator whom Moore had long seen as the only solution for the country. Troops were now ordered to protect repentant rebels from reprisals, so that the rebellion did not reignite.[15]

When the remaining rebels had been captured, Moore wrote to his father from Dublin to explain how he had achieved this.[16] To move as quickly as the rebels, the British abandoned all but their vital equipment and slept on the ground in heavy rain. Moore wrote that, with his rank, he could have avoided this discomfort by commandeering any house, but preferred to encourage his men by sharing their hardships. After three weeks of this strain, he went down with a combination of fatigue and fever brought on by perpetually sodden clothes. Help was, for once, given to him in the form of five regiments of veteran British troops, including Lord Huntly's Highlanders, who could run over the mountains almost without effort and fight immediately upon arrival.

Moore was given total command of this force, responsible only to Cornwallis, and within three weeks had forced 1,200 rebels to hand in their weapons. When the last 500 diehards of the insurrectionist force were cornered in the Glen of Imall, Moore urged his commander to permit a show of leniency. The surrounded men were offered an honourable surrender with written free pardons instead of the massacre they expected; this they accepted. In this manner, with additional strict prevention of the plundering of the population by the troops, apparent calm was restored. Moore went to Dublin imagining that he would now be sent for reassignment to London.[17]

However, assured that the Irish would rise again were the French to land, the latter belatedly sent the promised new invasion fleet in September. While it was much smaller than the initial attempt which had been swept aside by the weather, this fleet did actually get as far as anchoring in Donegal Bay. It was immediately engaged by a British squadron, which captured the single line-of-battle ship, the *Hoche* and three frigates. The remaining five frigates escaped back to Brest. The greatest victory, from the British perspective, was to find Wolfe Tone, the founder and leader of the United Irishmen, aboard the *Hoche*.

Though he was dressed in French uniform, with papers proving him a long-term French citizen, he was tried by court martial and sentenced to be hung. Preferring not to await such a public disgrace, he attempted to cut his throat, but merely severed his windpipe. Meanwhile, a writ of habeas corpus had arrived from the King's Bench, where the right of the army to court martial a civilian had been successfully challenged. Unfortunately for Tone, son of a coachbuilder but educated to be a lawyer, his lack of faith in any justice for him in Ireland had sealed his fate, for he died of his self-inflicted wound a day later.

Moore called on the Viceroy on the 17th of that same month, only to find him making notes from a huge wall map of the country. To the amazement of all, the French had sent another fleet to the same spot as their recent defeat and were successfully landing troops in the safe and defendable harbour of Kilalla Bay at the southern entrance to Donegal Bay. Indeed, they must have sailed at the same time, but arrived unnoticed, hidden in the square inlet, running well inland, but at no great width. Beginning on 24 August, they had been unloading unreported and were now as far inland as Ballina, advancing south down the Moy River, with the people rising in great numbers to pick up the arms which the French gave out, enough for 50,000 men.

An army was ordered to assemble at Athlone, in the centre of the country, to await the moment when its numbers were so superior to the invaders and rebels that success would be virtually certain. Meanwhile, the French advance was kept under close scrutiny, but left alone.

Accidentally, this served the British interest very well, for finding that, after losing what must be supposed to have been the other half of the invasion force to the British navy, the French veterans numbered no more than 1,100 men, led by a mulatto General. The Irish, who had swelled their ranks to 20,000, given time to think, did not have much faith in this number to lead them to victory against a full British army and they gradually began to drift away, leaving only 5,000 diehards to march onwards.

Unfortunately, General Hutchinson did not obey his orders and marched at the invasion column with three militia regiments. The French took them by surprise and the militiamen either ran away or joined the French upon surrendering, supplying them with nine field guns and ample munitions.

Next to be defeated was General Lake, first at Castlebar and then again, once regrouped, at Hollymount in Connaught. The rebels began to take heart and grow again in number. Athlone could not be defended owing to the topography and the British line regiments marched forward to make a defensive position at Ballinasloe on the Suck River. Once this was achieved, they and Dublin were safe, but they had to admit that they had no idea of where the Invasion column actually was. When Lord Cornwallis arrived, he informed Moore that his last information was that they had fortified Castlebar for defence and were busily training their Irish recruits.

Based on this information, the Viceroy gave Moore the honour of placing him in command of the best regiments to form an Advance Corps and cautiously move towards the enemy. Three further columns would follow on with triple the number of troops in reserve. Camped near Castlebar, Moore was astonished to have his brother James, the military surgeon, join him. He had heard that John was down with a fever and had travelled for three days to find him in order to act as his personal physician. Moore protested perfect health, but a surgeon could never be superfluous before a battle.

The reserve columns arrived at Hollymount on 3 October, totalling 10,000 experienced troops, and it was planned that Moore should storm the town of Castlebar the next day, with the Gordon Highlanders attacking in the first wave of assault. At dawn word came that the French had marched away to Swinford to the east, but their purpose in so doing was unknown. However, their destination was assumed to be the port of Sligo, for this was the only objective of value in that direction. For three days Moore's column marched around the countryside, trying to position themselves to advantage according to the reports of their scouts. Decisive contact was made at Collonney, but only in the unfortunate manner of the invaders cutting down 300 of the Limerick Militia, who had advanced without orders.[18]

Risings were reported at Longford and Westmeath, but inexplicably the French did not make for this area to gather strength. Rather, they headed into Sligo County, which was known as staunch Orangemen's territory. The result of this was that they suddenly found that their Irish recruits had melted away, knowing they were in hostile country.

General Lake had his revenge for his humiliation at Castlebar, for, after only a partial engagement with the French rear near to the bridge of Ballintra, they surrendered at a hamlet named Balinamuck in the direction of Sligo. However, rumours of a fleet containing reinforcements having sailed from Brest kept Moore in place.[19]

Moore had been confident that Nelson's victory at the Battle of the Nile would have made the enemy seek to conserve its ships and give up these Irish adventures. However, the harbour and inlet where the defeated force had landed were still in French hands, so a real danger existed. Two ships, and then six more, appeared suddenly in Donegal Bay on 20 October, with up to 7,000 reinforcements and stores, but the British navy was waiting for such an eventuality and they were attacked and dispersed. Captain Graham Moore with the *Melampus* was the hero of the battle when he engaged two enemy frigates of superior force and captured the one whilst driving off the other.[20] The Moores had at last fulfilled the hope expressed in John's childhood letter to his midshipman brother, "I hope that in some years after this you and I will thrash the 'Monsieurs' both by land and by sea."[21] The brothers later had the chance to congratulate each other during a brief meeting on Wexford Quay.

The last alarm was when a report came of yet another large fleet leaving Brest, but soon after it was observed to be heading for the Mediterranean.

A beneficial side effect of these continued invasions was to make patriotic young Britons flock to the recruiting centres to volunteer against the strong possibility of an invasion of their motherland. Each was worth three of the scum coshed and tricked into joining. The size and quality of the army increased dramatically.

Again, as in St Lucia, Moore's success was the cause of his being selected as the most competent man to continue the pacification of Ireland. While General Stewart sailed off to retake Minorca, with rumours of action in Italy, Moore was bitterly disappointed to be left in the rain and mist of garrison duty at Athlone. The winter of 1799 dragged by and the depth of his despondency may be judged by the fact that he made no entries in his journal for a full six months.

Meanwhile, the King had refused to sign the Union Bill which Pitt had steered through first the Irish parliament and then the

British. The King objected to the clauses for Catholic emancipation, which he claimed were contrary to his coronation oath of a Protestant parliament. These clauses, which had assured Irish support and would have totally calmed the country were struck out. Pitt resigned on principle and the King signed.

Union between Britain and Ireland occurred, but with the Irish once more seemingly tricked out of their rights as full citizens. Pitt, upon resigning, stated that "the omission of these clauses will cause conflict for generations to come". He was rarely known to be wrong.

In Athlone Moore was suddenly animated by the arrival of an order to report to Dublin, there to receive details of a secret mission that the Minister of War wished him to carry out. The journal entries were immediately resumed.

CHAPTER TEN

Holland

The 'secret expedition' is often considered to have been a farce, beginning with the fact that it was reported in the newspapers, the giveaway being a grand parade of the army at Lord Romsey's Kent estate. The review was taken by the King and the Royal Princes, accompanied by the exiled Prince of Orange and his father, standing next to the Duke of York, now Commander-in-Chief of the army. The symbolism so implied could not have been more clear. However, the part that was secret, initially, was not the planned invasion of Holland, but the fact that a treaty was in preparation with the Czar of Russia to send troops to assist, with Britain to pay the costs. Moreover, the objectives of the invasion were indeed kept secret, for they expanded according to the degree of success of each phase.

The prime objective was the destruction, or better still the capture, of the remaining Dutch fleet, which was under French control as the occupying power. Should this be accomplished, a march to liberate Amsterdam was to follow, with the landing of adequate reinforcements. Once Amsterdam was in allied hands, the Prussians had secretly agreed to issue an ultimatum to France to withdraw from the country or face a Prussian invasion from the east.

The timing was correct, for Napoleon was still trapped in Egypt and the Austro-Russian forces had driven the French out of all Italy, apart from Genoa. The other argument was to land these same British troops to take Genoa from the coast, so finishing the business in Italy rather than opening a second front. Hindsight shows that this would indeed have been the best course of action by far, but hindsight makes geniuses of all historians!

Initially, the command was to be entirely in the proven hands of Sir Ralph Abercromby, who immediately requested the transfer of Moore. Sir Ralph was so myopic that it was said of him that he could not distinguish a man from a tree. However, through a graduated telescope he could see perfectly and was a decisive tactician. He needed Moore's fearless ability to ride through a battle to execute these tactics and inspire the men. Once the treaty was signed with Russia, pressure was applied to give the nominal command to the newly appointed Commander-in-Chief, the Duke of York, as a chance for glory. He knew little of the business of soldiering, apart from parades, so it was decided by Pitt and Dundas to comply with the King's wish, but to prevent disaster by placing the issuing of strategic commands in the hands of the council of war and leaving the separate command of the left wing of the army to Sir Ralph. Thus the expedition was doomed from the very start, for never in recorded history has a battle been won with orders issued by a far-off committee.

In August 1799 Moore was promoted Major General and given command of five regiments under Sir Ralph. Moore considered only the 92nd Highlanders and the Royals as being worthy troops; the line regiments which accompanied them he graded from weak to unfit for service. Regardless, to be under Sir Ralph's command could not have pleased him more.

On 8 August the troops, and as many of their wives as could be embarked to care for them, began to board the slow transports at Ramsgate. The officer corps would join them later as they neared the operational area. With the troops set sail, Moore was given the honour of an invitation to dine privately with Mr Pitt and Mr Dundas, Secretary of War, at Walmer Castle on 11 August. The whole plan of the invasion was revealed to him and also the number of troops to be initially employed, these being 17,000 British aided by an equal number of Russians. Mr Pitt was confident that the Dutch would side with the British and view them as liberators, for his spy system had assured him that they were disaffected by French occupation. It was obvious that, should Moore survive this campaign, he was being probed in depth at a personal level, the better to assess his aptitude for greater command responsibilities in the future; he had been taken notice of at last.[1]

Once the staff officers joined the invasion fleet it became obvious to Sir Ralph that his plans to land on islands to the south of the Dutch fleet's fortified base of Texel and the Helder were impossible, owing to the continuous high seas. Exchanging the advantages of an unopposed landing for the lack of a long march to the objective, Sir Ralph now decided to land directly beside the Texel naval base and make up by audaciousness what was lost by surprise. Indeed, any element of surprise was now lost, for the invasion fleet had been cruising off the coast for a full week, waiting for the storms to blow themselves out.[2]

Amazingly the British landing, which was all confusion, was merely observed, but unopposed, by the Dutch garrison at the Helder fortifications. Mr Pitt's confidence that the Dutch would desert the French seemed to be borne out by this lack of opposition. However, it was merely that the Dutch knew the problems of fighting in the sand dunes and allowed the British to march out into the open plain towards the forts before attacking with cavalry and artillery. A "hot action" ensued, with 450 British casualties. The position was regarded as so precarious, owing to the Dutch resisting vigorously, that it was decided to gamble all on a night attack on the forts and, should this fail, to re-embark the troops next day.

The advancing columns of British were astonished to see the defenders of these strongly built forts marching away in retreat as they neared. The next day a greater surprise elated them when news came that the sturdy Dutch fleet, which they had seen sail away as they took possession of the protecting batteries, had surrendered to the Royal Navy without a shot being fired. The huge magazines of the Helder were quickly destroyed and Moore was given command of the garrison of the forts. The first objective of the expedition had been very easily achieved. All now hinged upon the attitude of the Dutch people and troops as the invaders marched inland against their capital.

Proclamations of the fact that the Anglo-Russian force had come as liberators and not as conquers were nailed up and given out as handbills, but the Dutch were apathetic. It appeared they were content with the reality of Republican freedom that came from the French; they certainly showed no wish to risk themselves for the restoration of the House of Orange. The invaders, therefore, found themselves facing 8,000 Dutch troops strung out along the coast and a French garrison at Alkmaar of 5,000. If the Dutch were not about to turn their weapons on the French, they had shown little interest in defending the country after the first battle. The invaders were 35,000 strong against 13,000 defenders and, therefore, in theory they were quite able to march on inland to Amsterdam. That they did not was for the most mundane of reasons – they had not brought either the special wagons to transport the heavier guns or normal ones to carry food and munitions, much less the horses to pull them. The local peasantry had loaded their wagons and moved inland, taking their livestock. When Marlborough had marched from Holland to Blenheim a century earlier, wagons, and even depots of replacement boots, had been planned meticulously ahead, but this time the expedition was organized by a committee.

The enemy showed no inclination to attack, until more ships arrived on 9 September with the Duke of York and his ten thousand men of nursery rhyme fame. The defenders then attacked along the entire front. The British, being in defensive positions, easily threw them off, killing a great many. In Moore's section alone he counted some 2,000 French dead. British infantry and field artillery had stayed behind the rim of the dyke of the Zype Sluys canal and let the enemy come on in formation until, at the last moment, they rose up and decimated the French ranks with musket balls and grape shot.

In this action Moore had his finger broken by a musket ball, which then glanced off his heavy brass telescope, so avoiding passing into his chest. Of necessity, his letters were for a time written for him by Anderson and the diary entries stopped. In one such letter he wrote to his father on 18 September, reporting that "The reinforcements have landed and the Duke of York accompanies them . . . The grand push will probably be made in a day or two . . . it is doubted that we will meet with much resistance until we reach Amsterdam." How wrong, for once, he was proved to be.[3]

The advance began on the 19th with 40,000 men, but the advance of the right wing, composed entirely of Russians, was completely routed by the French outflanking them, cutting them off before they could organize a stand, some four miles north of Alkmaar, at Bergen. Two Russian Generals surrendered and all the guns were taken, along with 3,000 Russian troops and 1,500 British.[4] The French breakthrough was halted by the advance of two Guards regiments, who in turn took 3,000 Dutch prisoners.[5]

In a letter to his mother on the 28th Moore explains that "The canals and dykes were more frequent here than hedges in England . . . This prevented the movement of British troops on the left coming to the assistance of the Russians. The British movement had, however, successfully turned and encircled the enemy's right wing, and taken the village of Hoorne . . . All movement, especially artillery, must be on the raised roads, and was thus obvious to the enemy well in advance."[6]

At this point his hand became usable once more and the journal entries began again, with this pessimistic note: "The natural strength of this country [for defence] is such that, without a general uprising of the people, it is in vain to hope to conquer it."[7]

On 2 October, after waiting for two days for torrential rain to stop, Sir Ralph's right wing and the Duke of York's left wing were given the task of retaking the ground previously lost by the Russians. Hopefully, the Russians were to hold the centre. Moore was delighted when General Abercromby gave him the honour of leading the vanguard along the shore, a column of 10,000 men with adequate artillery. Initially he was successful and the French lost some 2,200 men to large bayonet charges. However, they retreated inland, razing bridges and cutting other avenues of attack. Meanwhile, they had quietly brought up whole battalions of reserves and deployed them gradually, first to hold and then push back the British advance at Egmont.

During this engagement in the 4-mile-wide sand-dunes, Moore was shot through the thigh. He then had his mount killed, but pushed on with his men for a further five hours. While he was limping along, still advancing, the Duke of York had been advised to leave the fighting, as the risk of his capture was too great. The British troops were disheartened to see their Commander leaving the field and, at this moment, a massive French counter-attack threw them into a disordered retreat. Moore was so far forward that he and his men were almost cut off, but fought their way back to the main retreat. Moore made a perfect target in his General's uniform and bullets flew about him like bees, until one fired at close range hit him in the face. James, his brother, confirms in his account of Moore's later treatment that the ball entered below the eye and exited behind the ear and not the reverse, as has been commonly stated, so proving that he retreated still facing the enemy. On foot he was not the near impossible weaving target that he had so often presented to the enemy and the fact that the ball passed clear through, touching no bone, was a near miracle. Moore fell to the ground, however, stunned by the impact. Believing that one side of his head had been blown clean off, he lay contemplating that dying was not so difficult after all.[8] It was now that the kind treatment of his men was repaid, for two infantrymen recognized him and pulled him to his feet, making him regain consciousness. They then supported him as he staggered off the field. A horse was found and he was led ten miles to the rear for treatment of his wounds.[9]

The Russians had again failed to take their objective of Bergen and the 92nd Highlanders were sent in to stop the French advance. The Duke of York's column now won the battle by rallying and advancing to take the day's objectives of Bergen and Alkmaar.[10]

Upon hearing of the serious nature of Moore's head wound, the Duke of York immediately sent his personal physician to attend him. On 3 October the Duke asked his military secretary, Brownrigg, to write to Moore's father to reassure him that his son would live and that "His conduct in the serious action of the 2nd has raised him, if possible, higher than he stood before in the estimation of the army. Everyone admires and loves him, and you may boast of having as your son the most amiable and best General in the British service; this is a universal opinion."

Sir Ralph Abercromby also wrote: "The General is a hero . . . he is an ornament to his family, and to his profession."[11]

Moore himself now almost upset the million to one chance of a ball traversing his head, missing both bone and vital tissue, but now at odds of only two to one. In his naturally confused state, after such major trauma, he awoke and reached out for a beaker of whey on the bedside table, only to pick up, and swallow at one draught, the beaker of salts of lead used to dress his wounds. Immediately the burning sensation told him of his error and he calmly called to Anderson to pass him a quill pen to thrust down his throat to assist in vomiting up this deadly draught. Further instructions were given to bring water and olive oil, to wash out and then soothe his inflamed stomach lining.[12]

Once evacuated to London and placed in the care of his surgeon brother James, he made a swift recovery and was up and walking within five weeks. In mid-November he was able to join his parents at their country home at Richmond.

The whole area of Alkmaar was cleared of French troops by General Abercromby's column some days after the battle of the 2nd, but here the advance ended in stalemate. The British held a strong defensive line based on the Zype Dyke and from there, first an armistice, followed by a capitulation, was negotiated, there being rations for only two days and no money, as the war chest with 142,000 gold sovereigns had been lost in a shipwreck.

The British forces were allowed to evacuate in exchange for 8,000 French and Dutch prisoners held in England. The Dutch fleet was left in British hands, but, more importantly, denied for French use. So ended what became known as the 'Helder Expedition'.

Had its objective been limited to the maintaining of British naval supremacy by the seizure of the Dutch fleet, as originally planned, it would have been hailed as a brilliant success. The greater burden of a grand strategic advance, which was added on by the politicians without sufficient planning and logistical support, turned it into one of the British army's few resounding defeats.

Nothing was learnt from this lack of an adequate commissariat department, for the same failure to provide transport wagons would hamper the later campaigns in Portugal and Spain. Moreover, ten years later, when the British again landed to advance on Amsterdam, under the dubious command of the 2nd Earl of Chatham, in the Walcheren Campaign, the same failure to advance while it was possible to do so occurred for the same basic lack of logistics.

On 9 October Napoleon had managed to land once more in France, disgraced, but he quickly organized an army to cross the Alps and retake Italy, where Genoa had still not fallen. The result was that he returned a hero and was proclaimed as First Consul of France, with virtually dictatorial powers.

Moore's reward was to be named by the King as regimental Colonel of the 52nd, with the responsibility of training 1,000 new recruits by his own particular methods.

CHAPTER ELEVEN

Eventually Egypt

The resignation of General Stuart, owing to the lack of reinforcements with which to hold the now reconquered Minorca, concentrated the minds of the Ministers once more on the Mediterranean. He was also furious that, even though the army was to come, there was no consideration of his plan to seize the Maritime Alps, so cutting off Italy. Napoleon, however, thought it an excellent strategy and soon proved Stuart's arguments to be sound.

The initial aim of the fleet, with 15,000 men in transports, was to be the taking of Genoa from the French by a seaward attack and landing, while the Austrians came in from the landward side. Unfortunately, when the fleet arrived off the Italian coast, they were informed that the French had already capitulated, on the condition that they and their arms were transported to France.

Cut off in Genoa, they were of no strategic benefit to Napoleon. However, once they had been transported back to the Mediterranean coast of France, these veteran troops were immediately added to the force which crossed the Alps 35,000 strong and defeated the Austrians at Marengo. In this manner not only Genoa was conceded to France, but also Piedmont and Milanese, with Tuscan neutrality guaranteed. The road for a leisurely march onwards to take southern Italy lay open.

Thus, instead of occupying Genoa, Moore was sent as Military Commander of Minorca, with the Hon Henry Fox as Governor. Despite the fact that the Governor was the brother of Charles Fox,

Pitt's political bane, the two men got along well. Moore had been left with two divisions to train in his new light infantry tactics. Whilst there, Moore also made a friend of the energetic and fearless young Colonel Paget, fourth son of the Earl of Uxbridge, who would ride with him to his fate at Corunna.

Meanwhile, Sir Ralph Abercromby as C.O. of the army in the Mediterranean, had sailed to Malta to await orders, after despatching a regiment to garrison Messina in reply to the Queen of Naples' request for assistance. After the frustrated mission to Genoa, Moore had gone ashore at Naples where he met his old comrade Nelson, now made a Lord for his victory over the French in the mouth of the Nile. Moore, however, was not impressed, "finding Lord Nelson attending upon Lady Hamilton . . . so covered in medals that he looked like a prince of an opera . . . he cuts a melancholy and pitiful figure."[1]

During October he was sent to destroy the arsenals of Cadiz and burn the Spanish fleet moored there. He had with him the whole fighting fleet and 10,000 men in transports, but the navy had not thought to mention the well-known fact that a constant S.W. wind blew into Cadiz at that period of the year. To avoid being driven ashore, the fleet cruised 7 miles off the coast and began putting men into the flat-bottomed landing barges while under sail, for they had also forgotten that it was impossible to anchor there with the wind in that quarter. Regardless of the fact that such a landing from ships in motion had never been attempted and that a gale was blowing up, Moore had 3,000 men into the boats when the order came to cancel the operation. At that moment plague was raging in Cadiz, with 300 deaths a day, so it was fortunate that the army did not make contact.

In a letter to his father Moore tells of Sir Ralph's fury at being made such a fool of by being recalled in the middle of a difficult landing. The reason, however, was that a despatch had arrived at Gibraltar diverting six battalions to reinforce Lisbon, while the rest of the fleet, with 15,000 men under Sir Ralph and Moore, invaded Egypt to expel the French and end their Indian aspirations. Moore at last felt that he was being employed in events which affected the strategic balance at a world-wide level, for the French had not been abandoned by Napoleon in Egypt after their fleet's decimation by Nelson. A governor had been appointed and settlers sent; they had every intention of remaining and improving the overland routes to Asia, ready to win back their previous colonies there once Europe was under their control, as its dominant power.

Indeed, so seriously did the British in India take this threat that 5,000 native troops were assembling under General Baird to attack the French rear by sailing up the Red Sea to land at Suez. The British were, meanwhile, to establish an army on the coast near Alexandria, at a landing site to be chosen at Sir Ralph's discretion.[2]

Moore's divisions arrived at Malta on 22 November, intending to assemble all the equipment and stores necessary for success in Egypt. To their surprise, they found that the island was expecting an attempt at invasion by Russia, aided by Sweden, Denmark and France once the Baltic ice melted in the spring of 1801, the excuse for this expedition being that the Czar, Paul I, had been elected Grand Master of the Order of the Knights of Malta.

Before this expedition could be put together, however, Nelson sailed into the harbour of Copenhagen and decimated the Danish fleet. The Czar then died, which effectively put an end to Napoleon's Northern Alliance. British naval power once more dominated both the Baltic and the Mediterranean. However, the laxity of the blockade of the Egyptian coast meant that supplies were easily slipping through to the French, even as the British joined forces to train for the landing.

The whole fleet now sailed for Marmoris Bay on the Turkish coast of the Aegean, some 40 miles from Rhodes. In total there were 200 transports for the army, which consisted of 16,000 men, backed by the firepower of the Mediterranean fleet. The Ministers considered this a match for the French forces in Egypt; Sir Ralph most decidedly did not, but, regardless, began to plan how to use

1. The Duke of Hamilton (centre) with Dr Moore and the young John. From the original painted in Rome by Gavin Hamilton c. 1776.

2. William Pitt the Younger at the time of Moore's entry into Parliament. From the painting by James Gillray.

3. Admiral Hood accepting the keys of
Toulon. From an engraving of c. 1790.

4. General Paoli of Corsica
(British Library).

5. A typical Mediterranean Martello tower *(photo author)*.

6. A private of the West Indian Regiment at the time of the Napoleonic Wars
(British Library).

7. The Battle of Wexford *(National Library of Ireland)*.

8. The French attempt a landing in Bantry Bay. From an engraving by H. Warren c. 1798.

9. 'The Liberty of the Subject'; the 'crimps' system of forced recruitment at work. From a drawing by James Gillray, 1779.

10. 'The Irish Rebel Army in Action'; another cartoon by Gillray. Note the word 'Liberty' inscribed on the sword.

11. The Battle of Aboukir Bay; engraved by J. Rogers from the original painting by J. S. Copley.

12. General Sir Ralph Abercromby falls wounded at Alexandria. Detail from a painting by R. Polland *(British Library)*.

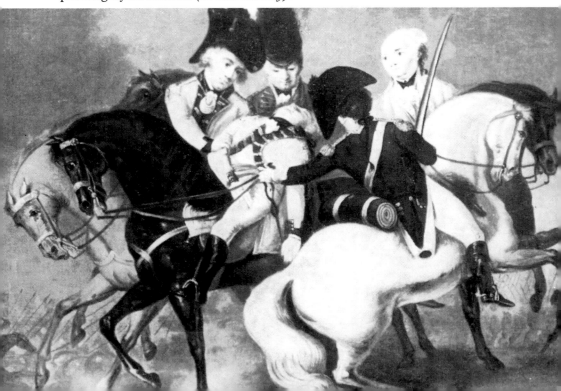

13. Maria Carolina, Queen of Naples
(British Library).

14. Caroline Amelia Fox
(British Library).

15. Lady Hester Stanhope, from an engraving by R. Hammerton.

16. King Gustavus IV of Sweden
(British Library).

17. Manuel Godoy, from the painting
    by Goya.

18. Jacques Louis David's allegorical
    painting of Napoleon at the time he
    was confronted by Moore.

19. The capture of General Count Charles Lefebvre-Desnouettes at Benavente by the 19th
    Hussars *(British Library)*.

20. Napoleon takes on the Spanish bull in the 'Plaza Real de la Europa'; Gillray, 1808.

21. Napoleon produces a new batch of Kings for Europe; Gillray, 1808.

22. The trail to Nogales from the bridge at Constantino *(Collectionistas of the Royal Greenjackets, Corunna; donated by Liberia Arenas)*.

23. John Hookham Frere
(British Library).

24. The old city of Salamanca.

25. Lord Castlereagh.

26. Marshal Soult *(from a print lent to the author by Barrie McGinley Jones)*.

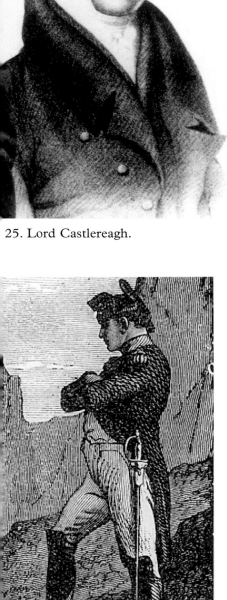

27. Napoleon watches the British Army's retreat.

28. The contemporary Battle Plan: see p. 199 *(Barrie McGinley Jones)*.

29. Sir Thomas Lawrence's painting of Sir John Moore, 1804
(National Portrait Gallery).

30. A model of the Battle of Elvina before Corunna

(By courtesy of the Regional Military Museum, La Coruña

31. A photomontage by the author: the last defenders of Corunna – left, Royal Greenjackets; right, Galieian Regiment of Artillery; top centre, Moore's tomb as it is today.

32. An engraving from the 1840s of Sir John Moore's tomb
(Amigos of Sir John Moore, La Coruña).

superior tactics, and the proven valour of the men in landing under fire, to carry the day against a foe superior in both numbers and artillery. In addition, the bureaucrats in London had not seen fit to send any horses for the dragoons, while the French had superb cavalry at their disposal. When Sir Ralph realized this obvious omission in the fleet inventory he was told that horses would be supplied to him locally. Lord Elgin sent 400 poor specimens which he had obviously bought unseen. These horses were totally untrained for military use and could only be used for messengers or to move light guns. The usual lack of wagons that plagued every British landing was also noted, vital items which could easily have been disassembled for transport. The result was that 200 sailors carried supplies to the army on their backs nonstop after the landing, resulting in constant shortages, the most serious being in munitions. A British army was supplied with what non-military officials in London assumed it would need and had to make the best of it. The French Generals, meanwhile, requisitioned what they knew local conditions required and were given priority in receiving the items.

The reality of the situation, that they would gradually discover once ashore, was that the French still had 32,000 of the specially selected veteran troops from the 40,000 with which they had arrived. In addition, they had 1,000 pieces of artillery, with ample supplies of munitions, and a large experienced force of cavalry. Admiral Sidney Smith, who had helped the Arab defenders win the battle of Acre against Napoleon by fighting the guns of his squadron to both seaward and landward from the harbour, had given these figures, quoting his Arab sources, but was dismissed as an eccentric, prone to exaggeration. The British soldiers were never made aware that they were so outnumbered.[3] Objectively, however, as half of the French were tied up in the suppression of the native armies, they could not appear together at one place to confront the British, and a camel can be used to pull a gun or carry supplies as well as a horse. Such conditioning factors must be taken into account when reading the complaints which Moore sends home concerning the British army's unequal task. The cavalry was expected, by treaty, to be supplied by the Turks and the Egyptian Mamelukes, Egypt's previous governors.

To assess just what was the value of the Turkish army, Moore was sent to meet the Vizier and his provincial army, currently awaiting events near the port of Jaffa in Palestine, today's Tel-Aviv. He reported back that he found "a plague-ridden army, burying 200 men each day . . . with no real knowledge of French strengths or positions . . . led by a weak-minded old man with no military experience . . . overall, a wild ungovernable mob."[4]

The result was that any participation from this quarter was left out of future calculations. The Sultan had, however, promised 5,000 Turkish regular troops under his Capitan Pasha once the British were ashore with a firm foothold.

The Vizier did have some figures to give to Moore of the French force on the coast at Alexandria. He claimed that there were 15,000 troops, half of them being cavalry, with fifty field guns. The only reason that the Vizier had not attacked them already was, he claimed, that the ships with the barley for his cavalry horses and marching rations for his men had yet to arrive. Moore did not believe either claim and, despite the wind being in the wrong direction for the safe anchorage of the huge fleet, blowing onshore, it was decided to cease the practice landings in the Gulf of Makri and proceed to Aboukir Bay to seek the best spot for the actual landing, close to their supposed first objective of Alexandria. They arrived on 3 March 1802, in a storm, and anchored 7 miles from the coast in only 6 to 8 fathoms, with even shallower water between the fleet and land. In all, the French had been given two months' warning in which to prepare. The storm would give them five days more to make defences behind the landing beach and, to make matters worse, a French frigate capable of raking the approaches with grape had slipped in to anchor under the battery of the fort at the left end of the bay. The soldiers were nevertheless in high spirits, for this was their first confrontation against purely French forces during the present war and they were eager once more to prove British superiority man to man.[5]

Moore, while still concerned at the lack of cavalry, could at least count on the fact that he would have behind him the best veteran regiments of the British army and not raw recruits as previously. Indeed, his main fear was not the enemy, but rather that the rumours of parliament being eager to sign a peace treaty with Napoleon would come true before he and Sir Ralph could drive his forces out of Egypt.[6]

Moore and Sir Ralph took soundings from a skiff and reconnoitred the beach and its strongly defensible dunes until the most advantageous landing site was decided upon. During the night the transports came into only two to three fathoms of water, but were still five miles from the shore. At 6 am on the morning of the 7th a small boat sailed in to mark the landing point and sailors stoically began to row the flat-bottomed barges to the shore, each with fifty soldiers seated on the floor. When they were near to the shore a hail of grape and ball, and then musket shot, began to fly among them, but only two boats were sunk and some dozens of men wounded. The soldiers huzzaed to encourage the tired sailors and two shallow-draft gun-boats opened up to either side of the barges to make the enemy take cover, while a bomb ship lobbed mortar shells over the dunes into their ranks. The landing point was chosen as being out of range of Fort Marabout and the frigate on the right-hand point of the bay, but Moore fixed his gaze on a sandhill at whose base they would land, for at its 60-foot summit were placed three enemy guns to rake the beach, just as he had predicted.

Landing at the base of this hill placed the invaders below the elevation of the guns and the first companies of the right wing ashore were to follow him in scrambling up the steep sand slope to put these guns out of action. The formidably large Grenadiers surged up the slope and in minutes the guns fell silent as the artillerymen were put to the bayonet. Three light infantry regiments, meanwhile, fanned out to take cover in the dunes and engaged the French hidden there. Within a few minutes the British infantry had not only gained the beach but had pushed back the elite of the 'Invincible Army' of Italy into the dunes, despite the fact that they were aided by artillery and cavalry. The beach was thus cleared by Moore, with an initial force of 2,500 men. The left wing, commanded by General Oakes with a similar number of men, had come ashore a little later, once the guns were taken. The 42nd Highlanders formed the shock troops of this wing and, as well as line regiments, they were accompanied by the Corsican Rangers and the Foreign Corps.

Fort Marabout was now cut off on its peninsula of rock and the combined 5,000 British caused such slaughter to the defenders that they broke and retreated to the fortified heights in front of Alexandria, some four miles distance. In theory the city lay open with no reserves to defend it, but the slow task of manhandling the guns and horses ashore in sufficient quantity to attack it took three days. Fort Aboukir fell to the British on the 18th. However, overall casualties so far had been 1,300 men and seventy-nine officers.[7] The engagements had been won entirely by infantry, with a single brigade of artillery, which, Moore stated, "amounted to nothing".[8] The guns of the forts were turned about to fire on the fortifications before Alexandria and more British guns were unloaded, together with the rest of the stores.

Unfortunately, the decision to unload every last item before attacking the city took seven more days, which were hardly justifiable, as no supplies were needed for a long march prior to the battle. The error of proceeding in this textbook manner was dramatically underscored on the 21st, as the British finally prepared a dawn assault. The French Commander in Egypt, General Menou, arrived with 6,000 infantry, plus cavalry, from Cairo, as reported by the Arabs, but ignored by the British as exaggeration, too busy unloading supplies to send out long-range scouts. In true Napoleonic style this relief army did not stop to rest or go into the city. Rather, it was flung immediately upon the British, who were moving in to attack.

Now they were faced with 11,000 defenders when the new force was added to the soldiers under General Friant in Alexandria. A deserter claimed that this amounted to only half the men defending Cairo and shocked the British, who believed that they faced half this number. Sidney Smith, whose plan to attack the city from the lightly defended rear by immediately sailing down the canal from the Nile had been dismissed as too adventurous, had been proved right in his claim of the quantity of French reserves. He could now claim that had his landing plan been followed the city would be in their hands, as they had previously outnumbered the defenders 3 to 1.

The British were dug in to the left of the 'Roman Camp' whose still-standing walls formed a redoubt. Amazingly a providential supply of precious water had been found by digging in these ruins, until a Roman aqueduct was found still running with copious fresh water with no obvious source. The French attacked again and again, but, having become accustomed to easy victories against the Ottoman troops, they were shocked at the volume and accuracy of fire of the British. The only brigade that did break into the ruins with cavalry were trapped in the roofless palace of the Ptolomeys and killed to the last man and horse by the Highlanders. At the end of the day they retired to the city, leaving behind 1,200 dead, including three Divisional Generals and 500 irreplaceable trained cavalry horses.[9]

The British could claim a victory, but they still could not advance to the city for lack of cavalry and field artillery to match the reinforced French defenders. The British casualties, killed and wounded, were 1,300, which, added to those already sustained, was some 14% of their entire force, with the main objective still unobtainable as a result of their unnecessarily slow advance.

During the early part of the action Moore had been shot through the thigh muscle, the ball drilling a 3-inch hole between entry and exit point. Ignoring the pain, he fought throughout the day, as did his aged commander Sir Ralph, who had also sustained a thigh wound, but with the nearly spent ball lodged against the bone. Not to preoccupy his men, he had not allowed anyone to know of his wound until after victory had been achieved, and only then was it discovered when he fell from his horse, fainting from loss of blood. The General had also been slashed across the chest by a French Hussar who tried to capture the short-sighted commander when he had separated himself from his escort. A timely shot from an infantryman had, however, put an end to the Frenchman.

Both men were taken to the ships for medical attention and each was assured that his wound was not mortal. Unfortunately, the ball that had entered Sir Ralph's thigh had not had enough force to break the bone, but, worse still, had run along it and could not be found by probing. A week later gangrene set in and he died the next day. After his death the ball was found to have lodged under the flange of the hip joint. Admiration must be given to the stoic endurance of a man nearing seventy, a great age in those times, who remained on horseback directing his troops while ignoring his wounds when most men of his age were seated in an armchair and not a cavalry saddle. Eulogies to him were published in the newspapers and his wife created a Baroness with £2,000 a year as a pension.[10]

Moore, aboard *Diadem*, was greatly affected to learn that his gallant and competent mentor had died on *Foudroyant*. He wrote a moving eulogy to Sir Ralph in a letter to his father, also describing the battle on 28 March.[11] Now that lists had been made, it was found that the French had left 4,000 dead in the three assaults against the British lines, whilst the overall casualties of the British were 1,300. The inability of the British to follow up the retreating French and take at least the outer fortifications of the Alexandrian heights was, Moore claimed, once more owing to lack of adequate means of transport. At the end of the battle they were actually out of munitions at the front and, with hindsight, the lack of cavalry and mobile field gun teams would have made advancing into open country extremely dangerous, had the French turned to reform their cavalry squadrons.

Moore was on crutches for five weeks and was taken up-river to a house near Rosetta to rest and recuperate. Despite initial inflammation, owing to cloth having been driven into the wound, careful draining and dressing saved the leg. He impatiently awaited despatches and his chance to rejoin the action before it was over. The faithful Major Anderson, his ADC, was sent home, with his own wounded arm hanging useless by his side.

CHAPTER TWELVE

The French Expelled from Egypt

General Hutchison now took over the command and was not pleased with his position. All senior officers with any talent were out of action with wounds and he faced a well-fortified enemy who had been reinforced to equal his own numbers. It therefore seemed the most expedient course of action to have the Sappers cut the thin strip of land dividing the seawater lake of Maadieh from the lower, Nile-watered, lake bed named Mareotis, so flooding 150 villages. However, from a tactical point of view this often criticized action was later to be of great benefit, for also flooded was the canal that supplied the city's cisterns with fresh water. Moreover, the main concentration of the fortifications were constructed to overlook what had been a flat plain. Alexandria was cut off from three sides and weakly fortified in what had been the rear, now the only avenue of attack. The British objective had been to cut themselves off from cavalry charges across the cultivated lake bed; the other factors were a bonus, which would be exploited later.

General Hutchison was now pleasantly surprised when transports containing 6,000 first-class Turkish regular troops arrived from Constantinople. These reinforcements enabled him to leave Alexandria cut off, once the new force occupied Rosetta along with 1,200 British troops. The whole of the Delta was now in allied hands, as was the coast to either side.[1]

Unbeknown to the officers, other than Moore and the new Commander, there were secret orders which directed Alexandria to be contained, while Cairo was taken first. It had always been intended that, with the capital in allied hands, the army could return to reduce Alexandria with ease, owing to its vulnerable position on the coast, where supply was no problem for the besieging army.[2]

Amazingly, the officer corps came near to mutiny when ordered to march along the Nile to take Cairo, when previously the only known objective had been Alexandria. Moore was approached to assist in detaining the unpopular General Hutchison, but his vehement refusal to entertain even the idea stopped the mutiny at that point. To maintain morale, Moore kept this episode to himself; also, there were already too few competent officers left active to begin a court martial of most of them. The disgrace to the army of this near mutiny only leaked out years after Moore's death.[3]

With groans from the ranks in their thick serge uniforms, General Hutchison, unaware of the disloyalty of his officers, marched off along the Nile in the June heat, heading for Cairo. Supplies had been unloaded in advance along the river bank and awaited the column's arrival under guard. Such advance planning for their welfare changed the men's opinion of the uninspiring figure of their new leader.

Following his tactics, the French were met with and beaten at Rahmaniya, a strategic communications crossroad. In number they were equal to the British at 4,500, but had the advantage of many cavalry squadrons and superiority in quantity of artillery. After a hot one-day engagement, the French retreated inexplicably during the night to Cairo. The same day a message arrived stating that the Vizier's army had crossed the desert to beseige Cairo and had beaten a French column of 5,000 who had swept out to meet them. The Turkish Vizier's army had previously been viewed as a picturesque joke by both sides and at first both the British and the French prisoners refused to believe the despatch. However, once it was confirmed, the British column made haste to reach Cairo before it fell to the Vizier and put them to shame. With his initial victory, the Vizier's army of 9,000 plague survivors had been joined by thousands of capable Bedouin cut-throats, who had come to loot the city and massacre the French. They swelled the numbers outside the defences to 21,000. During the nights the French became demoralized as the force continually beat upon their kettle drums and wailed high-pitched war chants.

The British arrived and set up camp across the river from the native armies, with 1,500 of the best French defenders as prisoners wasted by their commander when sent out to skirmish with the advancing column. To join them came a column of 1,200 superb Mameluke cavalry, the elite of the previous garrison of the city, who had merely retreated into the desert. News also came to both the British and the French of the advance of General Baird's Indian troops across the desert from Port Suez, where the wind had changed and finally allowed him to sail up the Red Sea. Any relief to the French from this port was now quashed.

The inspiring French leader, General Kléber, had been stabbed to death by an assassin in June of 1800. The men had felt as loyal to him as to Bonaparte himself and, had he still led them, doubtless they would have fought valiantly. However, the defenders under the lacklustre General Belliard were not prepared to face such odds for a land that they had come to hate. The day after the British arrival the French garrison agreed to surrender. The terms for which they asked were the same as those offered by Sidney Smith after their retreat from Acre, namely repatriation to France with their arms, munitions and mobile artillery. The British government had reluctantly confirmed these terms after Acre, and so there was a precedent. The alternative was some weeks of siege with the British army sure to be infected with the plague by the Vizier's men. The majority were already suffering from ophthalmia, which had developed on the sandswept march, making the sighting of a musket impossible. The terms were, therefore, agreed to and the French marched out in perfect order on 10 July to put themselves under the protection of the Royal Irish Fusiliers.

Meanwhile a column of Albanian troops of the Sultan's army had arrived to take control of the city to prevent the Bedouins entering to sack it, they being more the Sultan's long-term enemies than the French.

The temperature now stood at 120°F and General Hutchison went down with fever. Moore was sent for and took command of the march back to the coast, even though his wound was barely closed. He undertook this march with some apprehension, for the French outnumbered his men two to one and had been allowed to keep their ammunition to dissuade the Arabs from massacring them. The Vizier thought it ridiculous to return 8,000 veteran troops to France to fight again and had beheaded all the French he had taken prisoner to prove the point. Indeed Moore described the French as "fine stout fellows, all in good spirits". The 5,000 French sick and wounded were transported the 200 miles down the Nile in 300 native boats, along with General Kléber's coffin for burial on French soil.

The march to a holding camp near Rosetta took fifteen days, with strictly no fraternizing ordered between the French and their British protectors, who marched on either side. The column was headed by fine Syrian cavalry, while to the rear rode the Mamelukes with various infantry brigades from the Turkish armies. One evening Moore invited Brigadier General Morand, the French Commander's youthful ADC, to dine with him to pump him for useful information as to French military organization and war aims, once the wine took hold of his garrulous tongue, which Moore had noted. Much useful information was gleaned, along with the fact that the common soldiers, who cared nothing for the grand design upon India, were on the point of mutiny well before the arrival of the British. Even their commander, General Belliard, saw the British as their only insurance of a safe passage back home before the men resorted to mutiny.

95

Later French accounts confirm this as being the state of mind of the French army in Egypt.[4]

While on this march news reached Moore that British reinforcements had landed, so that when Alexandria was finally attacked it would be with 16,000 British troops. The last of the French from Cairo were embarked on 31 August, even taking their horses, but the British relieved them of sufficient of the best animals to mount three regiments of Dragoons and make the field artillery horse-drawn at long last. Attention was now fully turned on Alexandria, where General Menou was proclaiming that he would defend the city to the last man.

Menou was also Governor of the colony of Egypt, to which 10,000 French immigrants had come. Had Nelson not destroyed their fleet, 100,000 were ready to take over the rich lands of the Delta. Menou had taken his task so seriously that he had converted to Islam and married an Egyptian baker's daughter.

The siege began on 16 August and the harbour mouth was soon under British control. In this way a relief fleet, which Menou hoped would reach him through the blockade, could be of no use, even if it slipped past the British.

The plain before the city having now been converted into a 6-foot-deep lake, the defences had been partially removed to strengthen the landward eastern side, where the attack was now expected. The plan was, therefore, reversed and the attack on the outer fortifications made by using the landing barges to row across the new lake at dawn. The French, surprised, were quickly overwhelmed and the outworks reversed to breach the city walls. The expected relief fleet, rumoured to have six ships-of-the-line out of Toulon as its defence, turned away as the whole British fleet sailed to intercept it. Thus, Menou was without hope and, as the siege proper had not yet begun, he could still honourably ask for terms, having made at least a token resistance. The same generous terms were given as had convinced Cairo to capitulate. The French surrendered Alexandria on 1 September and Moore generously sent a detail of men to bring out Menou's wife, who

96

was in hiding for fear that her fellow Egyptians would murder her.

Immediately the city had surrendered 3,500 men were sent to garrison Corfu and 7,000 to reinforce Sicily. The 10,000 veteran French soldiers from Alexandria were returned to France, bringing the total once more at Napoleon's disposal from Egypt to 23,000 out of the 40,000 he had used to invade the country.

To Moore's indignation, he was ordered to command the garrison of Egypt as the only reward for his efforts. The aversion which he held for such duties when action was taking place elsewhere was well known, which added to his displeasure. Citing a letter from the Duke of York stating that he expected to see him in England once his wounds were healed and, in addition, had urgent private affairs to settle, Moore applied to General Hutchison to substitute General Baird to command the garrison. Baird agreed and Moore gratefully sailed for England on 23 September. After having his brig dismasted in a sudden violent storm, he arrived, via Malta, at Southampton on 10 November, to be greeted with the news that the new Prime Minister, Addington, had taken the easy route of signing a peace with Napoleon on 10 October.

Moore left with a ceremonial sword presented by officers who had served under him. The British Government appropriated the collection of priceless Egyptian antiquities that had been collected by Napoleon's experts and housed in the French Institute at Alexandria. 'Cleopatra's needle', an obelisk covered in hieroglyphics, was also taken from where it stood near Pompey's Pillar and may still be seen on the Thames Embankment.

The intention of the British to remain in the country with the Sultan's tacit consent was dashed in 1803 when the leader of the Albanian troops left to police Cairo, Mehemet Ali, announced that he was taking control of the whole country from the decadent Mameluke dynasty, proclaiming that he acted in the interests of the Sultan. The British were politely asked to leave, which they reluctantly did. However, the British determination to dominate the land route to India resulted in their attempting to seize Alexandria as a base from which to control the country in 1806. The expedition was soundly defeated, however, by Mehemet Ali's new army, trained by French deserters and equipped with the latest European weaponry. Ironically, the defeat occurred on the same ground where the British had previously decimated the French. The debate as to Mehemet Ali's actions ceased and he was proclaimed Pasha of Egypt by the Ottoman Sultan soon after he had massacred the Mameluke Beys.

Mehemet Ali has been given by historians the title of "The Founder of modern Egypt". The dynasty which he founded continued into the 1950s, until the army coup which sent King Farouk into exile. Events escalated into the nationalization of the Suez Canal when its British-instigated 100-year lease expired in 1955, triggering the ill-fated Anglo-French invasion, with disastrous consequences for Britain's status as a world power.

CHAPTER THIRTEEN

Sicily

After Pitt's death Lord Grenville was made First Minister. Under Pitt he had been Lord Chancellor and was also married to Pitt's cousin Ann; the continuity of Pitt's sound policies was, therefore, felt to be assured. The King also consented to a government for nation salvation, which he had refused while Pitt was alive. Thus came about the 'Ministry of all the Talents', with the previously vetoed Charles Fox entering as Leader of the Commons and also Foreign Secretary. Though he had doubled Pitt's problems when in opposition by decrying the war effort, now that his attempts to end it honourably had proved fruitless, he turned to pursuing it with as much vigour as Pitt.

With all the grand alliances torn apart by Napoleonic victories, Fox's strategy was to assemble a large force in Sicily under his brother, General Fox, to be used to disrupt the enemy, as and when opportunity arose. General Fox had been Governor of Gibraltar, and, with the knowledge so gained, was well suited to be made responsible for all Mediterranean political affairs and also military C.O. of the entire zone. Moore was promoted to be his second-in-command, with the rank of Lieutenant General. The force was to be based on the existing garrison of the island, taken out by General Sir James Craig, which was still preventing the French from crossing the Straits of Messina.

Craig was now invalided back to Britain and command of the troops in Sicily given to General Stuart, of whose true command abilities Moore thought poorly. While he had gained some glory at Aboukir, and more in the rout of the French at Maida, in Calabria, Moore knew that the victories had come about by the field commanders taking their own initiative for lack of orders from Stuart, who had merely looked on as if paralysed with indecision.[1]

Moore arrived on 5 August 1806 in time to be received in high spirits by the men back from the amazingly successful raid into Calabria. There, 4,000 British infantry had routed an over-confidant General Reynier, who marched straight at them with 7,500 French veterans and 300 cavalry. The British used no tactics other than not retreating as expected; rather they cut the massed French to pieces in a confined valley, allowing the whole region to rise up in revolt.

Moore's first task was to put to sea again in search of Admiral Sidney Smith, who was supposed to be protecting the force at Sicily, but was so under the spell of the Queen of Naples, who promised him a Dukedom, that he was busy ravaging the west Italian coast at points suggested by her Majesty. These were of no value to Britain's interests and were undertaken without orders. When Moore finally came up with the rogue squadron, he forcefully but tactfully ordered Smith back to Palermo to await General Fox's orders. The lenient reining in of the adventurous Admiral may well have been tempered by the fact that he was a cousin of Lady Hester Stanhope, whose friendship with Moore, when at her uncle Pitt's side, was rumoured to have grown into a serious romance, at least as far as she was concerned. Smith was also a national hero for his part in the defeat of Napoleon at Acre.

At this point Moore wrote to the Duke of York confirming that Sicily should be defended as a pivotal base, or even annexed as a colony, but that neither could be achieved with the present half-measures,[2] the more so as the peace that France had signed at Tilsit, after the defeat of the Russians, included the offer to the Bourbon Queen of Naples to exchange Sicily for the Balearics once the British were ousted.

Returned to Sicily once again, Moore found that the British

Minister to the Neapolitan court, Mr Drummond, was also so under the Queen's spell that he was placing her wishes above the interests of his country. Her ability so to manipulate high-ranking men on both the French and British sides may better be comprehended when it is explained that she was the sister of the late French Queen Marie Antoinette. The demand now was for men to assist the Neapolitan part of her Kingdom of The Two Sicilies against the new French advance southwards, after their decisive victory at Jena. Unlike Nelson and Smith, Moore could not be moved by charm or promises of Neapolitan titles and he firmly convinced the newly arrived commander, Fox, to have no treaties with the Queen, but rather to defend what was defensible and leave Naples to its fate, for it was as much allied with France as with Britain, depending on the side currently winning in the area. The Queen was most put out to be rebuffed, but, to raise Moore's morale, a further 6,000 troops arrived as reinforcements to the garrison; Sicily was to be held as an eastern Gibraltar.

In the ever-changing alliances of this, the real first world war, Britain now found itself briefly at war with its longtime ally Turkey. The Ottoman Empire had seized the unprotected province of Moldavia in retaliation for Russian incursions into its northern European territories. Britain had now signed a mutual defence pact with Russia, after her vast army's surprise drubbing by Napoleon in the snows of Eylau. Russia saw this as an opportunity to put Britain to the test as an ally. A demand was made that the British fleet be used to raid Constantinople and burn the main Ottoman fleet moored there. Such an action would allow the Russians freely to enter the Mediterranean from the Black Sea. While this operation was in progress, it was decided that, in the confusion caused to the Turks, the British should also seize Alexandria as a base for naval warfare and control all Egypt by the menace of its garrison.

Moore recorded that they could succeed at one enterprise or the other, but that, with the resources at their disposal, to attempt both simultaneously would most likely result in the failure of both expeditions.[3] Unfortunately, the Ministers in far-off London felt that they knew best and both assaults went ahead, only to be disastrously defeated by troops that were regarded as a joke. Once again Moore had been proved correct and the government wrong. The Ministers acknowledged his wisdom to the King, but hated him the more for their humiliation.

Only 8,000 British troops returned to Sicily, which, even added to the 7,000 Sicilian soldiers, meant that the island could barely now be defended and that all offensive action in Italy must cease. The new Secretary of War, Lord Castlereagh, ordered General Fox to hand over his command to Moore and return home. The reason given was that his weight made him bodily unfit for active service.

It was at this point that Moore came nearest to marrying, for he had fallen in love with his Commander's 17-year-old daughter, the beautiful and intelligent Caroline Fox, and the feelings were reciprocated. As her father was being recalled, Moore was forced to declare himself to the General or end the romance. One consideration was that Captain Graham Moore R.N. had made a pact with his brother that neither of them would marry until the war was over, for they had seen the ruin of many a young family when the father was killed in action. The other factor, which Moore gives in a letter to his friend Anderson, was the great difference in their ages. With the nobility of character and consideration for others which was typical of the man, Moore finally told her that "the differences in their ages would not lead to her long-term happiness, even if it mattered little now."[4]

Temporarily broken-hearted, she later went on to marry Sir William Napier and displayed her adult genius by easily breaking Napoleon's army staff code, where the best male brains of Europe had failed.[5] Later Wellington himself stated that by allowing him to read despatches encrypted in the Grande Chiffre she had contributed more to his ultimate victory than any person in Britain. When the coded French state archive was captured in Paris, this later revealed the true identity of 'The Man in the Iron

Mask', for Louis XIV and XV had also used this 'unbreakable system'[6] until a soldier's wife became bored with her household duties and began casually to look over the unintelligible enemy messages. An interesting aside to history, seemingly missed by past biographers of Moore.

Moore had mended his relationship with the Queen of Naples and consolidated the fortification of the island to have some hope of defence when a secret despatch came to inform him that the King of Prussia and the Czar had agreed to unpublished additions to the Tilsit treaty. The Ionian islands were all ceded to France, including the British island of Corfu, thus rendering the strategy of fighting from Sicily no longer feasible on a long-term basis. The orders were, therefore, to embark all British personnel for Gibraltar once the last evacuees arrived from the Egyptian débâcle. To allow the disentanglement of the British establishment from the island a force of 10,000 men was left to assist the Sicilian army, but only until they could decently be called elsewhere and not left to be captured in the inevitable defeat that must await the island.

Upon arriving at Gibraltar Moore was immediately given the task of entering Lisbon to extract the Portuguese Royal family to the safety of their Brazilian colony before a flying column of French seized the helpless city from the north, the country elsewhere being already in Spanish hands. Moore arrived to find that his work had already been attended to by the eccentric Sidney Smith and his own level-headed brother Graham. The most logical course seemed to continue on to London for reassignment.

Little did he imagine the reception that he would receive from the Ministers, who were outraged at his supposedly high-handed treatment of the Queen of Naples and the British Minister to her court. However, for once a solid defence of his actions was made directly not only by the Duke of York, as Commander-in-Chief of the army, but also by the political branch in the unlikely form of Castlereagh.

Canning was not, however, convinced and took further against

Moore as a commander as a result of the next wild scheme of the politicians that he was now required to execute. After the Machiavellian intrigues of the Queen of Naples, he now found himself destined to go to the assistance of the certifiably mad King of Sweden.

CHAPTER FOURTEEN

Sweden

The only country now left in Europe with forces worthy of an alliance with Britain was Sweden. Meanwhile, British goods were banned from import into Napoleon's continent, while the British Navy in reply blockaded the commercial ports, preventing exports from his domains. Napoleon's strategy was to force Britain to spend its vast gold reserves in buying goods, instead of trading them for manufactured items. It had long been Britain's policy to subsidize continental armies to raise men to fight the French, for Britain's small population meant that there were never sufficient young men available to man a huge navy and an equally large army. Such was the case with Sweden, who was to be given £1,200,000 in gold to help her fight the common enemy.

In addition, in May of 1808, Moore was sent with 10,000 troops to reinforce the Swedish mainland against possible invasion, while its own army fought the Russians in Finland and on the border with Norway. The only orders were for Moore to proceed to Gothenburg and then use his own initiative as to how to proceed. The only specific orders concerned what he must not do. He was not to leave the coast or move along it to any area where he could not instantly be re-embarked. Neither was he to place his men under the command of the King of Sweden.

While Moore would be available at Gothenburg to assist in land defence, Vice-Admiral Sir James Saumarez would cruise the Swedish coast with a British fleet to deter any would-be invaders from Russia or Denmark. Moore was from the first wary of the erratic and illogical behaviour of Sweden's autocratic King and wisely kept his troops aboard their 180 transports in the harbour while he went ashore to establish an H.Q. and find out what the King required of him. HMS *Mars* and *Audacious* protected the transports by straddling the harbour mouth.

The cautious approach proved to be correct, for the King wished Moore to use his men not in the defence of his homeland, as agreed, but to attack Zeeland and also invade Norway. Moore rightly claimed that he could do nothing that altered the reason for his army's presence until he had conferred with London. Immediately he wrote to Castlereagh, strongly advising against such use of the force. The exact words used were doubtless those repeated in a letter to his mother.[1] Moore informed her that "the [Swedish] force is so small and weak that any aid I offer will not enable the Swedes to resist for any length of time . . . The King had considered my force under his sole direction; against this I remonstrated and, as I have no power to depart, I was glad to refer the whole matter home, sending a full report with Col. Murray, Quartermaster General."

The Ministers in London now had a blunt and frank report confirming what had previously been stated by Moore, that no good could be done in Sweden; now they must decide for themselves. To his mother he confides that "The Ministers had a singular ignorance of the state of the matter".[2]

In his diary Moore could be even more blunt and he wrote that "The Swedish king, whilst honourable, was an autocrat without the ability to govern; with either a very weak or a deranged mind. The King governed directly, so that in effect the country had no government. The King refused to accept the force on British conditions as ordered and wished, for he would have no foreign troops on his soil unless at his command. Moreover, he sought to use the force for his wild plans of conquest, when there was little hope of even defending his own country with it."[3]

On 11 June Colonel Murray returned with replies from the

Ministers in London. The Duke of York and Castlereagh both wrote personal letters marked secret, which agreed with the position taken by Moore to the Swedish King's demands and commiserated with him over the difficult position in which he found himself.

King George III, however, sent an official despatch no doubt designed to soothe the feelings of a totally autocratic king on the part of one who tried his best to be one. He told Moore to place his command under the orders of the Swedish King whilst actually in his dominions. All the personal letters marked secret, therefore, meant nothing, for the King still held the last word as the ultimate Commander-in-Chief to whom the men swore allegiance. Naturally, this came as a most unpleasant surprise to Moore. The periodically mad King of England had sided with the permanently deranged King of Sweden!

On 11 June Moore made his way to Stockholm for an audience with the King. He took the position that his instructions were still inexplicit and contradictory, but it made little difference, for the King heard only what he had decided he would hear. Gustavus ended the audience by ordering Moore to take his force to Finland and join the Swedish troops in an attempt to take the province of Viborg from the Russians. He declared it to be Swedish and it was therefore within his dominions, as the English King had stated.

Moore explained to the Commander of the Swedish forces why this was impossible, but was told that, whilst he was in the right, it was his problem to convince the King of that fact. Not daunted, Moore returned and remade his logical argument, but the King merely accused him of disobeying a direct order and demanded to know, if he was to do nothing that was required of him, why was he there at all. Moore again patiently repeated that, semantics aside, his basic orders were to protect Sweden whilst the Swedish army was totally committed in its fight with the Russians. To this the King replied, as if the proposition was being put to him for the first time, that he would not allow foreign troops to land on Swedish soil. Moreover, he did not need any assistance in the first place. Gustavus then directly ordered Moore to take his fleet of transports and use the men to attack Norway.

Moore bluntly told him that he supposed that the King was only giving the order to be able to state that Moore had once again refused to obey, for the King well knew that the answer, and the argument to support it, must be the same as that already given in relation to Finland. The King exploded into an apoplectic rage, and just at that moment, as if in a stage play, Colonel Murray begged leave to enter. A message from King George was read out stating "that if the most unreserved facilities were not given to land, General Moore was to return to England . . . He was surprised and dissatisfied upon learning of this hesitation to receive the British troops [on Swedish soil]."[4]

At last Moore had some definite orders from the British King himself, but the problem now lay in disentangling his force in a diplomatic manner. However, King Gustavus now issued an order forbidding Moore to leave Stockholm without his written permission. Moore immediately sought an audience to have this order clarified, whereupon the King accused him of breaking all his country's promises. He then began to rage against Moore in such a violent and incoherent manner that his insanity was fully unmasked. Amid his onslaught was a call for Moore to be placed under arrest.

For once in Moore's career the politicians who had placed him in such an untenable situation stood firmly behind him. The British Minister to the Swedish court wrote to the Minister of Foreign Affairs to advise him formally that, if the arrest order was not immediately retracted, the consequence must be a state of war between the two nations.

Not waiting for a reply, the Minister advised Moore to ride at once to Gothenburg by secondary roads. He left on 27 June and felt a great sense of comfort on boarding the massive bulk of the floating fortress that was the *Victory*.

After a final conference with Admiral Saumarez and General Hope the whole force sailed for England on 4 July, leaving the Swedish King to his folly. Unfortunately, this later included blaming Moore's arrogant attitude for the inability of the two nations to work together. To some of those in London who had sent off the expedition with no real knowledge of the state of Swedish affairs beyond its place on a map, Moore would by then seem an ideal scapegoat. Memories of Corsican and Sicilian affairs would be used as prior examples of "some truth existing" in King Gustavus's inventions.

Chapter Fifteen

Iberia Seeks Assistance

Prior to examining Britain's decision to send aid to its oldest ally, Portugal, followed by its greatest land commitment of the war to date, to assist its oldest enemy, Spain, it will be of use to review the state of world affairs leading to those decisive months in 1808 from the perspective of these two countries.[1]

Under the Treaty of Utrecht of 1713, which ended the War of the Spanish succession, the government of France and Spain became a family affair between the two Bourbon Monarchs, united in their hostility to Britain.

Some genetic time mechanism then played the trick of rendering both the fourth Bourbon King of Spain, Charles, together with the Sixteenth Louis of that line in France, inclined as much towards borderline imbecility as their ancestors had touched on wisdom. Unfortunately, both were still absolute monarchs, who ruled with the assistance of the nobility and the church.

Charles, being slothful, not only allowed his wife to direct him in all decisions of state, but then sought the second opinion of his court favourite made First Minister, a burly guardsman named Manuel Godoy. Unbeknown to the king, Godoy was the lover of his Queen, Maria Louisa of Parma. In this manner the Queen's governmental advice was always concurred with by Godoy, adding little touches of his own. To advance him, and to prevent the King from considering their relationship, Maria Louisa pushed the Monarch into encouraging the marriage of her lover to the King's own sister, the 17-year-old Condesa de Chinchon.

The French Revolution's anti-monarchist propaganda made Spain resort to an alliance with its foe of centuries, Britain, in support of Louis XVI, and war was declared on his decapitation in 1793. Unfortunately, the French swept the Spanish and allied Portuguese Royalist armies aside and occupied the country as far as the Ebro. Godoy represented Spain at the subsequent peace conference of Basle in 1795 and earned himself the title of Prince of Peace. However, the reality was that the country had retained its autonomy by being bound to French Republican interests, regardless of the results. Soon the proud Spanish began to feel humiliated.

The final blow, which would light the fuse for the revolt of 1808, was the decimation of their fleet, along with that of the French, by the outnumbered British at Trafalgar in 1805. The Catholic population of Spain were already horrified at the removal of the Pope by the French, and the establishing of a republic in the Papal States. The seizure of the Spanish protected states in Italy, ruled by the Duke of Parma, came as a further affront from a supposed ally. Godoy fell from both bed and power as a result of being unable to prevent this brushing aside of the Queen's family in the considerations of the alliance.

For now, however, Bonaparte as First Consul, saw Godoy as still a useful tool in Spain, and demanded a new treaty in 1800, restoring him to power, as a dictator. He punished the monarchy by demanding it cede Louisiana and six ships-of-the-line, as a reminder of who really ruled behind Godoy. It was as far back as this point that the common people of Spain began to weigh the promised freedoms of the Republicanism, slow in their implementation, against subservience to a foreign power, the more so as Godoy enriched himself enormously at their expense. The establishment, naturally, hated him as a Republican reformist and turncoat puppet dictator under Napoleon.

There was, however, initially little opposition to Napoleon's next request that Spain invade and annex Portugal, who refused to close her ports to her ally Britain. Godoy led the invasion forces in person and was barely resisted.

The Spanish reward was to rule the country for Napoleon's benefit and to send from the joined treasuries 6 million francs per month to aid the French war effort, some 250,000 pounds Sterling of the time. Such sums came from the South American and Pacific colonies, and the British set out with an alacrity equal to that which they had shown in the times of Drake to capture the treasure ships on the Atlantic crossing, the advantage that was now enjoyed over their Elizabethan ancestors being the complete naval supremacy of the ocean.

An internal rivalry now began to manifest itself in Spain, as Prince Ferdinand, the heir apparent, began to gain followers in a movement to oust Godoy, force his weak father to abdicate and rule in his place. However, all such plotting was pushed aside when the Convention of Fontainebleau of October 1807 saw Godoy agree to dismember Portugal, with a French army being allowed to pass through Spain to occupy Lisbon.

The Portuguese Royal family, the Braganzas, as previously mentioned, fled to Brazil under British naval protection. The hope of French naval reinforcement was given a last devastating blow when all of the ships-of-the-line of the Portuguese navy sailed with their Monarch.

Godoy next had Prince Ferdinand arrested for a supposed plot to murder both himself and the Prince's parents, backed by the nobility and approved of by the people. The popular unrest, known as the Mutiny of Aranjuez, gave Napoleon the excuse to send reinforcements to bolster General Andoche Junot in Northern Portugal. The Spaniards now began to hate the French which Napoleon had not taken into account, for in all of his previous conquests the local peasantry had welcomed his armies as liberators from feudal oppression and provided supplies.

Godoy now found it expedient to become patriotic, but the

King forbade him to organize armies against the French. Popular uprisings ensued, which resulted in the King abdicating in favour of Prince Ferdinand.

Napoleon's reply to this was to invite all the parties to attend him at Bayonne for a conference of reconciliation. The reality was, however, an occasion of utter degradation for the Spanish monarchy and people. The Prince was forced to sign back the throne to his father, who then laid it at Napoleon's feet to dispose of as he thought fit. Thus came to fruition Napoleon's long-term plan to place his own elder brother Joseph on the throne of Spain, matching his brother Louis as King of Holland, soon to be followed by Jerome in Westphalia. Napoleon made no secret of the fact that he saw the boundaries of France as those of the Western Roman Empire of Caesar.

When Murat, later King of Naples and Napoleon's brother-in-law, arrived in Madrid to form a regency until Joseph came for his coronation, the Spaniards finally snapped and briefly took over the city. The arrival of Murat also brought the news of the exile of King Charles and Godoy, whilst the popular Prince Ferdinand was under constraint as the guest of Talleyrand in France. There were an estimated 500 deaths on each side before the French regained control.

The aristocracy had fled into exile with their Monarch, as had the intellectual class, many of whom were liberal reformers, but not collaborators. It fell to the bourgeois and yeomen classes to organize the common people, and remnants of the army, into a true plebeian revolt ironically against the now imperial ambitions of the Commander of the same revolutionary French army which had swept across Europe in the belief that it was ridding it of kings.

The uprising took place on 2 May 1808 and, whilst the people's militia could not overcome for long the French army in Madrid, they waged successful guerrilla warfare in the provinces. In July the unbelievable happened, for a militia force defeated, and made prisoners, an advancing French Army of 18,000, led by Dupont, at Bailen in Andalusia. In Valencia they repulsed a French assault on their city by 17,000 men and all Europe rang with the news that for the first time since 1793 a French Army had been defeated, and by mere irregulars with no central command. The Spanish people now surged on to Madrid and drove out King Joseph, who had just established his court and ironically proclaimed the popularist Constitution of Bayonne, which gave the Spanish populace a freedom equal to that of the French. If Napoleon, not unrealistically at that moment, saw himself as the rebuilder of the Roman Empire, his knowledge of that empire must have made the Battle of the Teutoberg Forest spring to mind at the mention of Bailen, and the ultimate boundary of the Rhine become synonymous with the Guadalquivir river in Andalusia.

Enraged, Napoleon, by now imagining himself to be truly some Leviathan, bestirred himself and declared that he in person would descend on Madrid and restore his brother to the throne; the Spaniards would either bow down or die.

It was at this point that Lieutenant General Sir John Moore was sent from Lisbon, at the request of the Spanish Ambassador in London, to assist in forming a centre on the northern front as a pivot to hearten the people of Spain as they organized into regional militias to resist the French, no matter how many came across the border. A central 'junta' or national organizing committee, was formed near Madrid at Aranjuez, headed by Count Floridablanca, to coordinate the regional militias' movements.

Again tasked with facing odds more impossible than those of David against Goliath, Moore remained confident of the reports concerning the ability of the Spanish militias and calmly sought the appropriate stanza from his pocket Horace, the childhood gift at Potsdam, which he still carried, to reflect the moment.

The penultimate stanza of the ode 'Martiis caelebs' was most appropriate, as was so much of Horace's patriotic irony to Moore's life. It calmed him to muse on how most situations had not changed in 2,000 years of warfare.

> Now at long last our ancient Spanish foes,
> Enslaved and chained, beat out their angry heart,
> The tired Celts prepare to unstring their bows
> And from these windy plains depart."

CHAPTER SIXTEEN

The British Perspective

Prior to entering into an account of the actual events which led Moore on to his fateful march from Lisbon to Corruna, it will be useful to review the British conception of the strategic position it held in relation to the enemy.

Britain began the war, in 1793, with an army of only 20,000 men, many of these being used as Marines. The country's real strength lay in its naval power and its worldwide commercial wealth. The European continental powers could thus be swayed by 'Pitt's gold' into alliances whereby their armies fought the land battles.

France, with an homogeneous population twice that of Britain's 14 million somewhat rebellious total, could always raise superior land forces. Filled, as they now were, with Republican fervour to liberate all Europe, each French soldier in the initial phase of the war was worth three of the reluctant conscripts that he fought against. The most that was expected of the British army by an ally was that it could swiftly alter the tactical situation by landing a well-equipped, disciplined force of up to 20,000 men anywhere that its fleet could gain access. Such limited actions from seaborne landings could set fire to a fleet, blow up an arsenal or cut off an army from its base using an expeditionary force.

However, apart from driving the French from Egypt, no significant land victory had occurred in 15 years of vastly expensive warfare. Rather, 100,000 men had been frittered away collecting sugar and spice islands, to keep the heavily taxed city merchants content. All other attempts to date had been ill-conceived assaults such as the Helder, Boulogne and Tenerife.

When Napoleon's 'Continental System' shut British commerce out of Europe after Trafalgar, Britain turned to trading with Spain's rebellious colonies, even occupying Buenos Aires. In this way she lost barely 6% of her exports and found a new source of hardwood trees for most shipbuilding requirements. The destruction of the combined French and Spanish fleets made such trade virtually inviolate, while Napoleonic Europe's great trade ports were blockaded, costing France 80% of her customs revenue.

While Britain consolidated her world naval supremacy, which she was to hold for a century, Napoleon was decisive in turning from plans to finish Britain by invasion to removing the menace of the land alliance to his east. Only five weeks after Trafalgar he had beaten the Russians and Austrians at Austerlitz. The Austrian ruler was also the Holy Roman Emperor; thus, with the occupation of Vienna, the ancient symbolic throne ceased to exist.

At this moment Pitt died, the depression into which he was thrown by total victory at sea being turned into total defeat on land possibly affecting his will to fight the initially minor ailment with which he took to his bed.

The immediate successor to Pitt was Lord Grenville, but the premiership soon passed to Lord Portland, who made Canning his Foreign Secretary. His introduction to the weight of Pitt's burden was to hear that Britain's one remaining powerful ally, Prussia, had suffered crushing defeats and occupation at the hands of Napoleon after only thirty days of fighting between mid-October and November of 1806.

Continuing the sweep of annihilation to the east, Danzig fell in May and Russia was beaten at Friedland in mid-June. At Tilsit the Emperors of France and Russia met on a barge on the River Niemen and divided Europe between them to the exclusion of Britain. The Czar told Napoleon that he now hated the British with equal passion, for they had led to his defeat by not opening a second front in the Mediterranean as promised.

Britain's only allies were now the mad King of Sweden, Portugal's demented Queen and the untrustworthy Queen and weak King of Sicily, that island being held only by the presence of the British garrison of a mere 10,000 men.

All of Europe not under Ottoman control was now ruled by Napoleon and his brothers, or puppet republics set up to serve him. The Czar was given the opportunity to make peace between France and Britain, on the condition that if Britain refused to yield, Russia would herself declare war on her, which occurred.

Portugal was seized for disobeying the Berlin Decrees and continuing to open its ports to Britain. Portugal had effectively become a British protectorate by refusing to renegue on its ancient alliance, whilst claiming neutrality in the renewed war. Moore initially became involved in the country with his previously Sicilian-based army against Junot's flying column of 28,000. Of these only 1,500 exhausted, virtual skeletons of men and horses staggered into the city on the afternoon of the day that the Royal Family and its fleet, whom they had been sent to capture, sailed out of the Tagus for Brazil. With the escape of the Royal family, Moore was ordered to sail on for Southampton instead of returning to Gibraltar as planned.

In the force sent to relieve him, under Lord Cathcart, was the 3rd son of the Earl of Mornington, a Major General Wellesley. Moore had heard of him only as a result of the fact that he had combined the political post of Irish Secretary with the command of a brigade on active service in that country. To have one foot placed so powerfully in both lanes of the racetrack of promotion was an unusual combination, especially for a 'Sepoy General' of only 39 years.

The Spanish now invaded Portugal from the south and for a time General Junot, created Duke of Abrantes, became Viceroy, while preparing the country to receive Eugene Beauharnais as the King nominated by Napoleon.

When, in 1808, the seizure of Lisbon was being contemplated, the army imagined that it would be led by Moore, or possibly Wellesley. Sir Arthur Wellesley was a true politician's General, whereas Moore had openly condemned the establishment for providing incompetent but well-patronized officers. Moreover, he also freely gave his opinion that government corruption and incompetence in Ireland were almost totally responsible for the alienation of her people.

In other postings he had warned the governing classes that their privileges also implied duties to those they governed. The safety and very existence of this class lay, he claimed in fulfilling these duties as strict obligations. Such liberal and highly moral statements were seen as comments on the self-serving Tory government of Britain, in particular on Dundas, Camden and Bathurst. Pitt had to some extent shared Moore's views at heart, but Pitt had now worked himself to death, partly in this selfsame struggle of patriotism over greed. Wellesley was, overall, a product of his times, while Moore was a century too advanced in his thinking to please many Ministers.

The insurrection against the imposition of King Joseph in Madrid saw the Spanish army leave southern Portugal, which immediately reasserted its independence, backed by Britain. After the defeat of his army in Andalusia, Napoleon sent a further 91,000 troops to reinforce the remaining 75,000 men under Murat. However, these were inexperienced conscripts, easily slaughtered by the guerrillas. The reality was that France held only the Spanish territory within the range of its cannons. The 'Spanish Ulcer' had begun to trouble Napoleon, even before the arrival of the British. Rumours of the planning of uprisings in the east meant that, for now, he must keep his veteran troops to garrison the occupied lands. The British had calculated that, even were Spain to remain unsubdued, the total requirement of first rate troops needed to police Napoleon's Empire would be one million, a figure not attainable even by the genius of the master of Europe.

If he could be provoked into sending several hundred thousand first-rate veterans into Spain, it was hoped that uprisings in the conquered nations, especially Austria, would occur. In this way the whole house of cards that was the House of Bonaparte might well come tumbling down were Britain to blow hard enough on the one card which she could still reach.

On 4 July 1808 Spain signed a treaty of alliance with Britain. It was in that same month that Dupont, with 18,000 men, surrendered them, and more importantly all their weapons, to General Castaños in Andalusia; Valencia defied a siege and Saragossa held off 17,000 French with only local volunteers.

By the end of August the French were back to the position of a decade past, holding only North West Spain above the Ebro. In the attempt to place Joseph on the Spanish throne 40,000 French soldiers had died. The brother who would be king maintained himself meanwhile on Spanish soil at Vitoria.

The Spanish peasantry did their best to deny any foodstuffs to the French and virtually all supplies had to come in from France over hostile Pyrenean trails, with possible ambush at every curve. Even these 'secret' routes were closed in winter, with only two roads open at either end of the mountain chain, close to the sea for observation and attack. Napoleon was to learn the truth of the old epigram that, "In Spain large armies starve, and small armies are beaten"[1]. The British, however, with command of the seas, could be resupplied by dozens of routes around the coast of the peninsula while keeping the French landlocked by blockade. The characteristics of the war would be one of attrition, for until the folly of the invasion of Russia, virtually unlimited manpower was Napoleon's to command, if not always of good quality. However, such forces could not come together in one place or time for more than the swift victorious clash with obligingly concentrated traditional armies that had been the norm until Spain gave the word 'guerrillas' to the world.

Moore, having been present in the initial act of the war, in the holding of Lisbon until the Royal escape, left two symbolic battalions with the reinforcements. It was at this point that he sailed to London to receive orders, while the Portuguese island of Madeira was occupied as a rear base. When Moore arrived in Southampton on 29 December 1807 he heard that the now Lieutenant General Sir Arthur Wellesley had also returned and was busily assembling an expeditionary force at Cork to retake Lisbon, if not all of Portugal.[2]

CHAPTER SEVENTEEN

A Competent or a Compliant Commander?

In June of 1808 Wellesley set sail for Gibraltar to unite his force with the troops returned from Buenos Aires and was expecting, indeed hoping, "to be placed under the brilliant command of Moore". Though his brother Henry was in the Cabinet and another brother was Governor General of India, both of whom were owed many favours by Canning and Castlereagh, Wellesley knew that his age and lack of European campaigning must place Moore before him by every scale of reckoning. Moreover, he was five steps below Moore on the seniority lists, after Lord Paget, and did not expect the command as even a remote possibility.

Moore's greatest defect in the minds of Ministers was the fact that he had so often pointed out the defects of given courses of action, thinking only objectively as a soldier, and, after being overruled by political considerations, be proved right by events. He also made clear by his liberal and moralistic comments on the causes of the revolts in St Lucia and Ireland that brutal repression was the cause and could not be the long-term solution. The Duke of York and the King delighted in Moore's frank and blunt appraisals, surrounded as they were by dangerously sycophantic advisers, and would have gladly given him the command of the Portuguese expedition, as indeed they had promised to the late Pitt's niece, Lady Hester Stanhope.[1]

Canning, however, was still galled by the Swedish fiasco, which had made him look foolish, while Moore again appeared before the nation as the silently suffering military hero, victim of politicians' bunglings on maps with no contours, figurative or otherwise. To the surprise of all, with the future of Europe at stake, Canning named two elderly political appointees to the command of the expeditionary force, as being the Generals with most seniority – Governor Dalrymple of Gibraltar for political matters, and, to handle the actual fighting, General Burrard as his second. Burrard did not even consider himself more than an average field commander when young, much less now at 73 years. He had last seen active duty 14 years previously, but he had not been involved in the actual fighting. Dalrymple had never before commanded as a General, but at least knew something of affairs in the peninsula.

Moore only confirmed the Minister's opinion that he would have been a spoiler and exposer of their politically rather than patriotically motivated planning when he sought an interview with Castlereagh to know his orders and expressed his opinion with his usual bluntness. When informed that both he and Wellesley were to proceed to Portugal and place themselves, for unspecified duties, under the geriatric commanders, Moore protested at such vagueness. Protocol demanded that, as the C.O. of both the Sicilian and Swedish armies, were he to be passed over now for men considered retired, the minimum he should expect was an explanation. Castlereagh still avoided giving him any reasons and Moore for once became openly furious. Without any of the normal formalities Moore stood and left, but told the Minister as he walked out that "I hold a feeling of the un-handsome treatment that I have received from you". Moments later he reopened the door without knocking and added as a post-script: "Remember, my Lord, I protest against the expedition (with its present commanders), and foretell its failure".[2] They would never meet again.

After Moore had laid down his life to assure his army's escape from Corunna the King accused Castlereagh of purposely under-supplying Moore's expedition out of personal spite at finally being again forced to eat his words. The grovelling letters of denial make pathetic reading.

When Castlereagh's own time came, he opened both jugular veins with his razor rather than explain to the Commons why he was stated to be the victim of a homosexual prostitute's black-mail. It cannot help but be conjectured whether he recalled the unflinching heroism of John Moore's last moments and un-blemished honour in life before himself taking the coward's way.[3]

Wellesley was, however, determined to show his own ability. The orders of engagement allowed him to attack the enemy if sighted from the moment that they were signed. While still at sea, some 25 miles north of Lisbon, near to an anchorage for Vimiero, news came to him by frigate of Junot's main army having regrouped there. Junot was surprised when Wellesley, with a British army of 18,000, suddenly landed at the mouth of the Mondego River. The French were in disarray and without supplies, and were beaten first at Rolica on 17 August and more decisively in the second encounter when they attacked Wellesley's well placed camp at Vimiero on 21 August. How-ever, in the afternoon General Burrard arrived in time to claim credit for the victory and forbid that it be followed up by chasing the disorientated French inland. Moore was ordered not to con-tinue disembarking his newly arrived force of 10,000 to hunt down the French, as Wellesley had intended after his initial victory. Several factors must be stated on Burrard's side, as hitherto he has only been accused of over-caution. Moore's army had never left the ships in Sweden and had then sailed straight for Portugal, pausing at Portsmouth only long enough to take on supplies. The men could hardly walk; their muscles had been wasted by such a long confinement and the cavalry horses were in even worse condition. Moreover, the main objective was the capture of Lisbon and Burrard therefore ordered Moore to join General Spencer's force marching on Lisbon from Cadiz, the idea being to put Moore ashore at Ericiera to cut off the 3,000 French left in the Lisbon fortifications before Junot could march back to join them. Next day 'Dowager' Dalrymple arrived to take command and it was then that the real chaos began.

Moore finally came ashore on the 24th, his first action being to send Wellesley, whom he had yet to meet, a warm note of congratulation on his splendid victory. The losses to the British in dead and wounded had been 800 men, whilst the French had lost 2,000 with fifteen out of twenty-three cannon captured.

Junot, meanwhile, was left with the chance to regroup and thus be in a position to ask for the same terms of surrender which had so angered the British public and parliament after the French defeat in Egypt – namely, transport to France with all the men's arms and loot. These terms were granted to him on 30 August by the venerable British Commanders at the Convention of Cintra, with predictable results once the news of the conditions of surrender reached Britain. Sir Arthur Wellesley implicated himself by signing this document, but Moore kept out of it, stating that he wished he was rid of the whole absurd campaign.[4]

The facts which seem to have escaped those who so scathingly criticized this agreement are that the French still held the three forts dominating Lisbon and the surrounding countryside, with their cavalry unscathed by the defeat at Vimiero. Moreover, it had been discovered that the total of all French forces in Spain had been 24,000, spread about to hold down the country. Moore could not understand why they did not unite and fight the inferior British force at Lisbon. The British did not have men to lose in a long seige, or time before the equinoctial gales cut their supplies. The removal of the French from Portugal was the objective. If it was achieved with as little bloodshed as possible then the long-term view of events, with the advantage of hindsight, make the Cintra Convention seem an extremely sensible course of action. Finding their army in command of Portugal and still intact, the Cabinet was able to consider marching on to aid the Spanish revolt, which had never been part of the initial plan. Had they fought for Lisbon the army would have required resupply and replacements and could not have marched until the next spring, which is to say not at all, for Napoleon would have swept up all Spanish resistance and been before Lisbon with all the resources of Europe to call on in January 1809. There can be little doubt that his eagle standards would indeed have "flown from the ramparts of Lisbon in three months", as he had boasted when crossing the Pyrenees against all allied calculations, for a winter campaign.

Sir Hew Dalrymple had now set up a regency in Lisbon, but the British reinforcements and the French prisoners awaiting repatriation made their own arrangements as best they could, for Sir Hew had no idea where to place or how to organize encampments, never having commanded an entire army before. Moreover, it was now autumn and the rains had begun. Wellesley wrote a scathing letter on the army's state to Moore, but Moore declined to conspire against the commanders, preferring to await the opening of the Ministers' eyes by the reports of others.

Meanwhile, the navy was also giving an unpleasant surprise to the Russian Atlantic fleet, which was riding out a storm in the safety of the Tagus at Lisbon. Russia had formally declared war on Britain at the beginning of the last week of October, but no steps had been taken to inform its fleet, and so, with the British fleet in the river mouth in receipt of this information on 2 November, the Russians were surprised to be asked to surrender without knowing that they were at war. In this manner over a dozen fine ships-of-the-line, plus frigates and transports, were denied to Napoleon's new alliance and added to the Royal Navy's existing 100-plus two- and three-deckers with a promise to return them when peace was made.

Junot's easy terms of surrender predictably angered the British public and Dalrymple was recalled to explain himself to parliament. Meanwhile, in the army encampment at Queluz, outside Lisbon itself, Wellesley sought out Moore and they met for the first time. Wellesley found all that he had heard of Moore's manner and bearing to be true and swiftly pledged him his loyalty. To put acts behind these words he immediately set off for London by fast frigate to bring all of the political influence that he could muster to have Moore named as Commander of the expeditionary force. It was obvious that the elderly Dalrymple would not be returning; the command had only been for the expedition to liberate Portugal and now Castlereagh had ordered a march on into northern Spain. Dalrymple had told Moore that this was absurd gibberish, typical of politicians comfortably at home. He also told Moore that he was horrified at the prospect, for he had no maps or even knowledge of where the Spanish militia armies were, or their commanders. Regardless of the apparent liberality of the Cintra armistice, and the outcome of the enquiry into it, he made plain that he would decline to take an army over the mountains into the unclear situation in Spain, especially as winter approached.[5] All seemed to be agreed on the weakness of the British when negotiating this armistice, but Sir Hew made clear to Moore that he had not been so weak, for the fact that the French still held all three well-stocked fortresses overlooking Lisbon and its harbour must surely be taken into account when he reached London. Better that the French walked out, on 3 September, with all the King's plate and the Bishop's artworks than lose many of the then relatively small British force in attempting to beseige three cleverly constructed defences of an Imperial capital.

Wellesley may well have also written ahead on the state of affairs, for Moore was named as Commander on 25 September, whilst Wellesley docked only on 6 October. Thus it is impossible to give him definite credit for influencing events, but the intention was clearly made to Moore. Moore had agreed that he wished for the command, but told Wellesley that he would enter into no intrigues to gain it and must receive it as his just reward from the King for past actions or not at all. The fact that Wellesley sought to convince Moore that the Cabinet was guilty of mere forgetfulness under pressure, and had not set out to slight Moore, suggests that he had been given the job of sounding out Moore's present feelings before the Cabinet attempted to rectify the situation by now offering him command.[6]

Wellesley, for his part, while ostensibly rushing back to London to try to make Moore Commander and serve under him, now applied for leave. He did not return, but rather went to Ireland to assist in gerrymandering the elections there once more. On the same day that Castlereagh wrote his unofficial conciliatory letter to Moore, which arrived with the King's order that Moore take command, he also wrote to Wellesley. In this letter he stated: "My first concern is for your reputation, my second is that the country should not be deprived of your service at this critical juncture.[7]

The reality of the political situation concerning Moore's surprise appointment, after his inappropriate verbal abuse of the Minister of War, was that the march into Spain would either be a disaster or a glorious achievement; mostly it was a leap into the unknown. The army and the Duke of York wanted Moore to command, and thus Castlereagh was appearing to give in to democratic pressure. The whole strategy was to goad Napoleon to take the best of his army into Spain, hopefully for long enough to allow Britain to encourage insurrection in Austria and Prussia, and so have him at war on two fronts once more. Moore had no political weight at home now that Pitt was dead, and the Duke of Hamilton had followed his father's example of a decline into drunkenness.

Thus, if the command that he had so vociferously demanded led not just to Portugal but on to the plains of Leon and a confrontation with Napoleon himself, with his 'Invincibles' behind him, no blame could come to Castlereagh for Moore's possible defeat and convenient death. Moore was known to lead from the front and would be well out of the way of Castlereagh if he died a hero's death. Moreover, as Castlereagh had left all decisions to Moore's initiative, both politically initially and militarily throughout, once the realities of the situation revealed themselves Moore would be blamed for any disaster. Castlereagh could, however, claim the glory for any victory, however unlikely, with the odds he knew Moore would eventually face. Moore was presently useful, but expendable, and then, with Napoleon's reaction fully defined, the politically correct Wellesley could be sent to harass the French and keep them tied up in Spain, weakening the other fronts.

The one aspect of Wellesley's career in India of which Castlereagh knew was his experience in skirmishes against often superior numbers. To the aristocrats of the Horseguards he was, however, merely a 'Sepoy General'. The brilliant use of ground and firepower had always given him victory, and it was obvious that the war in Spain would not be one of set-piece battles in the previous mode of Frederick the Great's tactics, even though that had been the case in the war so far, with Napoleon remaking the rules of combat as they occurred to him.

All that Moore, for his part, knew or cared about was the fact that, by good or bad grace, he had at last been given command of a complete army, moreover one that was to make the largest land strike against Napoleon's Europe since the war had begun; he wrote in his journal that he only asked that he might acquit himself well.

The 75,000 troops still left in Spain had now taken a defensive winter position in a line from the Ebro to Vitoria. Meanwhile, intelligence was coming into Moore's camp from Madrid that a minimum 150,000 veteran troops were assembling to the French side of the Pyrenees, supposedly to await the opening of the snow-filled passes in the spring, then to be led into Spain by Napoleon in person. In London it was noted that the bait had been taken and secret emissaries left for Austria and points east.

The Spanish victory in Andalusia and the generalized insurrection throughout the country had made the British Ministers confident; enough, indeed, to be persuaded by Castlereagh to not only hold Lisbon as a base but to throw into the Iberian Peninsula 35,000 men, the largest land commitment since the days of Marlborough. Moore was to march out of Lisbon with a total of 22,000 men, supported by 5,000 cavalry and 5,000 artillery-men, while Lieutenant-General Sir David Baird was to join him with a force of 12,000, marching over the passes from Corunna. The strategy was for them to unite on the plains of Leon, and, together with the Spanish militias drawn from several juntas, or regional government commands, stand between the French and Madrid. The British were to act as a reserve behind the all-important centre protecting the plains leading from the Ebro to the capital.

The decision to use two columns instead of sailing to Corunna and descending together down to the plains beyond Astorga was Moore's, taken for the logistical reason that so large a force was impossible to supply, strung out in the mountain passes. Moreover, a French advance could easily bottle it up behind those very passes, where cavalry were useless and infantrymen could only form firing lines of a dozen in the narrow roads cut into the steep mountainsides by the Romans.

Baird arrived with his transports off Corunna on 13 October, but was annoyed to find that the junta of Galicia had still not finished the debate concerning the landing of foreign troops on its shores. The arguments continued and were referred to the still forming Central Madrid Junta. No decision was made for a month and the British were finally allowed to land to assist their forces on 4 November after three centuries of pillaging the same coast. Thus, the criticism of the time wasted at Lisbon was point-less, for Moore could only hope to cross the border mountains before the worst rains, but could not enter the country until given the same permission. Technically the British and Spanish were still at war until the new government formed and voted other-wise. The vote occurred just as Moore was regrouping his columns at Ciudad Rodrigo, ready to cross over to Salamanca. He was obviously at exactly the right place at the right time, thus arguments as to prior events were, and are, pointless.

Moore's achievement in being there at all before the rains made it impossible to move was no small feat in itself. The lessons of the Helder and Aboukir had still not been learnt and both columns of the army found it impossible to find sufficient transport wagons or draft horses. In Lisbon the problem was particularly acute, for the previous Franco-Hispanic army of occupation had taken all available weapons and horses to carry their supplies and loot when the insurrection against the French had begun in Madrid. Neither had Moore been provided with a war chest of silver dollars with which to purchase his requirements. Luckily, his reputation as a man of scrupulous honour extended even to the traders of Lisbon, who accepted his word for later reimbursement by the British Ambassador. General Burrard, still commanding the garrison of Lisbon, handed over all his remaining £25,000 to Moore, who in turn sent on to Baird £8,000, for he was also penniless on his arrival at Corunna. The final result was that the column cut a comical sight, with every hackney carriage of Lisbon commandeered and stuffed with supplies, accompanied with every size and shape of wheeled vehicle not already taken by the invaders. These were mostly ponderous ox carts, crude and slow in the extreme.

The greatest problem was for the artillery. While the guns were mounted on wheels, these were not intended to transport the enormous weight of the larger pieces over mountain passes, only about the actual field of battle. Special carts existed for long journeys, with a sling below the axles for the barrel to give stability, as the weight was below the centre of gravity of the wheels. The gun carriage and dismounted wheels travelled in the upper cart. Munitions were also normally transported any distance in carts with racks to prevent movement of the layers of balls, with powder in rainproof trailers pulled behind. Lacking such transport, Moore had to send his guns by an easier and longer route into Spain, using the main road to Madrid, detouring to the southern Tagus valley, travelling on their actual wheels in the hope that they could survive. There would be time for the wheels to be repaired for action again when the forces all met up at Salamanca, or so it was hoped. Junot had already proved that this was a risky move by sending artillery from Ciudad Rodrigo to Abrantes the previous year, only to have the pieces arrive totally unusable. Meanwhile, the guns were unprotected by sufficient infantry and cavalry, and vice versa. The risk was calculated, however, for hostile forces were then well distant, with the Spanish militias in between. The present enemy was the weather, for the rains were beginning and the unmade roads over the mountain passes would soon be knee-deep in mud.

CHAPTER EIGHTEEN

The Advance into Spain

Moore had not been the initial Commander and thus had been unable to offer his usual sobering comments as to the more probable realities when the first exuberant reports of Spanish determination and fighting strength reached London. The British press and members of parliament were the first to raise demands that British aid be sent to assist this gallant insurrection, sparked off on 2 May in Madrid. Indeed, Moore was still in Sweden at the time and, pausing only briefly at Portsmouth to resupply his still embarked army and travel to London for instructions, had gone on to Portugal with no more real knowledge of the state of affairs in Spain than the other commanders.

One fact was obvious to him, however: if he did not get the army on the march instantly he would have no army to lead over the mountains. The men had been allowed to drink as much new wine and to eat all the citrus fruit that they could obtain. The obvious result to unaccustomed stomachs had been diarrhoea, followed by dysentery. The latrine trench was only 500 yards from the hospital and the slaughterhouses for the troops left their residue unburied in a pit to spread the stench of putrefaction and multitudes of flies. All the ingredients were there for an outbreak of typhus or cholera at any moment; indeed, several suspected cases were reported. The stench was overpowering to new arrivals who made their way there through hillsides covered in thyme, myrtle, rosemary and wild lavender bushes. Such was Wellesley's main camp around the abandoned royal palace of Queluz,

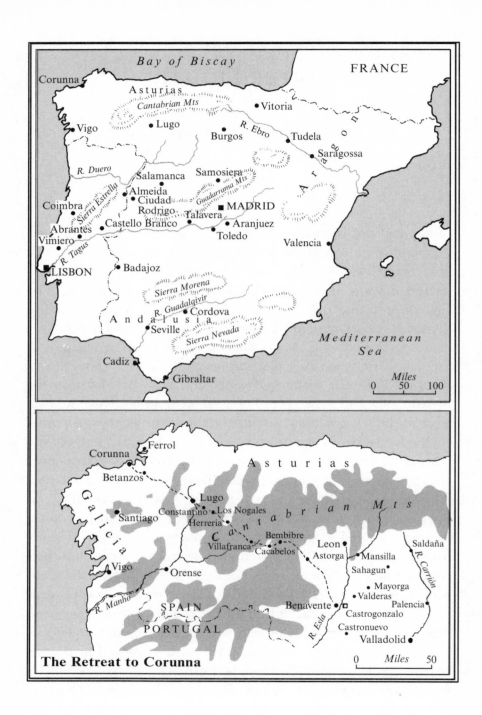

The Retreat to Corunna

redecorated by Junot for Napoleon's choice as King of Portugal, Eugene Beauharnais, who was destined never to enter it.

Moore found little comfort in the efforts of the commissariat department, for whilst they were "full of zeal they had no experience of supplying an army marching off to do battle".[1] The army marched with the hope of obtaining what it lacked as it progressed, as and when money was sent to do so. The transport ships, under the command of Captain Bligh, had brought sections of huts, ready to assemble for the garrison, to prevent a winter in tents outside Lisbon. Why carts could not have been brought from Britain in the same way can only be explained by the fact that it was the responsibility of another department with less imagination.

Moore had received the names of the Spanish generals of the armies of the provincial juntas when still in Lisbon from Colonel Bentinck, sent to liaise with the Central Junta as it formed. They were General Castaños in Astorga, General Cuesta around Salamanca, General Llamas in Valencia ready to move north, General Blake, an Irish mercenary, on the plains of Leon, with Palafox, a general of 28 years old and of little experience, in reserve at Aragon. The Central Junta itself was described as having little control over the provincial armies, whilst being lethargic in all it attempted. No overall military commander of these armies existed, resulting in continual arguments among the regions.[2] The favourite for the position of Generalissimo was Castaños, the victor over Dupont's army in Andalusia. The head of the Central Junta, Count Floridablanca, favoured his appointment, but the post was never filled, the main cause of the subsequent disasters. The Junta now moved from Madrid to nearby Aranjuez, to be less distracted by social obligations. No attempt was made to make contact with the British army, marching in to strengthen the Spanish centre and act as a reserve, not even by the supposedly competent Castaños, who was to hold the centre. Moore had no idea where he was, much less his proposed tactics. The Central Junta was supposed by the individual armies to be liaising with the British via that country's Minister, but they had too many problems of their own to make any individual responsible. Meanwhile, Moore marched on towards Salamanca in the hope that some authority would make contact, but all believed that there was plenty of time, for no army campaigned in the snows of midwinter. Moore was still wary, for he did not underestimate Napoleon's genius for overcoming all odds to take his enemy by surprise.

Moore had camped his men away from the rest of the army on a hill near to the abandoned palace of the Prince of Brazil, which he used as his Lisbon HQ. The vanguard of the army marched out from there on 27 October 1808. The general order of the day was that all consumption of non-regulation alcohol was henceforth banned, with which the army amazingly complied. Moreover, all the women and children of the soldiers' families who had accompanied them were now to be left behind, where rations would be provided for them. Unfortunately, this order was largely ignored, despite warnings as to the hard nature of the mountain roads; most paid the price of such loyalty to their men by freezing to death in the Galician passes. Moore had certainly ordered them to desist from following, which is often forgotten by those who write only on the retreat and its horrors. Indeed, these women were often the main element of the drunken looting bands, which were the curse of the rearguard actions.

Overall, Moore led into Spain an army of 30,000 men, including two regiments of cavalry and proportionately adequate artillery. The column to come via Corunna under General Baird was of 10,000 more overall, with five regiments of cavalry and, again, proportional artillery. Moore's command was, therefore, of an army of 40,000 men. Indeed it was the whole current British army and the knowledge of this fact was a tremendous burden for him to carry.

Just prior to leaving, Moore had written to Bentinck in Madrid on 22 October complaining of the total lack of maps of the roads in either Portugal or Spain. Not only must they rely on the word of local peasant guides, but, as the roads were explored as they went by Moore riding on ahead and calling up the units suitable for each route, this precluded the establishing of supply depots along the routes prior to despatching the men. Moore concluded by writing that "the politicians in London talked of going into Spain as if it was Hyde Park".[3]

Moore did not write his journal on a daily basis but brought it up to date when time permitted, thus in many cases the date of entries are not the dates of the events to which they refer. He closed his entry at Lisbon on the day of the march by stating that he "now cared little for the opinion of Castlereagh and other Ministers, although he would avoid vexing them if possible". If he failed, "then his own vexation with himself would be such that opinions of Ministers would matter little".

The next entry is at Villafranca on 27 October. Moore had left the actual marching of the men to the subordinate generals and, after scouting the routes, had ridden on with a small dragoon escort and his ADCs to Almeida to await the arrival of the two infantry columns. One marched to the north of the Sierra Estrella range via Coimbra, while the remainder went to the south via Abrantes and Castello Branco, the plan being for all to link up at Ciudad Rodrigo, just inside Spain, assess events and march on to join the artillery coming north via the Madrid main road, all then turning north to arrive at Salamanca and form order of battle.

While Moore was scouting the wooded sides of the beautiful Sierra Estrella, General Castaños was advancing with all confidence to confront the French, whom he still believed he outnumbered. The artillery had no alternative but to take the main Madrid road and Moore proved that this was a correct decision once the roads into the mountains deteriorated into mule tracks; he even had problems with the few field guns he had kept with the infantry columns. The argument concerning the decision to split up the army was settled by no less authority than Fortescue, who states categorically that Moore was correct. The only road possible for heavy guns was the one taken by General Hope. Moreover, the country could not have supported one long column of infantry, for it would have stretched almost from Lisbon to Almeida and have been impossible to supply; also, logically, it would have moved at half the speed along the narrow tracks.[4]

Rain and generally foul weather spoilt Moore's passage "through the prettiest country yet seen in Portugal"[5] and he did not arrive in Almeida in a good mood. The state of the garrison, which he surprised by arriving unannounced, was so deplorable that he was forced to hang one man for flagrant looting and deny the whole 6th Regiment the right to join his army, stating that he would not take such a drunken rabble into Spain to set the population against the British. Apart from alienating the local inhabitants, the Commander, Brigadier General Anstruther, had foolishly delayed the main army's northern column for several days to await Moore's arrival, when he should have resupplied it and sent it with all speed to the next assembly point of Ciudad Rodrigo.[6]

On 7 November word came that the French had received 20,000 veteran reinforcements, with a further 66,000, accompanied by 7,000 cavalry, expected to cross the frontier before the snow closed the passes. Moore became concerned that his army was still on the march in four vulnerable columns. However, his spirits were raised by the fine character of the Spanish people, whom he described as a far superior race to their Portuguese cousins, both in manners and the prosperity of their countryside. The border was crossed by merely walking his horse through a riverlet. When the army approached the ancient walled town of Ciudad Rodrigo the peasants lined the road to cheer the British into town, while the guns on the walls fired a salute. The countryside around the town was fine and open and intensively planted with trees from which cork was obtained.

The southern column was not neglected by the Commander-in-Chief; he had ridden with them the 84 miles to Abrantes before crossing over to the northern road to Almeida, via Castello Branco. Along the route he had stayed overnight at the houses of country gentlemen, but at Castello Branco he could not escape the invitation of the Bishop. He found him to be filthy in his person and impossible to communicate with owing to his lack of education. At that time the *lingua franca* of Europe's cultivated class was French and, as the Bishop had only a few words, they communicated in church Latin; but, even then, though the Bishop could recite the words, he understood few of them. In general Moore found the town poor and unpaved, with the countryside uncultivated. However, he was cheered by the arrival of a despatch from General Hope, leading the artillery column, that he was making good progress and expected to be in Valladolid by 30 November.[7] Moore rode on to Salamanca, expecting to have all his troops there by the 25th, ready to march for three days more to meet up with the guns.

From the point of his arrival at Salamanca on the 14th all news that Moore was to receive would be bad. When he made contact with the city authorities to arrange the billeting of his men he was informed that the Spanish centre had folded and that the French were in Burgos. Without a central command, the Spanish armies on the flanks did not swing in to encircle the break-through, merely staying uselessly in place, as the French galloped across the central plain towards the capital. The next day they were reported to be in Valladolid, a mere 60 miles away from the dispersed British columns. The lack of a coordinating central commander was directly responsible for this rupturing of the front. The army of Asturias under Castaños was not the army of regulars with which he had defeated Dupont in Andalusia, but in the majority untrained armed peasants, which at the time was unknown to Moore. He knew the armies of the various autonomous regions to be termed 'militias' by the liaison officers sent in June, but had imagined, along with the British Cabinet, that to imply that they were on some sort of a par with the English yeoman militias, all having uniforms, guns and training.

Indeed, much money and small arms had been sent to them from Britain in the intervening period.

Colonel Bentinck, Minister in Madrid, had until recently been merely reporting the Spanish self-confidant attitude, that they could beat the French by themselves and that the question of the British army's presence was whether it would arrive in time to share in the glory.[8] However, at last taking the obvious step of an actual assessment of the quality of these huge Spanish armies, he had sent one of his staff, Whittingham, with Spain's best General, Castaños, to review the troops of the centre army of Castile at Logrono. Whittingham wrote to Bentinck from the army's H.Q. at Calaharra on 28 October, at last stating the truth, which shocked the whole British military and political hierarchy. He wrote: "The strength is about 11,000 but for any idea of its composition it must be actually seen . . . a complete mess of miserable peasantry, without clothing, organization, and officers worthy of the name. The officers have no faith in the troops and what is yet worse, the men have no confidence in themselves."[9]

Moore had drawn his own conclusion concerning the civil population and entered in his journal on 15 November: "The peasantry and lower orders are enthusiastic and determined never to submit to France, but the enthusiasm is less as the class ascends." Indeed, it must not be forgotten that Whittingham's "miserable peasants" were all volunteers, who had come forward out of patriotism to defend their country. The fact that they lacked adequate arms, training and uniforms was the fault of their betters, most of whom had fled the country. A further consideration was that the Central Junta had no money, for the French-imposed King Joseph had taken the funds of the national treasury with him when chased out by the May insurrection. Britain was sending half a million Sterling, but it was now too late.

None of the Spanish generals had made contact with Moore at this stage, neither had the Central Junta, formed in Madrid since 26 September. The system that Moore was obliged to follow for information was that the diplomats in Madrid sent representatives out to ascertain the strength of the Spanish forces and their assessments were sent to Castlereagh in London, who relayed what he saw fit to Moore in the field by King's Messengers. Moore was well aware of this chain of misinformation, for he commented in his journal that "the reports were written by men without sense to see nor honesty to tell the truth to their superiors".[10] Moreover, as he did not know exactly where the various Spanish regional armies were he could not send gallopers of his own to liaise and ascertain the true strengths. Had he done so, it would have been regarded as a gross breach of protocol by all sides. Such was the absurd situation that Moore faced whilst trying to decide whether to order his columns to link up by forced marches or to retreat to Ciudad Rodrigo and await a clarification of events.

By 15 November he had decided to continue with the assembly of his army, as the French were not heading towards his columns, but had swung away to concentrate against Castaños's reformed army protecting Madrid, now barricaded and with its citizens armed, all swearing to fight to the last man.

To add to the problems Bentinck was now replaced in mid-crisis by an intellectual friend of Canning from his days at Eton, one John Hookham Frere, a career diplomat with no military experience, although it is often forgotten that he had filled this same post in Madrid from 1802–1804, so was not totally ignorant of the country, but under vastly different circumstances. In theory he could give Moore orders that outweighed the military decisions taken, were the political aspects considered to be of more strategic importance. Moore, however, was determined to obey politicians only to the point where the annihilation of his army appeared the only certain result; after that his responsibility to his men came first and that to the Cabinet second.

His most pressing problem was, however, the same as that with which he had left Lisbon, namely that he had been provided with no funds for the expedition and none had subsequently been sent. He calculated that by 25 November he would no longer be able to buy food for his army.

Frere had arrived at Corunna with Baird's transports and, finding the army also without funds, had begrudgingly given him £40,000 out of the half million he carried with him for the Central Junta supposedly governing the country from Madrid. Millions of Maria Theresa silver dollars were following close behind, he promised Baird. These did indeed come soon after, but when Moore was informed, and requested a half million from the two million received in Corunna, he was astonished to receive a reply from Baird stating that he had spent it all equipping his column and on supplies that would be left under guard along their line of retreat, and others which they would share when they linked up at Benavente. All at vastly inflated wartime prices, naturally.

The reason given for the shortage of money was that only silver dollars were acceptable currency in the peninsula and that the British treasury could not accumulate enough in so short a time. This line of reasoning is absurd, for international banking had evolved to such a stage that a promissory note by the British Ministers in Lisbon or Madrid would have secured sufficient sums short-term to alleviate the army's immediate crisis, with payment in sovereign equivalent to follow. Lady Hester Stanhope was able to draw sums of often one thousand pounds from local bankers in Constantinople, and even Beirut, only some two years later, merely by signing a draft on Coutts of London. To suggest that no money at all could be sent to Moore's army unless Maria Theresa silver dollars were physically placed in barrels in London, and that the British Minister in Madrid could not raise a penny, is the cause for suspicions that Castlereagh and Canning, through Frere, left Moore in this position out of personal spite, which are difficult to refute.

Moore's saviour was one of the few important aristocrats left in Spain at this time, the Marques de Cerralbo. Immediately Moore arrived in Salamanca the Marques offered him the use of his magnificent palace of San Boal, built in the manner peculiar to Salamanca, combining Gothic, Moorish and renaissance styles, with a double-gated wall making the central patio more private.

The Marques insisted that he would leave his butler to attend to the every requirement of Moore, his staff and all visitors, refusing any suggestion of payment as an insult to his hospitality. Moreover, the Marques suggested to a wealthy order of the city's nuns that it was their duty to assist an army come to fight the common enemy of church and state, Napoleon having seized one Pope, who died in captivity soon after owing to his advanced age, and then held his successor captive at Fontainebleau, pending his signing away virtually all his civil rights in the Italian Papal States. Thus, Moore's 47th birthday saw him with a splendid palace as his HQ and at last some cash in hand, for the nuns had given him the equivalent of £5,000 Sterling, enough to put his army into battle readiness with locally purchased equipment. The nuns also gave the British army permission to use several huge abandoned convents and their cloisters to dry themselves and rest. The local population also came to the convents to present all necessary food to the British troops, numbering 20,000 men, plus horses.

The men of the Marques's household were also sent out as intelligence gatherers for Moore. A report from Soult to Napoleon was read in this way and still exists in the Paris Archives. The conjecture as to who knew what, and when, concerning French strength can end at this point. During early November French strength had been brought up to 335,223 men, with 6,728 cavalry, and a ratio of artillery to men "never before seen in warfare".[11]

Moore was at last being treated as a man come to assist a country fighting for its freedom, but the army was uneasy. The veterans among them had only ever fought close to the refuge of the navy, which supplied all facilities and a quick route of sure escape if a battle was lost. Here, however, in the near centre of a huge country, with rumours as to the intention of the vastly superior numbers of French changing daily, it was easy to become nervous, but all still believed that if Moore led them they would not have their lives thrown away.

The only logical strategy was to await the arrival of Hope's column, with its twenty-four assorted heavier guns to add to the light field artillery accompanying the infantry and cavalry, and thereafter to retreat to the stronghold of Ciudad Rodrigo, sending messages for transports to assemble at Vigo to take off the whole army, if impossible odds were thrown at them. At the same time Baird's column marching from Corunna was told to halt, and them begin a slow retreat over the ground that they had covered, being almost out of the mountains and on to the plain of Leon. It was still totally feasible for Baird to reembark and sail around to reinforce the 10,000 British at Lisbon, for reinforcement or evacuation, as the Cabinet saw fit.

However, Moore's orders were to offer assistance to the Spanish armies in revolt against the French. Now that these armies had evaporated, apart from General Castaños making a futile regrouping before Madrid, Moore was left to divine what the Cabinet would have him do which could be strategically of use to Spain. One course of action that he was determined not to take was to go to Madrid and sacrifice his army in its futile defence, to do honour to politicians or add vain glory to the name of British arms. One fact is certain: Moore had done all he could to mend bridges with the British Cabinet, even cultivating Castlereagh's brother, Sir Charles Stewart, 3rd Lord Londonderry, who was a cavalry officer under his command. To the point thus far reached at Salamanca all Castlereagh's official despatches had approved of Moore's every move. The private correspondence, both to and from Moore, which he would cunningly refuse to produce before parliament, as being non-official, did the same, but only to this point.

It was obvious to Moore that he had been sent to aid a mere peasant revolt and that what served as the Spanish Central Government still continued to send gross exaggerations as to the

144

numbers and fighting ability of its various armies to London. The concept of a withdrawal to Ciudad Rodrigo and from there defending the passes into Portugal at that moment seemed the only logical step to take. Indeed, Wellesley was forced to the same conclusion when he retreated to the lines of Torres Vedras a year later. The one vital fact of which Moore was unaware at that time was that from 5 November Napoleon himself was leading this massive advance, thus every French soldiers' morale was lifted, so that it made them feel as if their numbers were doubled.

In mid-November, while still seeing tactical retreat as his only option, but keeping this opinion to himself, Moore addressed the assembled important citizens of Salamanca. The message was simple, given the fact, now known to all, that the Spanish armies had ceased to resist the French advance towards Madrid, the only way in which the British army could assist the Spanish people was if they could raise the whole countryside to attack the French at every point, as they had done the year before when they drove them up behind the Ebro. Rather prosaically, he was forced to end his address with an appeal for any transport wagons available and more food supplies.

News had come of the literal massacre of the army of the Conde de Belvidere defending Burgos, where out of a total of 13,000 Spanish regulars and 7,000 peasant auxiliaries, only 5,000 had been allowed finally to surrender, with the rest put to the sword. Additional bad news now came in that the northern army of Biscay, under General Blake, had been trapped at Espinosa on the Asturian border and defeated. However, they had escaped into the mountains after their defeat and would prove to be the only Spanish army which actually linked up with Moore to fight the French. It is not mentioned in the British accounts of the campaign that this northern army contained as its core some 15,000 of the best troops in all Spain. Moreover, they had been chosen by Napoleon and placed under the command of the Marquis of Romana to be sent to Denmark as an expeditionary force. Sir Arthur Wellesley had seen the wisdom of contacting this elite force, using a Scottish Benedictine priest, to advise them of the revolt against the French in their homeland. The whole force rebelled and was evacuated from Langeland on 21 August by the British Navy, but tragically they arrived at Espinosa only in time to join Blake's defeat. Their old commander from Denmark gathered the 9,000 survivors, however, and wrote to inform Moore of their existence north of the French rearguard near Burgos.[12]

On the 18th the news came that the French had swept through Valladolid, but had not wasted time on the small British force, whom they believed to be in retreat to Portugal as logic must dictate, but, rather, headed on to their initial main objective of Madrid to restore King Joseph to the throne. At that moment only three British brigades had actually arrived at Salamanca and the tail of the columns was still in Portuguese territory.

Moore waited, in the hope that his three columns from Portugal would converge before the French realized that the British were doing the reverse of that which the tenfold enemy superiority dictated and still advancing. The main cause for his concern at this time was not the French Emperor but the British Minister to Madrid, John Hookham Frere. This dilettante intellectual merely sat in his office in Madrid until forced to run south with the Central Junta and issued despatches to Moore which showed that he had no grasp of the reality of the military situation in the country, nor the political. One example from this time serves for all; when the French had sacked Burgos, massacred 15,000 Spaniards and were heading straight for Moore's HQ, three days' march on from Valladolid, Frere informed Moore that 11,000 French were advancing; the reality was 100,000! Fortunately by now Moore had sent out his own scouts to supplement the men sent by his host the Marques, ignoring political dictates over the safety of his army, and knew that it was Madrid which was to be attacked and not his still unassembled columns, which at that moment could do nothing to assist the doomed capital.

On 24 November Moore considered that, with so little truth in circulation, he must acquaint his ultimate master, Viscount Castlereagh, Minister of War, of the reality of the situation in which past misinformation from London had now placed him, merely by following orders based on these totally inaccurate despatches sent by the diplomatic corps. After describing the march to Salamanca and offering the possibility of falling back on Portugal, or, alternatively, were Hope and the guns cut off by the rapid French advance, of joining his guns to retire on Madrid, he continues: "The information which your Lordship now has renders it less necessary for me to dwell on the state of Spain, so different from the reports of officers employed at the H.Q.s of the various Spanish armies. They seem to have been most miserably deceived . . . Had the real defenceless state of the nation and its Central Government's character been known, I conceive that Cadiz and not Corunna would have been the place for disembarkation, with Seville or Cordova as the place of assembly . . . The Spanish armies are inferior in number to those of the French, and a great proportion of these are formed of peasantry . . . Even the armies of Castaños and Palafox united do not exceed 40,000 men . . . I am in no communication with any of the Generals commanding the Spanish armies . . . I am left ignorant of their plans or those of the Government . . . In this state of things it is difficult for me to form any plan for myself beyond the assembling of the army."

Moore also wrote to Frere in Madrid complaining of the lack of information of any description being forwarded to him, implying that Frere was simply not doing his job. He also again complains that "I do not have a shilling, as of the 17th. Lord Castlereagh promises millions in silver that are in passage, but also the necessity of [you] obtaining money locally." Frere sent no information and no money.[13]

Whilst wondering and waiting at Salamanca, Moore relieved the tension by writing to the only close female friend that he had, Lady Hester Stanhope. He had last written upon leaving

Portugal, saying how much her vibrant presence would have cheered the army "to see her prancing ahead 'à la Amazone'". Her reply, just received, was dated 26 October and mostly warned him of a plot within the Cabinet to place all the blame for the Swedish fiasco on his actions.

In his reply he told her not to concern herself with the plots of Ministers for past events: "They may have thrust me (for want of information) into a most critical situation here, and I believe that they will make no attack upon me until they see how I extricate myself. But at any rate, I should take no steps in my defence until I saw the attack begun, and then my defence will be in their and my correspondence . . . You must not be angry with me for not following your advice. I am not less sensible of the kindness which dictated it . . . If I ever have the pleasure of seeing you again I shall give you all my papers. They are in England."

Moore agreed to accept Lady Hester's youngest step-brother, James, as an additional ADC, although he already had more than enough with General Burrard also insisting on sending his son; neither would benefit from the adventure! He then allowed his private pessimism to show concerning the position that the government has placed him in through its ignorant enthusiasm: "I can refuse you nothing. He may then join me. He will, however, come too late: I shall already be beaten. I am within four marches of the French, with only a third of my force; and as the Spaniards have been dispersed in all directions my junction with the other two-thirds is most precarious; and when we all join we shall be very inferior to the enemy. The Spanish Government is weak and imbecile; and their armies have at no time been numerous, the country [population] is not armed, nor, as far as I can judge, enthusiastic. We have been completely deceived by the contemptible fellows sent as correspondents to the armies; and now perhaps the discovery comes too late."

The letter, written over three days, ends more gently on the 20 November 1808: "We are in a scrape; but I hope that I shall have the spirit to get out of it. You must, however, be prepared to hear very bad news. The troops are in good spirits, as if things were much better . . . Farewell, my dear Lady Hester. If I can extricate myself and those with me from the present difficulties, and can beat the French I shall return to you with satisfaction; but if not, it will be better that I should never quit Spain. I remain, always, very faithfully and sincerely yours, John Moore." He would never find time to write to her again.[14]

Word reached Moore on 28 November of the complete defeat of Castaños' army standing between the French and Madrid, which had been reinforced by General Palafox's last reserves. A total of 45,000 men including peasant auxiliaries had been swept aside by the French at Tudela. Now only the garrison held the capital, with Napoleon camped nearby awaiting their terms of surrender. The information came not from Frere, running with the Central Junta towards refuge in Seville, but from rumours among the local population on 9 December. Upon receipt of this news, Moore decided to halt Baird's retreat, allow his own army finally to unite and meanwhile await events in Madrid. Were the Spanish to achieve further miracles of defence by the civil population, as at Saragossa and Valencia a year ago, he might be able to assist them by attacking the French rear. Hope had sent a messenger on 5 December to state that he was near to Valladolid, having taken the road north at Villacastin to avoid Madrid itself, and passed unseen by the French. Baird also sent word that he was holding his column at Astorga, whilst bringing up supplies from Corunna. The French, he stated, some 9,000 strong, were staying in place under Marshal Soult, Duke of Dalmatia, to the N.W. of Saldanha, behind the River Carrion, a tributary of the River Duero, flowing on into Portugal until reaching the Atlantic. Obviously they were so placed in order to guard the French line of supply to the army before Madrid, he commented.

At last the Spanish commanders began to contact Moore's HQ. General Castaños wrote that, although beaten at Tudela, he was uniting 35,000 troops before Madrid to reinforce the 40,000 defenders behind the walls. The letter pleaded with Moore to join him or attack the French rear, but Moore remained adamant in his refusal to believe in any further claims of the Spanish ability to resist. He knew that if he did so his army would be annihilated when Napoleon arrived with his veteran reinforcements and the city's limited supplies of food and munitions inevitably gave out. He continued to wait and observe events and, while so doing, was visited by two veteran Spanish Generals, Esculante and Bueno, both in their seventies, who pleaded the same cause as Castaños. Moore declined to lead his army to certain entrapment in Madrid and, while he still intended to attack the French rear if Madrid withstood the siege, he committed himself to nothing. The elderly emissaries left convinced that he meant to retire on Ciudad Rodrigo and even reported this to Frere at the temporary seat of the evacuated Spanish Central Government in Talavera. Spies placed in the Spanish Government sent this belief to Napoleon as solid fact.

Frere had chosen most unwisely in his selection of a messenger, when finally he made contact, in the person of a French Royalist émigré known as Colonel Charmilly. The man was a notorious adventurer and swindler, who had just been declared bankrupt in England, and Moore refused to receive him initially. The note that he carried was, however, declared to be genuine. In this letter Frere demanded that Moore march to assist the defence of Madrid. The duplicity of Charmilly, whom Moore suspected of being a double agent, was such that whilst he had left Madrid on 2 December, when the army was already preparing to surrender, he had made Frere believe that the city would hold out for some time.[15]

So deceived, he wrote: "The report, just brought me by Colonel Charmilly of the state in which he left Madrid . . . so much exceeds everything which I had ventured to say of the spirit of the people that I cannot forbear representing to you in the strongest manner the propriety, not to say the necessity, of supporting the determination of the Spanish people by all the means that have been entrusted to you for that purpose. I have no hesitation in taking upon myself any degree of responsibility which may attach itself to this advice; as I consider the fate of Spain to depend absolutely for the present upon the decision that you may adopt. I say for the present, for such is the spirit and character of the country, that, even if abandoned by the British I should by no means despair of their ultimate success."[16]

When a government enquiry into the whole expedition was held this letter's existence would be denied by Frere, but Charmilly had taken a copy, which he published as a pamphlet in London, as even his black soul was affronted by the attempt to blame Moore, the dead hero, for any events not seen, with hindsight, as having been the best course to have taken.

The reality was that the population was ready to fight, but the duplicitous leader of the army in Madrid, General Morla, was secretly bargaining for advantage for himself both then and later, were he to deliver the city to Napoleon, the proof being that, as soon as decently allowed, he was given a high position in the French administration and kept all his property and titles. It is highly likely that the letter which arrived on the same day as Frere's, dated the very day of the end of negotiations with Napoleon for the city's surrender, was a typically Napoleonic trick to draw Moore's army into a well prepared ambush near Madrid. Morla persuaded the people's leaders that they could not hope to hold out against the French, now that Napoleon had arrived with his Imperial Guard, 'The Invincibles', and other strong reserves. To do so was to have the city sacked and plundered, with all men massacred; Morla returned on 4 December to state that the city would surrender.

Meanwhile, the French had occupied the high ground of the palace of 'The Retiro', from which to bombard the city if necessary.

Morla wrote: "The army which General Castaños commanded, of 25,000 men, is falling back on Madrid to unite with the garrison . . . The force which was at Somosierra, of 10,000, is

151

moving to the same purpose . . . In the city 40,000 more wait to join them. With this number of troops the enemy's army which has presented itself is not to be feared . . . If no force is immediately opposed to you the junta hope that you will join these armies or fall upon the enemy's rear . . . The rapidity of your excellency's movements, it is not doubted, will be such as the interest of both countries require." The letter was signed, "With great consideration, the Prince of Castel Franco, and Thomas Morla".[17]

Morla's treachery is explained by the fact that he was taken aside and quietly reminded by Napoleon that, under international rules of war, he could seize and execute him for breaking the terms of Dupont's surrender in Andalusia the previous year. For he had not returned the army and its guns to France, but, once disarmed, held them prisoner. A Basque town had been sacked in reprisal and all its 1,500 inhabitants put to the sword, so Morla had every reason to expect his life to be worth nothing unless he could buy it by delivering Madrid, and hopefully the British expeditionary army as well.[18]

Before being ordered out of the British camp, where he was inspecting everything in detail, Charmilly demanded an audience with Moore in person, insisting that if there was no reply given to the first note from Frere he had instructions to deliver a second.

"Mr Frere to Sir John Moore"
Dec., 3rd., 1808

"Sir,

In the event, which I do not wish to presuppose, of your continuing the determination already announced to me of retiring with the army under your command, I have to request that Colonel Charmilly, who is bearer of this, and whose intelligence has already been referred to, may be previously examined before a council of War.

I have etc., J. H. Frere."

The implication contained in Frere's second communication was that Moore, lacking zeal for his command, must be driven to do his duty by threats. Moore was furious and walked about the room verbally upbraiding Frere's ignorance and impertinence. Charmilly had to ask twice to be allowed to retire before Moore heard him through his burst of invective and coldly gave his permission, casting the offensive note into the fire. The formal reply that he wrote to Minister Frere dated 6 December was, however, merely calmly sarcastic:

> "I shall abstain from any remark upon the two letters from you, delivered to me last night and this morning by Colonel Charmilly, or on the message which accompanied them. I certainly at first did feel and express much indignation at a person like him being made a channel of communication of that sort from you to me . . . I shall thank you not to employ him in any further communication with me . . . It is impossible not to remark that, whatever enthusiasm exists in the country, a small proportion of it indeed belongs to the [Central] Junta; who would otherwise, I think, have found some place more central and less remote than Badajos for their residence.
>
> I have the honour to be etc., John Moore."

Moore pondered on how he might theoretically comply with his orders to place himself, and the army that the Cabinet had given him to command, under their hopelessly misinformed Minister's political instructions, to communicate with the Spanish Government and put his army where they saw it best used. The answer suddenly came to him from their only official communication, treacherously designed to lead him on to a defeated Madrid and a waiting Napoleon. In the letter from Morla was the phrase, "if no force is directly opposed to you, fall back and unite with your army, or take the direction to fall upon the enemy's rear". The meaning, as Madrid was known to be lost by the writer of the letter, could, unless he was proved to be actively Napoleon's tool, as Moore suspected, be construed as meaning that he was to unite with the remnants of Blake's army of Biscay and attack the French rearguard of 10,000 under Marshall Soult, which held open Napoleon's vital supply route from the Pyrenees.

Two results could come from this strategy. The first was that, once joined with Baird's men, now back at Astorga, the British would number 40,000 and could take Soult's force by surprise, by attacking whilst appearing to be retreating, and annihilate it. The British could then see if this ignited the whole country to rise, as it had done the previous year; if not, then the way was held and stores laid down for a retreat through the Galician passes, back over Baird's entry route to be evacuated from Corunna, the narrow mountain tracks making a perfect setting for a classic rearguard action, where the enemy could be kept from mass attack by the nature of the terrain with well placed marksman and light field guns.

The second, grander design, worthy of Napoleon himself, was to cause him great concern, that his supply route might be overwhelmed and his army trapped in the far south, just as had occurred to the army of Dupont the previous year. Napoleon had proclaimed when he crossed the Pyrenees that his eagles would be planted on the ramparts of Lisbon within three months. Thus he had revealed his next moves to Moore. He must move south with all speed, take Andalusia and receive the capitulation of the Central Government Junta in Seville, then swing to the north-west and on to Lisbon, held only by the British garrison of 10,000 men. It was to Lisbon that Moore must, therefore, logically be falling back, for its defence or evacuation. When, instead, Moore appeared at the other end of the country, Napoleon must turn back to reopen his supply route, so leaving the previously unconquered army of Andalusia time to regroup, and be assisted by the British via Cadiz, where they had 10,000 men already placed as a reserve.

If the French did return south to cross the Sierra Morena mountain passes and also the Guadalquivir River, it would be with an exhausted army, or not for another year.

In either case Moore's army could retreat with honour from their present predicament and, hopefully, live to fight another day, even reentering the war by sailing down the Atlantic coast to Cadiz. Moore would have fulfilled the general directives of the Cabinet, however ill-informed they were to the reality of the Spanish conflict. All this could be brought about with some reasonable chance of success, even though he still did not have a penny sent in official funds with which to put the plan into action, but at Astorga were the vast stockpiles of food and munitions upon which Baird had spent the whole two million dollars and claimed to have brought through the passes with great difficulty.

The decision made, the British vanguard marched out of Salamanca in fine order and high spirits on 11 December 1808 to the cheers of the population. The days were fine and clear and the men marched easily under a warm winter sun. The reverse applied to the nights, for, under a blanket of stars, the men shivered in the frost. One column made straight for Baird at Astorga, while a second, screened by cavalry, sought out the actual route of the French supply train between Burgos and Valladolid, basing themselves at Toro and Tordesillas on the River Duero.

The great strategic play, which would with hindsight decide the ultimate fate of Napoleon, and of Europe, had been conceived and now put in motion by Moore. If it was to succeed, the overall plan, and the various options to be taken according to Napoleon's reaction, could only be known to Moore and his closest confidants. The soldiers and junior officers could only be told that they were off to trap Marshal Soult, Duke of Dalmatia, or the 'Duke of Dalmation' as the British soldiers called him. The prospect was relished by them and they were all fired up with the pre-battle adrenalin release, plus the prospects of relieving the French rearguard of loot accumulated from two-thirds of Europe. Moore's only miscalculation was in not taking into account what would happen to all this built-up lust for battle if necessity instead required a tactical withdrawal, should Napoleon arrive too swiftly to defend his rear. His ability to cover ground at seemingly impossible speed and then throw his men directly into battle was well known, regardless of the casualties. A dictator need never be worried by the opinion of parliament or the people, nor must he plead for resources. All he must do to stay in power is to be seen always to be victorious.

CHAPTER NINETEEN

Napoleon Marches on Moore

A small event now occurred which gave all the advantage to Moore for just long enough to alter the course of history, as is often the case during the fog of war. A lone French messenger had been killed by peasant partisans near Segovia, north of Madrid. The patriotic but businesslike partisans had sold his document pouch and its contents to a Captain Walters for £20, reasoning that the documents must be of much value to the British by their large seals and the fact that the messenger was an officer.

The peasants' shrewdness was verified when it was discovered that among the documents were uncoded orders from Berthier, Prince of Neufchâtel, commander of the French army before Madrid, addressed to Marshal Soult, commander of the 2nd army corps at Saldana. The orders were for Soult to take control of Benavente, Leon and Zamora, for the purpose of making continual sweeps of this area, from the Galician mountains to the River Duero, and thus prevent the formation of partisan groups into large formidable bands, capable of attacking the supply route from Bayonne to Madrid as it crossed the Plain of Leon. Moreover, the document outlined the marching route of the French advance on Badajoz, now that Madrid was subdued, and gave Napoleon's personal H.Q. as some 4 miles outside of Madrid at Charmartin. The opinion was given that Soult could expect to meet no Spanish regular troops in the Plain of Leon, and, as for the British, they had already retreated into Portugal.[1]

Moore was overjoyed. For the first time in the campaign he had full knowledge of the enemy's plans and positions, whereas they were totally mistaken as to his own. Apart from the despatches to Soult, a captured French Colonel had sought to buy eventual repatriation for himself by giving away the true strength of the French column heading for Badajoz that Moore expected to draw off to pursue him. Moreover, Napoleon led the army himself, which was composed of ten army corps, the Imperial Guard elite corps and no less than thirty-six regiments of veteran cavalry. The treacherous French Colonel also confirmed that Napoleon still had no knowledge of the exact British position, although he was quite certain that they were retreating into Portugal.[2]

Moore had been planning on making his stand at Valladolid on about 15 December, there to await the French to be drawn to him, with Vigo as his escape route. The Berthier letters to Soult, combined with the treacherous Colonel's information, changed the tactical position entirely. Moore no longer had to announce his presence in the middle of the country astride the French supply route and await events. Now he could secretly march to Benavente, some 35 miles from his supply depot at Astorga, unite with Baird's and Romana's forces and then attack the still stationary army of Soult's rearguard by a surprise move due east, with a superiority of five to one. Moreover, the junction with Baird's forces would bring his force up to strength in the areas where it was presently weak, for with Baird had come three field batteries and three regiments of Hussars, the 7th, 10th and 15th.

All this information was dutifully reported to Castlereagh by Moore in a private letter outlining his changed plans and asking that most of the evacuation fleet prepare to move at his summons from Vigo to Corunna, as he would doubtless now retreat via the Galician passes once he had drawn Napoleon's legions upon him from the south. Moore also asked that General Sir John Cradock, who now commanded in Portugal, be informed. He ended the letter: "Unless the Spaniards make more ardour and energy in their own cause, all Britain's aid would be of no avail."

Canning had already written on 10 December approving all

these new plans of Moore's and his past actions, so tacitly under-lining Frere's previous misunderstanding of the whole Spanish theatre of war. Unfortunately, Moore would only receive this letter of encouragement when retreating through Benavente.

Frere now tried to cover himself by sending a messenger with a despatch which arrived on 16 December ordering Moore to undertake what he was already doing on his own initiative, namely a union with Romana's forces to hold the north-west of Spain.

Unfortunately, before the letter to Castlereagh, dated 16 December, could be despatched, reports came in that made it necessary to add a postscript, stating that the element of surprise was now diminished.[3] General Charles Stewart's orders were to search with his dragoons for enemy outposts and report the positions to Moore. However, when he came upon a detachment of French infantry accompanied by a large cavalry contingent sleeping around camp fires on the night of 12 December in the village of Rueda the temptation to annihilate them was too much for him. Stewart's men swept through the village either killing or taking prisoner the whole enemy unit, but, as is almost inevitable in such an action, some French went undetected and reported back to Soult that the British were sending raiding parties into the area of the supply route which he guarded. Moore now expressed the possibility to Castlereagh that were Soult to discover the magnitude of the British advance he might well fall back on Burgos to join Junot's 8th Corps, which was advancing to that city as a reserve of 3,000 to Soult's force.

On 17 December Moore had his H.Q. at Castronuevo, near enough to Benavente where Baird's advanced position was estab-lished with three brigades for him to ride over to report to Moore as the overall Commander. Unfortunately, he did not bring good news, for the French had moved at last from Saldanha and taken Leon, 30 miles to the N.W., but, while it dispersed the army of Romana that Moore was marching to join, it meant that Soult did not as yet realize that the entire British army was marching to confront him. Soult was still following orders to keep all Spanish forces from reforming into a real threat to the supply lines and not scouting seriously to his south-east.

The Spanish forces under Romana, though regrouped, had not been resupplied and had been forced to retreat on the main British supply base of Astorga. Their numbers had been brought up by peasant volunteers to 20,000, but they now were clogging the town and hampering British mobility. Baird stated that they were, however, in good order, with, surprisingly, no drunkenness. The peasantry was drawn from sturdy clean-living mountain village folk, he stated, and needed only arms and training to be good soldiers.

Moore had one message from Romana, declaring himself ready to advance to wherever he was required with 22,000 men. Baird brought another, of more recent date, declaring that Romana was now retreating with his force into the Galician mountains. A messenger was sent at the gallop by Moore to ascertain what Romana's actual intentions now were. Baird had a reputation for being blunt and outspoken. Thus, it is extremely likely that Romana's men were dispersed to the villages of the Galician foothills to keep the vital crossroads town of Astorga open for movement of men and material after his complaining of "their clogging up the town". If he complained of this to Moore, he was not a man to have kept quiet in the town that he commanded.

The lack of a clear understanding developing between Moore and Romana was also quite possibly a result of Moore's atrocious handwriting. Indeed, prior to this date Romana had asked Moore to write to him in French, for, while he spoke and read English fluently, he simply could not make sense of the English written by Moore. It certainly does not appear that Moore was aware of the significance of the references to the "10,000 picked men" who were with Romana as being the same hardened veterans who remained from the force of 15,000 that Napoleon had handpicked to serve on the Elbe front, so cleverly spirited away by Wellesley's intrigue from Denmark. Were this fact known to him, it is difficult to know why he should write in his journal on the 17th, after meeting at last with Baird to discuss tactics concerning Romana's position and intentions, that "In truth I placed no dependence on him or his army, and was determined to persevere in moving up to Soult in all events[4]

In the dearth of information sent to Moore by Frere and Castlereagh, and the previous superlatives constantly used to describe Spanish forces which then dissolved like morning mist before the onrushing French, the fact that these were indeed elite Spanish troops, who only needed fresh arms and munitions to increase his strength by 25 percent, was truly unknown to the British Commander. Moreover, Moore was well aware that one in five of his own men were criminals, forced into uniform and despised by him and his own elite brigades. Thus, only ignorance of the fact that Romana's regulars had been selected personally by the Master of Europe at the zenith of his power and glory can explain Baird and Moore failing to respect these troops and use them to their full potential.

Once having deplored the attitude of the British Commander towards the only Spanish troops who had made an effort to join him and showed a wish to fight, it must be also made clear that Moore had already rejected Castlereagh's offer of reinforcements. He had stated that to confront the French he would like six or seven thousand more cavalry, but that they were useless in the mountains through which he must inevitably retreat once the main French army and probably Napoleon himself were drawn from their southern conquest to attack him. The attack on Soult's 13,000 was as well done by 40,000 troops as 50,000, for it was the bait to draw off Napoleon, and in itself, even if a total victory was gained, served "only to add character to British arms".[5] After the battle, retreat before Napoleon was inevitable and planned. It would then be up to the whole Spanish people to decide their fate, after Napoleon's defeat of their last southern armies and Government had been disrupted.[6]

The next day snow began to fall and a violent wind then sprang up to push it into the faces of the British army as it advanced along the east bank of the River Esla. This tributary of the Duero ran due north to south, almost exactly parallel to its twin, the Carrion, some 30 miles to the east, behind which the fixed French positions were defended. The British marched between the two rivers to prevent a frontal attack being accompanied by a cavalry encirclement to the rear. The rivers in northern Spain were at this time of year great barriers, for they were fed by the constant snow and rain in the mountains and their few crossing points could be easily guarded, the rest being a rushing swirl of deep near-freezing water. A temporary H.Q. was set up at Mayorga for the night and the next day, 23 December, saw Moore in Sahagun, which he intended to use as his base to assault Soult, centred on Saldanha less than ten miles away, but with the River Carrion protecting the French forces. The trick would be to lure them across to attack the British instead of fighting a defensive battle, for Napoleon had heard of the British advance on 21 December; time was no longer on Moore's side. Moreover, the rest of the British army must come up, along with the supplies, before uniting and advancing to do battle.

The British vanguard was billeted in a vast deserted convent which accounted for half of Sahagun's buildings, the troops were busy drying out and greasing their weapons for the coming battle. Lord Paget and the 15th Hussars moved out on a night sweep, lest the enemy be quietly advancing upon them at night, as the British themselves intended to do two nights hence in a surprise attack on Soult's main army, crossing the river to get at the enemy if that was required.

Lord Paget did not come across a whole army on the move, but a very large French cavalry force about the same business as himself. The element of surprise fell to the British cavalry, however, and a force of between 600 to 700 French were totally routed. Whilst the majority were put to the sabre in the action, two Lieutenant Colonels and eleven other officers were captured, along with 140 troopers. Moore wrote in his journal that "it was

a handsome thing and well done".[7] The infantry were tremen-
dously invigorated by this overwhelming cavalry victory in the
largest skirmish with the enemy of the campaign, which had still
not given the British main army's position away.

The British press would later elevate this to a British victory as
"The Battle of Sahagun", but it must have been clear to Moore
and his army this was merely a large skirmish and a prelude to
the battle about to occur if Soult could be drawn out to fight, or
they attacked him the night after next. It was at this point that
Moore received a messenger with the news he had been hoping
for and yet dreading if it came too soon; Napoleon had turned
about in his march south at Talavera and was now amazingly close
at Tordesillas. His cavalry units had ridden on ahead and had been
quietly waiting close by, near Benavente, since 21 December.[8]

Napoleon had left his weather-proofed carriage to set the pace
and inspire the men. He had then marched on foot at the head
of 50,000 infantry in hail and sleet over the passes of the
Guadarrama Mountains. He had covered 200 miles of hard terrain
in continually foul weather in ten days in the manner that had
made him at that moment the undisputed master of Europe. He
intended to settle the matter of the small, but impudent, British
expeditionary force decisively and then return to crush the
Central Junta, still claiming to the world that it was the legiti-
mate government of Spain, ruling from Seville. Napoleon's only
comment concerning the British was that he wished that they had
come with ten times the numbers, so that he might defeat the
whole of Britain's military capability in one decisive battle. The
boast was widely put about and the echo would come back to drive
him and his bruised ego from Spain in a few days, never to return.

The night of 26 December, when Moore received reports
that Napoleon's infantry march had reached Tordesillas, some
60 miles or three days' march from Sahagun, was one of mental
anguish for him. The French cavalry regiments which had been
near Benavente since the 21st were already placed to cut off
Moore's retreat across the River Esla to Astorga and the road

into the defensible narrow passes beyond. During the night before the main British army's advance to be in place for a night attack on Soult's army, now reinforced by 3,000 troops from Valencia to 16,000 overall, Moore saw that it was totally impossible to engage in battle before Napoleon cut him off from the intended line of retreat. In fact if the army turned west at first light they had two days to get ahead of Napoleon's northwards advance. The reserve would then hopefully fight a prolonged rearguard action as the guns and the bulk of the army escaped into the passes. While the men slept, dreaming of the coming battle, Moore explained in a letter to go by messenger immediately to Broderick holding Corunna that he must retire without giving battle to Soult. Another was to be sent on from there by fast frigate to Castlereagh, again, unfortunately, as a private letter.[9]

For Moore, personally, the stratagem had succeeded perfectly, with Napoleon on his heels and not on those of the remnants of Spanish nationhood in Andalusia. Unfortunately the great trainer of soldiers by Rottenburg's concept of the troops understanding their objectives had not considered how to break the news to an army keyed up to annihilate the long-sought enemy. Indeed Hope's and Alten's brigades had already set off and had to be recalled in torrential rain that would continue for the first decisive days of the retreat, drenching the British, but blinding the French as to their exact positions.

Moore then sent a messenger to Romana, asking him to appear as a close-ranked army, and to make a stand at Mansilla, rather like a tethered goat, as a lure, for Soult knew the Spanish force to be dispersed near there. Amazingly his scouts, sweeping further out, had still not been able to find the main British position, even though it was poised like a tiger about to spring upon him, a tiger that Moore would soon have to try to jump on the back of, to calm and turn about. The ruse worked and the two-day advantage which allowed Moore's army to reach Benavente and the road to Corunna must be seen to have been bought with Spanish blood, as General Romana's 9,000 best men held the flank against Soult's full assault.

The decision made and communicated, Moore made the last entry into his journal, before closing it for ever. It read:

> "Generals Hope and Fraser retire this day to Mayorga, Sir David with his division will march tomorrow to Valencia, (village) and I shall follow Hope and Fraser, with the Reserve and two light corps, by Mayorga and Valderas to Benavente. Lord Paget, with the cavalry will follow me.
>
> "If we can steal two marches upon the French we shall be quiet. If we are followed I must close, and stop and offer battle.
>
> "At this season of the year, in a country without fuel, it is impossible to bivouac; the villages are small, which obliges us to march thus by corps in succession. Our retreat, therefore, becomes more difficult."[10]

General Moore then made his last communication to the odious Frere, which concluded, after a general summation of the situation, thus: "I wish it to be apparent to the whole world, as it is to every individual of this army, that we have done everything in our power in support of the Spanish cause, and that we do not abandon it until long after the Spaniards have abandoned us."

CHAPTER TWENTY

The Retreat Through the Passes

While Moore's journal ceased at Sahagun, his letters continued until the last day of his life; and there were others recording the tragic, and glorious, moments of this vast enterprise – the retreat and embarkation of Britain's fighting force. Spanish and French pens were also recording these events from their perspectives, as were many British officers of lower rank, and even literate private soldiers. Thus a more objective account of Moore's actions may obtained than had his journal continued.

One example, showing great perception of events, comes from Captain James Sterling, 42nd Royal Highlanders. He left a 'Memoir of the Campaign of 1808 in Spain' in manuscript form that was included by Maurice in his conclusions to his account of the war.[1]

Sterling wrote: "So eager were my men to come to a reckoning with Soult, 'The Duke of Damnation', that when told that they must go back to their quarters, ready to retreat in the morning, they threw down to a man their precious firelocks, that until then they guarded as their greatest treasure."

One fact must be clearly held in mind when considering the behaviour of the British troops on the march to their final embarkation at either Vigo or Corunna. In the elite regiments, apart from some initial disapproval at the decision not to press home the attack from both officers and men, discipline did not, in general, break down and the casualties during the hardships of the passes were few. It was in the line regiments, where men had been snatched drunk or by brute force from low taverns or the gutter, to be forced into uniform, that such 'soldiers' reverted to type. The looting of houses and wine cellars, with the resulting drunkenness, was indeed prevalent. The fault lay with the officers, who were themselves of a lower calibre, as a result of commissions costing less in unfashionable regiments. Once the fear of organized discipline being enforceable was removed the criminal element became uncontrollable. Moore had not trained or selected this army, but had inherited it in Portugal, troublemakers and slothful officers included. So he can hardly be blamed for the shameful conduct of those few who ran ahead to pillage and cause chaos. Moreover, at all times during the retreat he was at the tail of the column commanding the rearguard, and in almost constant skirmishes with the French pursuers.

The same Captain Sterling's manuscript proves that the junior officers were perfectly conversant at this stage with Moore's main purpose in drawing Napoleon north and that Soult was not the main objective. In proof of this he wrote: "These circumstances [Napoleon's closeness in great strength] caused our General to relinquish an attack which, although successful, could not have been of any ultimate advantage to the cause we were engaged in."[2] The accusation that the junior officers thought that Moore was running away from the battle he had come to fight, as the soldiers may have done initially, is rendered untrue.

Neither was Moore unique at this period in finding the British soldier eager to march resolutely to do battle against any odds, but to feel disgraced and turn into an uncontrollable rabble when ordered to retreat, even to regroup. Indeed, even the great Wellesley himself found that he had identical problems to those of Moore when he retreated to hold the lines of Torres Vedras and in the sacking of Badajoz and Burgos. The Duke of Wellington, as Wellesley became, later claimed that he did not establish true discipline in the Peninsular Army, even by judicious hanging and flogging, until 1810.[3] The argument that Moore's problems were owing to his being over-kind to his men is thus negated by the admission of the greatest disciplinarian of the period. Moreover, the sack of Burgos by retreating British troops was not until 1813.

The Spanish population of the villages through which the British began their retreat in such harsh weather did not help themselves from receiving bad treatment by hurling insults at the sodden troops as cowards who ran away while their General Romana fought the French. These peasants could know nothing of the grand stratagem or events in the south, but by slamming doors and shutters of houses and barns to the frozen soldiers they became the target of all the bad feeling of the men towards the nation that they had marched to save when it had done little or nothing to assist them in the process. The barred doors and shutters swiftly received rifle butts as visiting cards and served as fuel to warm the men who now pushed in where none would invite them. The precedent having been set by the elite Highlanders, it became the normal way to deal with reluctant villages, who had previously promised to shelter and feed the troops, via their magistrates, now in hiding.[4]

Baird's division, having knowledge of the route, took the vanguard, followed by the heavy guns that were Hope's responsibility. These at all cost must not be allowed to be captured, for at that time they represented the army's honour, as had the golden eagles of a Roman legion, a tradition encouraged by the Treasury.

Christmas Day of 1808 saw Moore with his H.Q. established at Mayorga, with the River Esla between his army and Benavente, on the road to Astorga, behind which lay the Galician passes. Until all the men under his responsibility had crossed the river Moore would maintain his H.Q. at this position. Heavy rains were still falling, turning the unpaved roads to foot-sucking clay, especially once the gun train had moved to the rear. The river was beginning to rise and it was only with the aid of boats that the infantry protecting the guns could follow their draft horses across the ford. The bridge at Castrogonzalo, some miles downstream to the south, was reported by scouts to be intact, with no French in sight. The rest of the army crossed the Esla by this means and without incident. The bridge was to then be blown up behind them by the Engineer Corps. The enemy had not as yet come in their direction in full force and the sudden move south confused them sufficiently for Lord Paget's and his cavalry to hold them back, despite having been in action now for three days and nights without rest.

Leaving the Engineers to their task, Moore crossed over and arrived in Benavente, still unoccupied by the French cavalry regiments, for it was a seemingly unimportant and unfortified town. Fortunately, these massed regiments had now headed north to aid Soult. The vast multitude of men and horses had bivouacked so close to it, without realizing its vital importance to the British plan to draw their Emperor to the north and then take that town as their first step to an escape to the coast, both Vigo and Corunna being accessible from there. Hope was now waiting there with his guns for orders as to the route he should take.

The army were allowed two days for rest at Benavente and from the H.Q. established there by Moore a General Order was read to all of the troops by their officers:
"Headquarters, Benavente, 27 December 1808.

"The Commander of the Forces has observed with concern the bad conduct of the troops at a moment when they are about to come into contact with the enemy . . . He is the more concerned at this, as, until lately, the behaviour of that part of the army, at least, which was under his own immediate command was exemplary and did them much honour. The misbehaviour of the troops of the column which marched by Valderas to this place exceeds what he could have believed of British soldiers. It is disgraceful to the Officers, as it strongly marks their negligence and inattention . . .

"The Spanish forces [Romana's] have been overpowered

169

and until such time as they are reassembled and ready again to come forward, the situation of the army must be arduous, and such as to call for the exertion of qualities the most rare and valuable in a military body. These are not bravery alone, but patience and constancy under fatigue and hardship, obedience to command, sobriety, firmness, and resolution, in every situation in which they may be placed . . . It is impossible for the General to explain to his army the motive for the movements he now directs. The Commander of the forces can, however, assure the army that he has made none since he left Salamanca which he did not foresee, and was not prepared for; and as far as he is a judge, they have answered the purposes for which they were intended . . . The army must rest assured that there is nothing that he has more at heart than their honour and that of their country."[6]

Meanwhile, while their humanitarian commander was appealing to the good he believed existed in the roughest of men, if kindly treated, instead of hanging the worse offenders as an example, the Engineers were still attempting to displace the massive stones of the Roman bridge across the Esla. Well maintained, it had resisted flash floods from the mountains for two millennia and was not easily thrown down by the uncontained black powder blasts of the period. While they were trying various positions and amounts of explosives, they were covered by General Stewart, with a picket of the Infantry Regiment of the King's German Legion and some brigades of the 18th and 3rd German Light Dragoons[7], who were in turn covered by sharpshooters of the rifle brigades. The explosions echoed across the Plain of Leon and drew the attention of possibly the most formidable cavalry of all Europe, the Imperial Cavalry Guard, commanded by General Count Charles Lefebvre-Desnouettes, the favourite ADC of the Emperor and nephew of Josephine. The magnificently attired and mounted cavalry swept down on the still-standing bridge 600 strong, like hawks onto startled rabbits, or so their master

Napoleon imagined from the vantage point of a low hill some mere hundreds of yards distant. The surprise that these Anglo-German 'rabbits' were about to give to the pride of his entire army was destined to change the course of history.[8]

Finding that a direct frontal assault against the bridge, with the infantry lined up before and on it, to be unwise without their own infantry to cover them, the Count led his men upstream to a swollen ford. There he valiantly plunged his horse into the raging stream, swimming it across into the opposite shallows, while calling on his men to follow. The Dragoons, being mounted infantry, quickly ran to their horses and galloped the 300 yards up river to cut off this valiant enterprise. General Lefebvre was also Colonel of this most elite of all French regiments and could hardly believe what was happening when mere dragoon troopers charged along the shallows into the river and cut himself and some seventy of his best men off from those following, who swam back to the opposite bank. A sabre cut to the head convinced him of the reality of the occurrence. He had been captured beneath the very eyes of the Emperor himself, who did not pardon failure, however valiant the attempt.

Not appreciating the rare fish that they had cut down in the river, the dragoons handed him over to the infantry to march to Moore's H.Q. for evaluation, taking only his magnificent sword as a trophy. Lord Paget's cavalry and field guns then came up to patrol the river for the rest of the day and night, until the bridge finally had two of its arches blown up.

Upon entering Moore's presence and proclaiming his identity, the shivering and now wretched man collapsed into a chair. Moore immediately began to clean and dress his head wound personally, while giving orders to Colborne, his Military Secretary, to search out from his baggage one of the dozens of sets of clean winter underwear that, together with similar quantities of shirts, filled Moore's most important trunk. A flag of truce secured the French General's voluminous luggage from across the river, and then the Imperial Guards, being without backing, retired after their humiliated master, who had shut himself within his waterproof campaign coach. He had proclaimed that he would fight Moore personally, for he was the only General left in Europe worthy of his personal attention. Now, at the first encounter, with only second-rate troops, vastly inferior in number to his vaunted Imperial Guards, he had been personally humiliated. Seeing that Moore would inevitably escape to the passes via British-held Astorga, he set in motion a plan to extract his person and honour from what was becoming a fiasco and not the triumphal sweep through Spain and Portugal he had foreseen. Marshall Ney was summoned with reinforcements to take Astorga along with Soult; the British, with their backs to the escape route to the sea, might well be capable of many more desperate defensive actions. Should these result in defeats for the French, then they must not be attached personally to the name of the all-conquering Bonaparte. That day the Imperial Cavalry lost 200 men, or one third of its strength, while the British took only fifty casualties overall.

Moore invited his captive to dine with him and, on the mere verbal promise that he would not attempt escape, handed him his own fine Indian sabre to fill his empty scabbard and so restore his honour and morale. He was then sent on ahead to be forwarded to England as a prisoner, and showed the worth of his honour by escaping in 1811, perhaps calculating that the man who had taken only his word and not a signed document as advised was dead.[9]

Meanwhile at Mansilla, General Romana was also attempting to hold or destroy the only other bridge over the Elsa. He placed three thousand infantry, together with four guns, to block it, but lacked professional engineers with which to destroy it. Soult's army had now been reinforced to equal that of the British and was determined to cross in order to block Moore's march to Astorga. The French light horseman charged the bridge repeatedly until they broke through the Spanish troops, many of whom were fighting while suffering from the first symptoms of typhus.

The small dam broke and Soult's army surged over. Once again, however, Romana's army had hindered the French for long enough for the British to be organized on the road to Astorga and safety. At this juncture the whole rearguard action was to be won or lost by the ability of the British guns and soldiers to get to, and hold, Astorga, before, with only Baird's column to defend the town, it was taken by the French. While British accounts speak only of Spanish defeats, the reality must once again be emphasized that it was Romana's men who fought the battle between Leon and Astorga against the main French force. The valiant encounters and rearguard actions of British troops and cavalry were in truth all only skirmishes of greater or lesser degree. Only at Lugo would Moore stand to give battle briefly, until the final reckoning before Corunna. Romana's exhausted, under-armed and overwhelmed force of 9,000 fought for three days to buy the time for the British to get to the passes.

Once on the road to Astorga, Moore finally decided that his main escape route must be via Corunna, for the simple reason that the Spanish naval port was massively fortified in comparison to Vigo, as it was likely that the army would have to embark whilst the French were held back by one last all-out rearguard battle. However, to prevent the French taking command of the road to Vigo, via Orense, and possibly cross over to cut off the passes to Corunna, Moore ordered General Craufurd with 3,500 men to take that route, these being Alten's German Legion, the 1st/43rd and the 2nd battalions of the 52nd and 95th. Thus the load on the impoverished resources of the Galician passes would also be lightened and the transport fleet at Vigo protected from any French surge to the coast, now they were arriving on the Plain of Leon in ever-increasing numbers, finally to total 100,000 men. It was this road that Rifleman Harris took, as did Sergeant Surtees of the 2nd/95th, and, while their experiences on the march were similar, those who quote their anecdotes are not truly recounting the march with Moore to Corunna, which was more severe climatically and

173

geographically. Nor was the march to Vigo at any time attacked by the French.

General Romana was also finally persuaded to take the 5,000 men under his command still fit to march away by that route, but some inevitably became mixed with the British column on the Corunna trail, to cause confusion to historians. He would finally circle back to Asturias and his men continue to ambush Soult's army of occupation in the region. Few of the original French force who followed Moore would ever leave Galicia alive.

It was at this point that a messenger came gasping up to Napoleon's carriage on a lathered horse to deliver an urgent despatch into the Emperor's hands only. Napoleon left almost immediately for Paris, after having ordered Soult to pursue Moore's retreat to Corunna, with the object of destroying the column with a 25,000-strong army before it could escape by sea. Marshal Ney was left to hold Astorga and the entries to the passes with 16,000 reserves, to prevent Romana's army following Soult to harass his rear. Romana's artillery, some forty-five good-quality pieces, was sent to safety with that of the British.

Napoleon was known by several derogatory titles at the time, one being 'The Great Dissembler'. It is, therefore, not surprising that many versions of the explanation for his sudden dash for Paris exist.

The realliance of Russia with Austria, which was rearming, is one. A palace coup of Ministers and Generals, using the Spanish fiasco as an excuse to end his dictatorship, is another. If any authority is to be believed it must surely be the French historian Lanfrey who volunteered to accompany the fallen tyrant to his final exile in St Helena for the privilege of writing down his memoirs and who came swiftly to hate him. He claims that Napoleon left out of pure pique when Moore was obviously about to slip out of his grasp, so that it might not be said that he personally had been outwitted if Moore got clean away after ruining his much-publicized plans for the subjugation of the Iberian peninsula.[10] Ironically, Moore never knew that Napoleon had left Spain and that his plan had succeeded even beyond his own expectations.[11]

When comparisons are made between Moore's handling of the command suddenly thrown upon his shoulders and that which followed, conducted by Sir Arthur Wellesley, it is often forgotten that Sir Arthur never confronted Napoleon in personal command in Spain. Moore calmly called Napoleon to him in an act of courageous defiance when he was at the height of his power, both personally and politically, well before his self-esteem was worn down by his own frozen retreat from Moscow.

The harsh climatic conditions continued to blind the French left to deal with Moore. Soult approached Astorga in a thick fog with great caution, taking two days to encircle it, for his scouts reported many thousands of fresh British troops about the area. The fact was totally the reverse, for they were the men that Romana had been forced to leave behind as too sick to march into the mountains. From the vast piles of stores at Astorga they had been given new British uniforms to replace the rags that they had been reduced to fighting in from Blake's defeat at Espinosa to the present.

The stockpiles of equipment at Astorga, so long held out as an incentive to tired footsore men to keep marching, could only be snatched at as the columns passed. What could not be handed out to either British or Spanish troops, or carried along because of the perpetual lack of wagons, was burnt or dumped in the river. Unfortunately, in the confusion half of the new shoes intended for the retreat were burnt when found to be piled under unneeded material. More unfortunate was the fact that the men of both armies got to the piles of navy rum barrels that had not been ordered to be either issued or destroyed. Rifle butts opened the casks and every available canteen and other container was filled by unstoppable troops. The erroneous belief, still common today, that alcohol keeps off the cold was universal then. Hundreds fell drunk into the snow with a rosy warm glow to their skins, never to rise again, as hypothermia swiftly took them. The effect of alcohol is now known to be that it circulates the core temperature of the body to the skin so as to shed the toxic alcohol as sweat. Thus, whilst appearing to warm the drinker, who is suffering from extreme body heat loss, it may well be the cause of his death, for the inner organs cease to function when a mere 2°C is lost around the heart.

All did not die so peacefully or painlessly. Many drunken stragglers who could not be prodded on by the rearguard were cut to pieces by the French, who finally realized, upon entering the town, that the British columns had a two-day start on them into the mountain passes and temporary safety from mass attack by their force. The British numbered 19,000 after Astorga.

Moore sent most of the cavalry ahead on to the escape route, retaining with the Reserve in the rearguard only the regiment of Lord Edward Paget, who fought unceasingly at the rear all the way to Corunna, despite becoming virtually blind from opthalmia. If one true hero lived to tell the tale, then Lord Paget must be the prime candidate. The rifle brigades of the 52nd Regiment, apart from the 2nd, sent on the Vigo road, were all kept in the Reserve, as were the 20th and 1st battalions of the 28th, 91st and 95th Regiments.

The Baker rifle, which they carried, with its long rifled barrel, was accurate to within six inches at three hundred yards in the hands of a trained marksman when standing and more so were it rested on a pack with the shooter lying prone. The gun's one disadvantage, that kept it as a skirmishers' weapon only, was that its rifling required the ball to be forced down the barrel, so slowing the reloading to once a minute, against a smooth-bore musket's five possible reloads in that time. Should this fact mean that the rifleman could be overrun by the enemy, while reloading, a sword-length bayonet could be fitted, including hand-guard, so turning the long gun into a weapon which could be used effectively as a lance. The French came to dread every turn in the trail, for a company of riflemen could be waiting in ambush and each shot meant a dead or seriously wounded man. The muskets that they carried were inaccurate at more than 50 yards, with a much lower muzzle velocity and penetration. Muskets were meant for volleys or mass firings, where some balls must hit the enemy ranks, but the trail to Corunna was too narrow for such tactics. The French also had sharpshooters, *tirailleurs*, but they were not concentrated and trained into a regiment such as the 52nd.

The quality of the British Light Cavalry was far superior to that of its French counterpart. Smaller in numbers, they were, however, mostly drawn from the upper classes, who brought their own horses, trained to jump hedges into the unknown when foxhunting, and were far superior in agility and manoeuvrability for this reason. The French cavalry were no more than mounted peasants and, with exceptions, could be compared more accurately with the British dragoons than with the hussar regiments.

When the rearguard entered the market town of Bembibre at first sight they thought that the French had encircled them and there had been a massacre. Piles of bodies of British and Spanish soldiers lay covered in light snow, with what appeared to be voluminous puddles of blood colouring it red about them. The truth was then realized, for the town held various *bodegas*, or wholesale wine warehouses, which purchased the crop of the peasants' vines and stored it in huge barrels of up to 15 feet in diameter, lying in racks in the cellars. The inhabitants had again mostly fled, locking their houses. It was Romana's men, infuriated by this treachery after fighting to protect the civilians, with the promise of food and shelter if in retreat, who led the British, breaking into the houses, and the thousands of litres of *vino tinto* lying below in the cellars. Even a few men from the elite regiments were found within the houses filled with snoring drunks, who were the more intoxicated owing to the fact that the alcohol had flowed into mostly empty stomachs.

The two items lacking from the supply dumps along the route were food and firewood. Hardtack biscuits had been brought to Astorga, but had mostly been seized by Romana's men, who had been fighting the French from Leon without rations. Flour was to be had at Corunna to bake more, but not the wagons to bring it up, together with the more important powder and ball. The officers and men asked for food in the supply dumps, but were offered cannon balls, mixed too often with more kegs of rum to keep off the cold. Again, it must be stated that the magistrates of the towns on the planned route of the retreat had been ordered by the Junta of Galicia to provide food and shelter, including firewood, as the successive brigades came long. Moore expected this and could only pretend stoicism when it was found that the magistrates and the inhabitants, with their livestock and wagons, had all fled to the mountains, the logic being that to help the British would mean that there would be a reckoning with the French who followed.

Moore was forced to waste a day of his advantage in the town quelling this riotous behaviour, driving the drunks who could stand out towards Cacabelos and then defending the town against the French dragoons who had now caught up. A less humanitarian commander would have left them to their deserved fate at the hands of the French, but it was this feeling of responsibility for even the lowest of the men in his charge that made Moore so special. Even when he marched on, he left a regiment of infantry to defend the town, whose buildings were still filled with unconscious drunks. When the infantry was forced to leave, Paget's cavalry remained to hold back the five French Dragoon squadrons, but were finally forced to gallop on to catch up with the Reserve. The French Dragoons came in hot pursuit, lopping the heads off the sluggish drunkards who staggered along to either side of the road. In the town, the French infantry massacred the remaining incorrigibles, regardless of sex or age.[12]

Twenty miles down the trail, over the ridge of the first high mountain pass, in front of the town of Cacabelos, was a very narrow bridge over a deep gorge, which slowed down the Reserve. The result of the day wasted in the defence of the drunken soldiers and their women at Bembibre was that the French Dragoons, seven squadrons strong, were now up to the rearguard of the 52nd

Rifles, who defended both sides of the bridge with 400 rifles and a battery of four cannon. The French managed to break over the bridge, but the riflemen, firing from the vineyard terraces to either side, killed the leading General and virtually all of the men who had galloped over with one shot for each life. A large force of dismounted chasseurs now recklessly came over, covered by the parapets, determined to seek revenge, but Moore sent more light infantry marching down the road and drove them back. The main French infantry column was now seen snaking down the hill opposite, but some well-placed shots from the battery sent them back over the ridge.

A virtual repeat of this action occurred at the bridge before Constantino, but now the French columns could be seen flowing along the road behind, from valley to valley. They were shot down in droves by the 52nd, but such was the pressure from the column behind that they had to spread along both sides of the bridge. The action continued until dusk, when General Paget took over the defence of the bridge, preventing any French from crossing until midnight, when he was ordered to gallop on to rejoin the rearguard.

At the next town of Villafranca Moore had organized a cache of food, pulled in wagons by men often with their shoes, lost to the sucking clay, but when he entered the town after a seven-mile descent from the heights of the Manzanal pass, he turned ashen-faced at the scene of wanton indiscipline and destruction before him. The more cunning had not indulged in drunken dalliance under the shadow of French sabres but had run on ahead of the marching columns. The street cunning of the slums told them that whatever pickings were to be had would go to the first to arrive. Moore had kept secret the fact that at the half-way point a huge cache of food did indeed exist, for he had ordered Baird to get salt meats and hardtack biscuits there, sufficient to feed the whole army for fourteen days, even if they must be carried on the backs of sailors and men from the Corunna garrison. The quartermasters' guard had, however, been overwhelmed by men in their own uniform, whom they welcomed, but who then held them at gunpoint, whilst they took all they could stuff into their emptied backpacks. They had then run on, leaving the broken barrels of meat to spoil without the preserving brine. Broken biscuit layered the floor like mosaic.

At the moment when Moore arrived the ammunition was being thrown into the river and such carts as had been pulled up, now serving no purpose with the supplies stolen, were being burnt. The exhausted men of the disciplined majority foraged for what lay about, for the chill air had preserved a certain amount. Uninvited, they pushed into every house until all were full to capacity. The remainder slung tarpaulins across the narrow streets and slept exhausted beneath them.

Moore sat astride his horse, with the enormity of the tragedy that his own men had wrought upon their fellow soldiers fully expanding in his mind, as he calculated probable deaths by fatigue-induced collapse owing to the theft of these vital supplies. At that moment he saw one of the renegade redcoats running before a group of Spaniards. The man was detained *in flagrante* with the leg of cured ham he had stolen over his shoulder. Thirty years of leniency and tolerance finally snapped and Moore ordered the man to be hanged on the spot.

Meanwhile a dragoon was dragged into the town square by a Captain Paisley, who had found him looting valuables from a country house, and had then been attacked by the man. Moore called a drumhead court martial and the man was instantly found guilty and shot beneath the swinging corpse of the hanged food thief.

The maimed victims of the French dragoons, rescued by Lord Paget's cavalry, drunkards and malingerers cut about and with missing limbs, were also placed along the walls, propped up to demonstrate the rewards of indiscipline chaos. The army were then marched past this gruesome display, lest any others might consider breaking ranks to take their chances alone, with the promised food cache now ransacked.

It has been written that Moore's retreat and unyielding rear-guard defence commanding the Reserve lost hardly a man to the French in the march to Corunna and this is largely true. The losses and suffering must be laid squarely with those ultimately responsible – the politicians. For, fearing a Cromwellian army coup against the worst of their own self-interest, they adamantly refused to have a standing army of any useful size. It was also they who sanctioned the 'crimps' system, the army version of the press gang, put out to private contractors. From this system came the vice-ridden scum that could be dragged or tricked from the slums of the country. To then proclaim the villainy of the common soldiery was comparable to cursing a dog for eating a half-decomposed rabbit when it was the known nature of the beast.

At this point Moore came as near to despair as at any moment of the retreat, which he had believed he had so carefully planned to save his army after wrecking Napoleon's plans. Seeing the French swarming down the road towards the town from a vantage point, he pointed at them and said to his staff in a bitter voice, "There they are, up to us now. They will not leave us until we reach Corunna, but follow us close."[13]

The frustration was made a thousand times worse by the fact that his protection of the rioting drunks had cost him his two-day lead over the French, while decent soldiers' food was being stolen by the criminal element of the army. Moreover, the French had come on faster and without fear, for they believed the British army to have totally disintegrated into the rabble they at first encountered.

The discipline and resolve of the Reserve, and in particular the deadly accurate fire of the 52nd Rifles, had blown away this belief at the bridges of Cacabelos and Constantino. Combined with Paget's cavalry charges, these actions had bought the army a night of rest, but now they had to be sent onwards before they were encircled by the enemy, at the same time holding the town. Moore stayed to command the rearguard action, filtering his

181

sharpshooters away a company at a time so as to disguise the strength left. At 11 o'clock in the morning the French gave up and made camp at a distance from town, and Moore rode on, knowing that he had again bought a day's advantage.

An incident now occurred that cost a minimum of 400 soldiers' lives, owing to the stubborn irascibility of General Baird. At Las Herrerias, on 4 January, Moore received reports as to the situations at both Vigo and Corunna. Until that moment he had held open the possibility of dividing the columns between the two ports at Lugo. Now he intended to stand and offer battle to the French as they came out of the passes on to the pastureland around Lugo. Should they refuse to engage there, Moore knew that he would have to turn and fight them as the troops embarked. The fortresses of Corunna were the most easily defensible from the landward side, but would require the whole army to allow embarkation and defeat of the following French simultaneously. Thus, he sent a despatch by his most reliable ADC, Captain George Napier, to Generals Hope and Fraser to halt at Lugo and prepare for battle, rather than take the road to Vigo as previously intended.

Napier came up to Baird's camp to request a fresh horse, while he briefly rested and ate, before galloping on. Baird, however, insisted in sending a fresh messenger of his own, despite Moore's orders for Napier to carry this important document direct to the Generals himself. The document was literally taken from him by force and off went Baird's picked man. Unfortunately, the valiant but obstinately blunt-witted Baird was no judge of men, for the messenger stopped at a roadside tavern and spent his expense money in getting drunk. Fully aware of the importance of the message, but not its contents, he sprawled over his horse and the vital despatch fell from his pocket. It was found by the roadside by the marching men a day later and luckily Hope, Fraser and the guns were halted one march down the Vigo road and double-marched back. Four hundred men died in the snow on the return march to Lugo and many more were so exhausted that they fell behind on the march from there to Corunna and were cut down by the French.[14]

On 5 January the Reserve entered Los Nogales, which lies just before the start of the last mountain passes. By a forced march of thirty-six miles they had gained a twelve-hour advantage over the following French, who would take two days to catch up. The road over this, at 6,000 feet, the highest mountain ranges in Galicia, dwindled to a track in which only one horse could pass in many places, with sheer drops to rivers in the depths below.

The next night was perfectly clear, revealing every star, but the beauty above was in proportion to the misery below. The track leading on down to Lugo had now to cross the highest pass of the Picos de Ancares range. Every animal and human was white with frost, for it was many degrees below freezing. Horses lamed in this brutal crossing were ordered to be shot, for a fully trained cavalry mount was a great prize to an enemy. Cannons could be cast far more quickly than the 18-month minimum training which was needed to accustom a naturally sensitive and easily frightened animal to the sights, sounds and smells of war. Men who would charge cannon and decapitate the gunners, then eat a hearty breakfast, cried openly as they fired a ball behind the ear of loyal animals whom they had grown to love.

The drunks and miscreants were no longer to be seen like frozen statues beside the roadway; now disciplined older volunteers were seen, whose legs had given out under them. If alive they begged to be given the same treatment as the horses and not left for the French peasants in uniform to hack slowly to pieces for amusement.

The women and children also now wished that they had obeyed Moore's order to stay in the sun of Lisbon. They too knew what fate awaited them before the French infantrymen would finally kill them.

Only one good thing had happened as they descended into Los Nogales, the Simla of Galicia – a well-ordered column of supply wagons was seen coming towards them. The Junta of Galicia had decided to send fifty wagonloads of fresh food and equipment to the now disbanded army of General Romana. The British officers explained that the army of Romana had left Astorga loaded down with every conceivable type of provisions from the British stockpiles and that over the pass were the equally starving and bootless French. The shoes, clothing, blankets and protein-rich hams and cheeses from this miraculous convoy, whose very lateness placed it where most needed, saved the lives of countless men.

Moving from the sublime to the ridiculous, a paymaster's clerk had come up to the half-blind and frostbitten Lord Paget to ask for assistance. The draft animals pulling his wagon had died of exhaustion and he required more for an important cargo. The long-pleaded-for casks of silver dollars, to the value of £25,000 Sterling, had at last come forward, but now they were a potentially troublesome burden. Soult's heavy cavalry could be made out descending a distant ridge, as mere dots, but obviously moving round the Reserves flanks, for the bridge at Herrerias had resisted two attempts to blow it. Pausing for a moment, Lord Paget called up men of the 28th Regiment and ordered them to hurl the casks into a deep ravine, not mentioning their contents. Unfortunately, the casks exploded upon hitting the rocks below and showers of bright new silver dollars covered the floor of the gorge. Many men, and especially women not under orders, risked all to clamber down to scoop at a hundred lifetime's wages that lay below. The more circumspect, whose regulation packs were anyway killing them by their weight, marched on and left them to their folly. When the snows melted, hundreds of impoverished mountain herdsmen became rich beyond their wildest dreams.

The ragged and bearded Reserve, still with a vastly lower percentage of casualties than the regiments in which discipline had broken down, now staggered into the relative warmth of Lugo on the plain below. They had fought almost constantly from Astorga and now looked incredulously at rows of perfectly aligned tents, with men shaving and whitening webbing to hang on trees to dry; it was of course the Guards Regiment which had marched over and back with Baird.

Soon, however, they would take their place among their ragged fellows as the order was given to form battle ranks and await the French from the vantage point of a low plateau facing the road out of the mountains. To this position some 3 miles back from the town naval stores were brought up and the whole army ate heartily while waiting for the famished French to march out to meet their reward for the exertions of the long trek. The British had grapes for them, and fifteen cannon to deliver them drawn up in their centre.

Moore chose this moment to vent his frustration in an address to the assembled army. Many consider this was unwise and unfair, for his execration fell on the ears of the loyal men who had stayed the course when it was meant for the villains now dead or already safe in Corunna or Vigo aboard the few transports that were already waiting. When filled and on course for England, from them spread the first covering lies as to the horrors that they had suffered under a Commander who would not stand and fight.

"General Orders
Headquarters,
Lugo,   6th Jan, 1809

"Generals and Commanding Officers of Corps must be as sensible as the Commander of the forces of the complete disorganization of the army.

"The advance guard of the French is already close to us, and it is to be presumed that the main body is not far distant; and action may, therefore, be hourly expected. If the Generals and Commanding Officers of Regiments (feeling for the honour of their country and of the British arms) wish to give the army a fair chance of success, they will exert themselves to restore order and discipline in the regiments, brigades and divisions which they command.

185

"The Commander of the Forces is tired of giving orders which are never attended to. He therefore appeals to the honour and feelings of the army he commands, and if those are not sufficient to induce them to do their duty, he must despair of succeeding by any other means. He was forced to quote one soldier to be shot at Villafranca, and he will order all others to be executed who are guilty of similar enormities, but he considers there would be no occasion to proceed to such extremities if the Officers did their duty; as it is chiefly from their negligence, and from want of proper regulation in the regiments, that crimes and irregularities are committed, in quarters, and upon the march."

It was from this moment on that certain officers began to form cabals to invent excuses that would all come to be placed against their Commander as the cause of the disastrous retreat – the more so once he was dead and they safely in London.[15]

Full bellies and the thought of at last standing and fighting did far more than their Commander's speech to restore order among the waiting men. Moore, however, went off aloof to his tent and could not be jollied out of his melancholic state by Colonel Graham's banter, which normally cheered him, but was now met with a silent stare. While other men would have broken completely and sooner, or ordered executions by the dozen, it was obvious that, after commanding the Reserve under almost constant attack, Moore was very near the limit of his nervous tolerance.

The trap was laid, but Soult, arriving on 7 January, was not foolish enough to come out of the passes with his whole army until he knew what opposition he faced. He was not sure if he faced the whole Reserve or the whole British Army. Thus, he came out with five field pieces and up to 12,000 troops to protect them, but no more at first. When he opened fire at the British centre, the reply was a salvo with all fifteen guns and so he had his answer. Here was a challenge to settle the issue, like medieval forces facing each other, massed into two huge groups. Had Moore been less fatigued and had he more faith in his men, it might have occurred to him that the way to draw Soult's unre-supplied, half-frozen men out to battle was to have had the centre fall back and return fire with only some three field guns. If Soult then believed that the main army were well on to Corunna or Vigo and the troops over the top of the plateau were only the Reserve he might have charged with all he had.

It had been made instantly clear that this was no mere rear-guard and so Soult did nothing with his initial force, apart from a diversionary feint to the 76th Regiment on the last flank, that was driven off by a bayonet charge, with Moore himself leading the 51st, his old Regiment. Then darkness fell. The next day the British merely watched from their elevated position as Soult brought out from the passes 17,000 infantry, 4,000 cavalry and fifty pieces of artillery. The British strength was 16,000 infantry, including 1,800 fresh troops from Corunna, 1,800 rested cavalry and forty pieces of artillery.

The two forces assembled into battle formations, but then stood glaring at each other until darkness again fell and Soult still had not given the order to attack. He had seen that the British were fed, rested and full of determination, while his own men were in as bad a state as had been the British when they emerged from the passes, or worse, for the British had utilized all the poor resources of the land, meaning that the French had to bring every-thing with them up from Astorga. Here, and ahead in the fortress of Corunna, were vast accumulations of supplies for the British. Given this situation, he decided that he would not give battle, but hope to catch the enemy at their moment of weakness as they sought to embark and fight simultaneously.

Moore was again forced to consider his position objectively. If he fought and the attack failed, the horrendous march would have been for nothing. If he gained a victory it would be costly and no annihilation of the enemy could be expected. Moreover, he would be left with many wounded to carry on to the fleet and escape.

However, with no opposition, the vast cavalry reserves of Napoleon, who Moore still thought to be at Astorga, could sweep through the passes to reinforce the remains of Soult's army, who would surely retreat, if losing, once more into the defensible passes, and Moore's victorious army would be cut down before it could embark. For Corunna was still thirty miles distant in a line drawn on a map, but over yet one more mountain range. Once more, to the fury of the uncomprehending troops, he ordered camp fires stoked up to burn bright and long, then ordered his army to take the road to Corunna at 10 o'clock that night.

So many accounts of particular incidents of disgraceful behaviour have been emphasized in the many accounts of the retreat to Corunna that one which demonstrates the other side of the character of the British soldier must be included to redress the balance. It was written by Moore's brother James. In the one flank attack made by Soult at Lugo, to test British resolve, a Major Roberts had voluntarily pushed through to the front rank to get at the enemy. Immediately he ran a French officer through the body with his sword. However, whilst his outstretched hand was about to withdraw the weapon, it was shot through twice by French infantry of the officer's company. Having discharged their muskets and mashed the Major's hand, they raised their bayonets to run him through. At that moment an Irish Private, Conners, stepped forward and, striking with the speed of a cobra, himself bayonetted the two Frenchmen with upward thrusts as they had raised their arms to stab down at the transfixed Major Roberts. Conners then cleared a path by bayonetting two more of the enemy and, pulling the Major's hand free, helped him through the line to safety. Moore witnessed the skirmish while charging to reinforce the line and Conners was rewarded with instant promotion.[16]

Trusses of straw were set out to mark the route from the battle positions in the plateau to the escape route, but, as if sent especially to torment him, Moore saw them blown away by a wall of sleet, driven by blasts of wind that the locals could not remember ever previously coming so suddenly and with such force. The troops blundered about the streets of the town half the night before all were set on the right road, again soaked, near frozen and utterly exhausted.

The next day the French cavalry came up to these hapless victims of the weather trailing behind the massed columns and cut them down as if scything barley. The biggest losses of the march were on that day, with 2,600 killed by the enemy or by exposure. Up to the day of this foul trick of the weather, despite all the hardships and folly, only 1,400 men had been lost overall.[17]

Moore decided to hold the French in front of the bridge at Betanzos, twelve miles from Corunna, to prevent the encirclement of his column when at their last gasp, as Soult obviously planned. The lengthy bridge could then have its brick and stone arches blown and again a two-day respite would theoretically be won. No sooner had he ordered this plan put in motion than a messenger came out from the port to declare it to be empty of transports. The gale-force north wind was preventing them coming south into Corunna. Moore immediately thought of Ferrol, on the other side of the estuary, with its entrance passage facing east, where the transports could tack in across the wind. He as quickly dismissed the idea, for the French would obviously not remain static on the other side of a wide river mouth, behind a blown bridge. Rather, they would be hacking away at his collapsing army as it staggered the last few miles along the alluvial plain. The only answer to the salvation of his men was to stand at Betanzos, blow the bridge and then fight his best men in battle with Soult before the walls of Corunna, but on ground of his own choosing.

Chapter Twenty-One

The Battle of Elviña

Sir John now rode ahead, as protocol demanded, and rapidly set up his H.Q. in a street in the unwalled part of Corunna, named the Canton Grande, within easy reach of the all-important harbour, still forlornly empty of troop transports. The number of the house was 13. A frigate had dropped a messenger to inform him that the transport fleet, with its twelve ships-of-the-line escort, was still attempting to tack round Cape Finisterre, which meant that it was a minimum of three days' sailing away, even if the strong northerly wind shifted to allow them to enter Corunna. It was obvious that he would have to give battle and, after the satisfaction of seeing his army, bearded, ragged and filthy, march into town by regiments in well-formed ranks, he rode out to survey the terrain. A distant explosion, followed by the cessation of rifle fire, informed him that the Engineers had finally blown the Betanzos bridge at the third attempt sufficiently to stop any immediate crossing. The Reserve could at last retire to rest and prepare, leaving the French temporarily impotent on the other side of the hopefully uncrossable and swollen River Burgo. From the other bank nearly the whole army had seen the French dragoons cut down the last 500 men of the column as they weaved with tottering steps the last few hundred yards to safety behind the lines of the Reserve, by then at the bridge and only a few miles from Corunna.[1]

The Galicians were in a high state of morale and seemed not to think of the inevitability of French occupation that must come as soon as the British embarked. Hot food and new shoes awaited the mud-encrusted soldiers. The population of Corunna impressed the British soldiers by their height, sturdy build and fair complexions. Previously they had only encountered the Spaniards and Portuguese of the south, short, dark and with traces of their Arab ancestors in their faces.

The night of 11 January 1809 saw the town seething like a disturbed ants' nest as they prepared to see off the French from their massive walls. Even young women joined the communal effort by carrying ammunition, balanced in baskets on their heads, up the steps to the ramparts. Had all of Spain been of this defiant mood, as promised, Moore's expedition would have run a different course. The stiff Atlantic breezes here did not allow the peoples' minds to drift into the dreamy lethargy of the sunny south and centre. Moreover, the encircling mountains had kept their Gaul and Viking blood mostly unmixed with the rest of the country's and they were fiercely proud of their unique identity.

Among the British the hatred of the French was now deep, violent and personal. Within the ranks discipline was total, for, apart from the rabble element now dead or missing, the British army, to a man, was filled with a cold desire for revenge.

Early on 12 January Moore began a survey of the terrain surrounding the harbour fortresses, for the French were retiring inland down the river to find a crossing place and would certainly return. The limited number of fresh troops, combined with the still effective core of the survivors of the march, still meant that he would be too thinly stretched, with 15,000 men, were he to attempt to hold the crests of the two parallel ridges which over-looked Corunna. The tactical advantage went to the army who occupied the higher of the two, the Peñasquedo at 600ft, but he had only men sufficient to hold the lower, 400ft Monte Mero. Obviously, he would be fired on from above, but the French had only shown light 4lb field guns at Lugo, such as were easy with their greater resources to pull over the passes. The fire from these

191

pieces at extreme range was a factor that he knew he must reluctantly accept, but he had a secret in surprise for the French batteries once they opened fire. Two of the heaviest shore battery guns of the harbour forts of Corunna, 32 and 42 pounders, had been wheel-mounted to traverse through 380° and, with more than a three-mile range, could return a devastating counter-battery fire; the French would not be able comfortably to concentrate their guns. Two more were in the process of manual reversal, at a weight of some 7,500lbs each.

A sprawling village, Elviña lay at the foot of the slope on the western flank below the heights that the British would occupy. A valley communicating with Corunna ran due north through the Monte Mero ridge, before the land rose again to command the route. This western side of the valley would also be occupied by the British. The village was a farming community and was intended to be used by the British as a redoubt, for its many stone-walled corrals would make ideal defensive positions to be held by riflemen.

The British left flank would be protected by the Mero and Burgo Rivers and the mud flats of the estuary, but the right was, it appeared, completely open to a sweep that could cut the British army off from the valley to Corunna. To reinforce the impression that this was not only a vital but also a weak spot, which he felt warranted extra protection, Moore planned to place a third of his disposable men to face it. What was not obvious from the heights was that this heath land was not simply undulating and over-grown with gorse. Covered by the prickly bushes were innumerable slabs of sharp-sided rock, washed down from the heights. No cavalry could sweep through this ground, only slowly pick its way, making ideal targets for the riflemen, who might use each bush as cover. Neither might infantry advance across the ground in a formidable charging line for the same reason. Any attack that came swiftly and in force would have to come by the tracks on the valley floor, and there Moore hoped that the disposition of his troops would bring them into a series of killing fields where his infantry could fire volleys at them, from one side and then another, using the maze of stone walls for concealment, then dropping behind them to reload after each volley.

Moore returned to the town, satisfied that the only options for attack by the French were those that would give them such obvious advantages from possessing the heights that they must mass their army there, and then advance down to destruction among the boulder-strewn heath before Elviña, which blocked the only way to Corunna. Skirmishers from the rifle brigades would keep any scouts from testing this ground on foot, but it appeared so straightforward from above that he himself would not have thought it necessary to scout it were he attacking, with so many other more complicated positions to investigate.

Moore in no way underestimated Soult and indeed they had a great deal in common. Born in 1769, he was eight years younger than Moore. His father had been the Notary of a provincial town; thus they both came from the professional middle classes. When the war with England began, Soult had been a law student, but, like Moore, had chosen to volunteer for an army career, rising by ability from the ranks. He had been made a Marshal of France in 1804 and a Duke following his directing the charge that had gained victory at Austerlitz in 1806. He was well-mannered and treated the officers captured at Corunna in a magnanimous fashion, even defying Napoleon's orders concerning their treatment as mere POWs. We know so much of his perception of the march from Astorga, and the battle before Corunna, owing to the fact that he was later sent as French Ambassador to Queen Victoria's wedding and became a good friend of the Duke of Wellington. They compared notes, as old adversaries will, and corresponded frequently. He died a much respected political figure of the reconstructed France at his country estate in 1851. In January 1809, however, he was still 'The Duke of Damnation' to the British.

During the night of 12 January and the morning of the 13th

a series of enormous explosions was heard as the British Engineers blew the many small arches of a lengthy bridge close to the city, over the mouth of the River Mero, near the town of El Burgo. This river ran at a right angle to the main River Burgo and then into it, but split into two as it did so, needing a bridge wider than that of the main River Burgo, for the tide flooded the area between the two channels. The bridge's destruction was vital, for it was the last serious obstacle on the road to Corunna. The more so as the French had remade with trunks and beams crossings of the half-blown arches of the bridge over the river at Betanzos and were now following on with two divisions and cannon. General Baird's division was marching out to block their thrust, aided by a stiff cannonade of grape. Lord Paget had reminded the Engineers, caustically, of their costly failures at Bembibre and Constantino, and that here there was powder by the ton. The French now gave up these attempts at bombardment from the Burgos road and marched up the main river some seven miles to where it narrowed and a small bridge existed at Celas. Here, with all their equipment, they slowly crossed and rested for a day at Alvaro village, then marched back along the track through Villabog to the heights above Corunna. They had taken only a day to detour, but that was all Moore required.

A mighty explosion shattered windows and threw tiles from the roofs of the houses in Corunna; even the supply vessels at anchor heeled over many feet and shock waves rippled the sea. The largest man-made explosion to date had just occurred as the Engineers detonated the main magazine, kept out of town in a store house on the very height of Peñasquedo, where the French were expected to arrive. The most informed sources, Napier and Blakeney, give approximately 400,000 pounds of powder as the quantity, contained within stout stone walls in 4000 standard 100lb barrels. It was ignited after a smaller store had successfully been blown, with a thick powder trail leading to the main store as a fuse. Like an ominous warning of things to come and with as

194

little idea of what the effect of so large a quantity of explosives igniting simultaneously might be a mile-high cloud rose behind Corunna. The novelty was that it was shaped just like a mushroom. It was captured by the sketch of Ker Porter, who was in the town, drawn the next day, as if viewed from the sea. The expansive lateral heatwave vaporized a sergeant and three or four men of the Engineers, plus several local inhabitants.

The seaward batteries at Corunna had their guns spiked and dismounted, should the French break through the fortresses' defences and fire on the transports as they manoeuvred to leave the harbour.

Next morning, the 15th, Moore was in the saddle early to inspect the positions of his men, for the French were expected by the hour. Noon came and the French had not arrived, but from the heights even Marshal Soult, scouting ahead, had to admire the marvellous sight that over one hundred large transports and warships made as they appeared over the horizon and then on, with the most favourable of winds, into the harbour of Corunna. Soult was too wise to attack now, for his troops would not all be there before the middle of the next day. The action was going to be one where hours would be as important as days, and minutes as hours, in deciding if all or none of the British escaped in the fleet, so timely in its arrival.

It was difficult for the men to believe at first, but the naval planning had not included enough of the specially constructed horse transport vessels, even though the animals had initially arrived by sea. The cavalry and commissariat were ordered to shoot all their animals, for trained cavalry horses, then the most valuable asset of warfare, must not be presented to the enemy, regardless of sentimentality, nor draft animals. The 80,000 horses lost by Napoleon during his ill-fated invasion of Russia would be a decisive factor in his later defeats. From a charger's birth to battle readiness was a three-year process.

The later, ill-informed outcry in England over the handling of the campaign was fiercer concerning the destruction of fine bloodstock than it was over the death of 4,000 men, mostly, of course, from the 'lower orders', as Napier tells us.

Whilst the horses were being put down, the cannons, the wounded and the infirm were loaded from the quays. Moore had given the command of the Adjutant-General's department, which controlled the embarkation, to his friend of years, Colonel Anderson, whom he knew he could trust not to bungle the operation while he attended to the French. New firearms were issued to the whole army from the vast cache in Corunna, along with fresh sachets of powder. The French would fight with rusted guns and what powder they had kept dry along the trail. Moore estimated that they could fight a full-scale battle, as attackers, for no more than one day, owing to this. Corunna had still retained sufficient for weeks of vigorous defence. The French would need a minimum of 100 hundred-pound barrels for a day's full-scale assault of this size with artillery, judging from past experience.

On the eve of the battle Moore was astonished to be asked to receive a delegation of senior officers not of his staff. The suggestion was made that a truce be negotiated with Soult to allow the embarkation of the army, without a mutually destructive battle of dubious outcome. The fortifications and stores would be offered intact, as a further inducement to the hungry French army. The precedent of the repatriation of the French from Egypt and again from Portugal, with their arms, would give Soult the authority to agree to this with honour. Moore was, however, sure that his plan would lead to victory. Moreover, he was not about to seek a way out of the battle at the request of the same officers who had previously complained that their Commander would never stand and fight.[2]

Exhausted by the exertions of the last three days, he had then thrown himself onto his bed and slept until evening. When he awoke, he learnt that Charles Stewart, Under-Secretary of War and Castlereagh's half brother, had not yet sailed. It was to Stewart that he had trusted the delivery to Parliament of a verbal first-hand account of his strategy against Napoleon, together with his reasons for not fighting at Sahagun or Astorga. Now, finding that there was time, he put a last justification of his actions in writing to Castlereagh, knowing that they were still not understood by the soldiers in his army nor, probably, by many parliamentarians. The letter ended with a painful mention of his officers proposing that he come to terms with Soult and of his refusal.[3] Neither Stewart or Castlereagh were to be trusted, however, and the debate over the expedition would only end when Canning challenged Castlereagh to a duel over his attempt to use Moore's honour as a political lever. The duel was fought on Putney Common. Both men survived the pistol shots, but Castlereagh's reputation did not.

The next day was spent in a series of skirmishes as Soult probed the British defences to map them and note their strong or weak points. The heaviest fighting on the 15th was when the French 15th Infantry Regiment, commanded by Laborde, advanced under heavy fire to place two field guns on the Palavea slope. From there they could fire effectively on to the estuary end of the Mero Heights and the left of the main British position. An attack to displace them was repulsed with heavy losses to the British infantry, for the French had also found a stone-walled corral of obvious use as a redoubt. The French morale was still high, for they were the pursuers and came in superior numbers to their enemy, now virtually devoid of artillery and cavalry, which they had seen loaded or put down respectively.

Night fell and Soult was content to wait until well into the next day to launch his main assault. By then he would have 20,000 infantry arriving onto the Heights of Peñasquedo, overlooking Monte Mero and Palavea above Elviña village. The other arrival would be two batteries, each of six medium guns, which he had succeeded in dragging over the mountains without Moore's knowledge. Moore was expecting to receive the fire of only light 4lb mobile ordnance at extreme range. The mix of 8lb and 9lb battery guns would cut down many in the British lines, only on average half a mile distant, with perfectly accurate fire from their elevated position and within range. Indeed, at three-quarters of a mile, which separated the two sides at the maximum, a veteran artilleryman could hit even a particular group of men. The key stronghold of Elviña village barring the way to Corunna was only three-eights of a mile from the French battery above!

The British mobile artillery had been loaded on board, with the exception of seven 5 1/2-inch howitzers, (approx. 10lb ball) on siege carriages, a heavy mortar and now four of the massive shore battery guns from Corunna's forts, reversed as counter-battery weapons. The light manoeuvrable 6lb field guns were all loaded, meaning that where the British guns were placed they stayed, whilst the minimum of forty French 4lb light guns could be wheeled about the battlefield to support the infantry.

Both commanders slept soundly that night, happy that the enemy would be walking into a surprise the next day – Moore, with the seemingly smooth but boulder-strewn gorse heath before his men, as a cavalry and massed infantry barrier, now full of riflemen, and Soult with his twelve medium guns, having twice the range that his enemy believed him to possess.

Major John Colborne, Moore's Military Secretary, had been sent out to check the truth of a gathering of French troops in a village some 12 miles off and to wake him upon his return. The French were there, but only enough to fill one house. Regardless, Colborne obeyed his orders and woke Sir John at 2.30 on the morning of the 16th. To occupy his time, he wrote to Rear-Admiral Sir Samuel Hood, in command of the fleet. It would be his last letter. In this he outlined his plans for the battle. The main concern expressed was that Soult would not attack the army but the fleet as it embarked, if he could place guns to fire on it, should he outflank the British positions and gain the heights opposite the town and harbour. Moore, therefore, lest it had not occurred to the Admiral, advised him of the importance of getting each ship under sail the moment it was loaded.[4] The letter proves that Moore had thought not only of the battle but the tactics following a possible failure to hold the French at Elviña. It is clear that his intention was not to annihilate the superior French army, but to hold them back until the main part of his own army was embarked, then rely on the Galicians to hold their walls long enough for those who had fought the rearguard action to scramble aboard the ships waiting in the bays on the other side of the peninsula on which stood Corunna Citadel, under the Tower of Hercules. The Galician Artillery and militia did not fail the British when that moment came, their honour meaning more to them than fear of French reprisals.

Moore then shaved and dressed, and, luckily for posterity, checked that his trunks were all packed and loaded, to be sent on to his mother's house. In the first grey light of the coming dawn he rode out to inspect and animate the men at the front. Passing Lord Paget, now virtually blind, and the invincible men of the Reserve Division, he gave orders that they were to board first in the final withdrawal as compensation for being always last in line from Astorga. Moore rode on to the forward defence line and, as he appeared through the swirling mist, the men cheered him, convinced that, now he was here to direct them in person from the front, they must succeed in holding, or even chasing off, the enemy. The day was clear and bright that morning; by mid-afternoon gunsmoke would blanket the entire landscape.

Attention was paid by Anderson's staff to reminding each regiment at the front which ship they must seek out and board when night fell again.

There was no sign of activity from the enemy, silent and invisible on the heights.

The contemporary indexed battle plan (plate 28) shows the initial position of the opposing forces, the British advance and the positions taken by the French to bombard the departing fleet and is worth careful study truly to understand the action.

On the heights to the left of Elviña the British held a near straight defence line of one and a quarter miles, beginning after the steep slopes coming up from the River Burgo mud flats and following the crest to those which descended down to the redoubt of Elviña itself. The first two divisions[5] of General Baird's command made up the right flank and General Hope's first two the left. The right flank's position was the weakest, around Elviña, and General Fraser's entire command was placed behind as a reinforcement. General Edward Paget still insisted on commanding the Reserve, which was out of sight of the enemy, with orders to move where required at Moore's orders. Along the main defence line twelve howitzers were spaced to fire grape, for mass assaults by the enemy descending from the heights in front and crossing the river valley were possible, even though dangerously uphill finally to reach the British. Howitzers were chosen, for their short thick barrels allowed a much greater elevation and could reach the French on the 200ft higher ground in parabolic trajectories, similar to a modern 5in mortar. Conversely they were also capable of being depressed to fire down a steep slope, whereas the French long ordnance could be approached from below, once close enough, but the double length of the barrel gave greater accuracy and range. Moore was confident that the rock slabs hidden in the gorse would protect Elviña from rapid mass assault. The French had shown that they possessed a minimum of forty light 4lb field guns at Lugo, which did not mean that other ordnance had not been concealed farther back along the trail.

The great British advantage was in the new 'Shrapnel' shells, first used at Vimiero, which exploded on impact and threw out grape shot. The French never developed this weapon in the Napoleonic Wars, their shells being merely hollow steel balls packed only with explosive and using a pre-lit fuse. (See note 8, p 233)

No movement was seen from the enemy and by late morning some rearguard regiments were ordered to march one by one to their assigned ships. Hope's 3rd Division, under Colonel Craufurd, took up position on the crest of the hill overlooking the harbour at San Diego Point, half a mile from the left flank's rear, opposite the town, for Moore's declared tactical logic inferred that, so late in the day, the French would hit the left flank hard to encircle it, while at the same time passing guns between the defenced heights and the River Burgo to bombard the ships loading and leaving. Nothing further suggested itself to perfect the defences and Moore took the opportunity to eat an early lunch.

Word came just before 1 o'clock that the French had placed four guns in a wood to their left flank and Moore, with his staff, decided to ride up to the heights above Elviña to assess the situation. However, two cannon roared in quick succession, just as they were about to mount – the signal that the main enemy advance had begun. All swung round and galloped out to begin the final reckoning with the French. Moore's only fear was that the winter sunset would come too early to allow for a complete rout of the French.

After a heavy bombardment, the French came down from the heights in three ordered columns, led by General Jardon, which, under a covering continuation of the bombardment, advanced to attack both British flanks and the centre simultaneously. Moore, in reply, sent Paget's Reserve to advance against the French lower heavy battery by circling round the British right along the valley's sides, to appear behind the end of the French left flank, drawing the attention of Soult away from the left of the British line and causing him to send troops to save his battery.

The Imperial infantry was attacking with its usual impetuous vigour and was concentrating on Baird's 1st Division, led by Major-General Lord William Bentinck. The Division consisted of the 1st, 42nd and 50th Regiments and held the right-hand flank of the main line of defence immediately above Elviña, which dominated both the British redoubt and the valley between the defended heights which led directly to Corunna. It was to this point of maximum danger, should the enemy concentrations effect a breakthrough, that Moore galloped to encourage his men by his presence. The French were, however, by now almost in control of the village, which would change hands three times that afternoon and be carpeted with corpses.

He arrived at such a speed that he had to force his charger onto its haunches to stop, but all was done in perfect control. He leant forward over its mane to assess the enemy's dispositions.

By contrast, Bentinck was mounted on a mule, which, he claimed, behaved as well as the pure-bred charger he had sacrificed, it being too stupid to be afraid. He was giving orders in a placid tone, as if telling his butler his requirements for breakfast – British *sang-froid* personified.

Moore's mount was magnificent and very easy to recognize among the few horses left, being cream-coloured with black mane and tail.

Major Charles Napier explained the situation and suggested sending in the Grenadiers to fire from the walled enclosures above the village of Elviña, which the French had now occupied. Moore agreed and Napier gave the order to Captain Clunes to "Take your Grenadiers and open the ball". The Captain was 6ft 5ins and as heavily built as he was tall. Clunes strode forward, his regiment of men of similar build following. So began the British counter-assault.

At that moment a cannon ball bounced between their horses, while another took off the leg of a Royal Highlander of the 42nd, completely removing it from the knee down. The man let out screams of such a pitch and volume that the whole section of the line about him began to open up and back away. Moore said, sharply, "This is nothing, my lads. Keep your ranks. Take that man away." Then to the victim, "My good fellow, don't make such a noise; we must bear these things better."[6] Napier was to hear no other words from his General and friend, but very soon Moore would prove that his words in the face of another's extreme suffering could be put into practice concerning himself.

Moore next saw that Paget had not fully succeeded in closing the British right flank against the French cavalry movement of

General Lahoussaye threatening to encircle it. He immediately spurred his horse to Colonel Wynch and ordered him to swing his Regiment at right-angles back from the line to cut off the French cavalry initiative, as if a gate had swung open to block a lane. Owing to the hidden rocks, the smoke from the firing inadvertently hid this manoeuvre from the advancing enemy, who were dismounting and, thinking they were attacking men from the rear, walked calmly into a devastating massed volley, which killed many and threw the rest into a confused retreat which spread to the infantry following behind.

Moore now returned to Bentinck's men at the weak spot to the rear of Elviña village where the retreating French were regrouping after their failed attempt at encirclement. "Remember Egypt," bellowed Moore at the 42nd Highlanders and, placing himself at their head, personally led them into the initial bayonet charge against the French firing from the corrals. The reference to the slaughter of the French in a walled enclosure at Aboukir Bay gave heart to the men and the French were driven from the stone corrals and on to the foot of the hill, where their main battery was. Here the advance was stopped by French sharpshooters, placed to select targets from behind yet another stone wall.

Now the 50th Queen's Own, led by Majors Stanhope and Napier, after an uncertain start swept through the village proper, completely clearing it of French. With Moore's encouraging shout of "Well done my Majors" ringing in their ears they ran ahead of the men into the lane beside the church. The aim was to continue on to the battery, avoiding the now identified sharpshooters' position. General Mermet had, however, seen the danger to the battery and blocked the lane with his Reserve. Turning the bend, Stanhope was shot dead instantly by a ball through the heart, while Napier was wounded five times, one ball shattering his ankle. A French drummer boy chivalrously stood over him, preventing the defenceless enemy officer from being bayoneted to death by an Italian. After being beaten and robbed by the French, he was taken prisoner, and believed dead for many months.[7]

The French Reserve noted that the 50th were checked in the village square, seeing their officers fall, and, seizing the moment, charged back into the village, reoccupying it. Moore responded by ordering the Highlanders, now without ammunition, to retake the stone walls with the bayonet alone, which they proceeded to do, but got no further, as the French reserve had solid control of the village centre. The 1st Guards Regiment and The Royals were sent in to reinforce the Highlanders, whilst a second Guards batallion attacked the enemy centre. Some confusion occurred at this point, for Bentinck thought that the Guards were to relieve the ammunitionless Highlanders, but Moore rode back to insist that they carry on the attack with the bayonet, telling them that ammunition was coming.

The crossroads that may be seen to the north-west of Elviña on the map, leading on to Castro village or back to Corunna, was easily recognized by a group of large rocks. Here, to the rear of the main action, officers had agreed to meet and confer, or send messengers. A French gunnery officer on the heights above Elviña had not failed to notice the comings and goings of cocked-hatted figures about this landmark. Naturally the British officers did not think that it showed a good example to the men were they to shelter behind these rocks and stayed visible to them and to the enemy battery at a range of five-eights of a mile. The astute artillery officer had ordered one gun to range in on the group of rocks and then to hold the gun ready for the moment when a number of officers re-congregated there. To his delight, the British Commander himself, so easily identifiable to all on his cream and black mount, now appeared by the rocks, as visible as had been Nelson on the deck of the *Victory*.

Moore was stationary there for some time, receiving reports from other parts of the line, but most especially waiting for news that the Guards and the Highlanders were still advancing through Elviña and beyond, with the Guards beside them. Major

General Hardinge galloped up to confirm that the advance was still successful and extended an arm to indicate their exact position to his Commander, for the dusk of a winter evening, added to the smoke, made everything unclear at ground level. Moore followed the pointing arm, turning until their two horses had their flanks touching, then without a sound suddenly vanished backwards, flung by the impact of a round shot[8], and landed at the feet of General Thomas Graham in a group conferring with John Woodford and Henry Percy.

At first Moore appeared unwounded, for his shattered shoulder, virtually severed arm and rib cage stripped of muscle all lay against the ground. It was only when Captain Percy lifted him to rest his back against a bank that the horrific nature of his wounds was revealed. Moore asked in a normal voice if the Highlanders were still advancing and, when Hardinge confirmed it, his face brightened.

Graham knew his duty, for one look at the Commander's injuries showed them as fatal, and he immediately galloped off to inform Bentinck that the command now fell upon his shoulders, General Baird having already been carried off the field with a shattered arm.

A medical officer had been stationed close to this liaison point and was now called, but Moore already knew his fate and told him, "You can do me no good". The surgeon removed the impacted uniform lapel from the wound and agreed, stating with frankness, "It is quite a hopeless case".[9]

Six brawny Highlanders of the 42nd were called to carry their Commander from the field in a blanket sling, for the jolting of a cart would cause additional pain and time was now obviously of no consequence. While he waited, Moore again asked, in a calm clear voice, "How are the Highlanders doing, who were so hotly engaged?" Hardinge was again able to inform him truthfully that they were still advancing, and Moore's face once more brightened and he lay back against the bank. Hardinge tried to use his thick silk sash as a tourniquet for the severed shoulder artery, which must have served to some extent, for Moore did not die from loss of blood for several hours more, content in knowing he had gained the day's victory.

The Highlanders appeared, grave-faced, to lift their fellow Scot gently onto the blanket, but as they did so the hilt of Moore's sword was seen to be entering into the wound and Hardinge made to unbuckle it. Moore, still with a steady voice, stopped him, saying, "It is as well as it is. I had rather it should go out of the field with me." Hearing Moore sound so strong and unaffected, Hardinge gave his opinion that with surgery and careful dressing he might yet be saved. In the same calm voice Moore answered that he felt that to be impossible and then told the Major-General to be off and tell Hope that he had been wounded and carried to the rear.[10]

The grim procession had not gone far when two senior surgeons, who had finished attending to General Baird, came running up to assist. Moore thanked them, but sent them away, stating that "they could do nothing for him, and were to better spend their time with the wounded soldiers who had some hope of surviving." The sun was now setting amid the acrid smoke that covered the valley, but the firing could be heard to be diminishing after a crescendo which was British howitzers obliterating Soult's final assault on the centre with salvos of grapeshot. After that the sound of small arms fire was predominantly distinguishable as coming from British weapons. Moore lay back in his blanket content to know that the French had been driven back up the heights, which meant that his army had all night to embark those not already aboard. He had drawn Napoleon off from his conquest of Spain and could now re-embark the majority of his army with all of his guns and could die knowing that, essentially, he had succeeded in his task.

Moore's ears had provided him with a correct picture of events on the battlefield. The Imperial Infantry, which had marched from Astorga, had been driven back, exhausted, up to the heights from which they had attacked by the men of the Guards brigades, reinforced by troops streaming down from the heights. The Guards were relatively fresh, one brigade only having marched to Astorga and back with Baird, well supplied and striding ahead of the mass of the army, whilst the other two had garrisoned Corunna. The Highlanders were also fitter than most, for cattle herding in a Scottish highland winter had much in common with the march through the passes. Life in a city slum, on the contrary, was not a good training for such exertion.

The superior number of French guns could not now fire to assist their comrades, for the fighting was now hand-to-hand, and to mow down the advancing British with grape would also kill their own men. When the French broke and ran for the plateau, the British were saved by being so close that they were under the battery guns' lowest angle of fire. They left by a sideways movement until out of the field of fire, then headed for the ships in darkness. The British dead were some 500 and the French left 1,500 corpses amid the gorse and rock-walled corrals: lists vary, but analysis shows this to be the closest estimate.

A procession formed behind Sir John's stretcher party, with the Chaplain of the Guards Brigades following behind. The General's French valet, François, had campaigned with him three times and was accustomed to seeing his friend and master return wounded, owing to his style of leading from the front. He was not prepared, however, for the state of his General on this occasion. Moore, noticing the look of fright mingled with horror on his loyal servant's face and, ever-conscious of the condition of his subordinates, said to him reassuringly in French, "My friend this is nothing". Then he smiled.

Colonel Paul Anderson had been awaiting his long-time friend in the dark street and Moore saw or sensed him in the crowd and called him to his side. Seizing Anderson's hand in a strong grip with his undamaged hand, he said in the tone of a man who knows the true frailness of his grip on mortality, "Anderson, don't leave me".[11]

Moore was now carried to the upstairs drawing room of the house which formed his H.Q. and laid out on a mattress placed on the floor. The house was in the Canton Grande, outside the walls, along the harbour quay. The worst ordeal was yet to come, for now the surgeons insisted in probing his wounds. He did not utter a sound, but his face took on the pallor of marble. Once they had concluded, Moore again overwhelmed the pain by his willpower and in a composed whisper to Anderson confided that he had always wished to die in battle, and not grow old.

Next, after a while, he asked, "Are the French beaten?" and, when Colborne stated that "There could be no doubt of it," Moore sighed and said, "I hope that the people of England will be satisfied. I hope my country will do me justice". He then instructed Anderson to "See my friends as soon as is possible and tell them EVERYTHING!" Moore then tried to compose a last message to his mother, but at the thought of her he was overcome with emotion and could only whisper, "I have so much to say but cannot get it out".

The surgeons again insisted on changing his position and now the only words of mild complaint during the near three-hour ordeal escaped his lips. He whispered, "It is a great uneasiness. It is a great pain." The initial numbing of the nerve endings from trauma and the mind from shock had now completely worn off, as had the adrenalin surge of battle. He refused opiates, however, for he stated that he wished to die with his mind unconfused. At this point he addressed all the people gathered in the room and said, "Everything that François says is right, I have the greatest confidence in him." Also, "Colborne has my will, and I have remembered my servants".

Now the newly arrived ADC James Stanhope entered the room, fresh from London with despatches and messages from his sister Lady Hester, who loved Moore. He entered with Captain Parry and the sight of the young men made Moore enquire as to the wellbeing of his other ADC, General Burrard's son, but a penetrating look from Anderson told Parry that the fact of his being mortally wounded was best left unsaid.

At that very moment General Baird was aboard ship having his right arm amputated. He had not allowed so much as a sigh to escape his lips, but when he was informed that Moore lay dying he burst into tears.

Moore's next utterance was that the Duke of York be asked to give the 31-year-old Colborne the Lieutenant Colonelcy that he deserved. Again he asked for positive confirmation that the French were soundly beaten and, this given, he lay back and said, "It is a great satisfaction!" Then he exclaimed to all, "I feel so strong, I fear that I shall be a long time in dying." Mercifully he was wrong, for this was that still inexplicable last surge of energy which is noted as a prelude to a conscious man's death.

All marvelled that he had lived for so long with such vast blood loss, but now he sank back peacefully as if all the pain had left him. He then beckoned young James Stanhope to come close and in a matter-of-fact way said, "Stanhope, remember me to your sister". These were the last words that he spoke and shortly afterwards his breathing slowed until it faded away completely. At that exact moment the 8 o'clock gun sounded.

All that night had seen furious activity on the quays, but the word of their General's death had turned the whole army into a model of discipline. While the most undisciplined men were no longer there, those who had survived seemed determined that his sacrifice should not be in vain. The entire army embarked in complete quiet and good order, such as had never before been seen, unless at Potsdam.

General Moore's body had been moved to the quarters of Colonel Graham in the Citadel at about midnight, while debate continued as to whether it should be prepared for transport to Britain or if it was truly his wish not to leave Spain if he fell in action. Colonel Anderson insisted this to be his friend and Commander's serious intention and, as by now men of the 9th East Norfolk Regiment had already begun the grave, the matter was settled. The site of the grave was fortuitous, for the day before an officer had been buried below the bastion of San Carlos, where it was thus proven that a decently deep grave could be excavated. A bastion is an arrow-shaped extension from a defence wall which allows the curtain wall to be raked by cannon fire if being climbed or breached. This is clearly visible on the map, inside the second defensive wall of the fortified peninsula. General Moore's grave was excavated to the landward side, overlooking the harbour.

No coffin could be found, but François insisted on dressing his master in his regimental dress uniform and, as the first glimmer of daylight was appearing, the body of Sir John was lowered into the Galician earth. A blanket covered his face and his heavy cloak was placed over him. Apart from the Chaplain, those present were Colonel Anderson, Major Colborne and Captains Stanhope and Percy. The General's body was lowered into the ground supported by the long silk sashes of the officers present.

Even while the grave was being filled, the French skirmishers could be seen advancing cautiously past the abandoned British camp fires, kept brightly burning all night in order to deceive the enemy. Moore had predicted that the French objective would be to try to sink the fleet as it left. However, the Galicians, commanded by General Alcedo, refused to surrender their forts and continued to counter-bombard the French battery established across the harbour overnight. The result was that only two ships were forced to run aground and all on board were transferred to other boats and the ships set alight. A strengthening wind blowing from the south-west sent the rest easily out of the harbour and later scattered the fleet along the whole southern coast of England as it turned to gale force. Two ships were sunk against the English cliffs with all 273 on board lost.

Once their allies were safely away, the Galicians held on until 18 January before surrendering to Soult, who treated them well. He immediately enquired as to the site of Moore's grave and ordered a rough plinth to be erected, "to mark the spot where so worthy an adversary lay."

"So it is true, in the long sleep of death
Our hero lies, whilst Honour with bright faith,
Truth and Justice unashamedly weep for,
Their one incomparable son."

Horace, the odes.
'Quis desiderio'[12]

Epilogue

Canning wrote to Lady Hester and offered a visit of condolence, knowing the deep feelings which she had held for Moore. The reply that he received sums up so well the way both he and Castlereagh had sought to trim their sails to public opinion as it changed for and against Moore's conduct of the campaign. For they made sure that all documents that put them in a bad light were suppressed, altered by obliteration of sentences or destroyed.

The date was omitted from her letter, presumably as a result of her grief for the death of her young step-brother Major Charles Stanhope and the man she had hoped to marry. By placing it in sequence with other letters from her Montagu Square house, however, it would have been written during the last week of January 1809.

Lady Hester to Mr Canning
Saturday Night.

"I disapprove of your past conduct to the dear General, and despise your present silence respecting him. Were you not gifted with eloquence, not to do justice to his glorious death? But if you FEEL like that vile Castlereagh, perhaps you do well not to tell the host of lies he did in the House, and hold a different language out of it . . . I am also morti-fied beyond description that you are not the public character I expected, [he had been a close personal friend of both herself and Mr Pitt in private life], and I am sure this feeling is not softened by your conduct to those I love . . . you cannot suppose it would be any consolation to me to see you.[1]

Lady Hester Lucy Stanhope

Lord Grenville, her uncle, had succeeded Pitt as First Minister in 1806 and she had also written to him demanding that the nation honour the General as he deserved, as would have been conceded by Pitt were he alive. Examples were given to him to the degree in which Pitt had relied upon and taken into account in his decision-making the military opinions of Moore. When her uncle also initially sat on the fence, in the matter of defending Moore against the covering lies of incompetent officers, diplomats and Ministers, she refused all offers of assistance from him. At the time she was without an income and he one of the richest aristocrats of the land.[2]

The other great friend that Lady Hester had kept after her social demise, caused by the death of Pitt, was the Duke of York, Commander-in-Chief. Unfortunately he was in the middle of his own crisis concerning the sale of army promotions by his mistress, unbeknown to him. But he at least came out with a public statement which ended with a poem of praise for the dead General.

General Orders
Horse Guards

Feb, 1st. 1809

"The life of John Moore was spent amongst the troops. During the seasons of repose, his time was devoted to the care and instruction of the Officers and Soldiers. In war he courted service in every corner of the globe. Regardless of personal considerations he esteemed that to which his country called him the post of honour, and by his undaunted spirit and unconquerable perseverance he pointed the way to victory.

"His country, the object of his last solicitude, will rear a monument to his lamented memory, and the Commander-in-Chief feels he is paying the best tribute to his fame by thus holding him forth as an example to the army.

"By order of His Royal highness the Commander-in-Chief."

After dozens of newspaper articles and statements in the House, on 24 February an opposition member, Mr Ponsonby, attempted to have the House call for an enqiry into the campaign, blaming Frere for inciting Moore to act when the Spanish armies had collapsed, when he could so easily have retreated into Portugal. He concluded a tirade of several hours by stating, to the wrath of Ministers, that "there is something in the Councils of England, in the application of her military force, that makes it impossible ever to place any reliance upon her military assistance".[3]

A Mr Tierny rose to speak next: "He lamented that the General had well known that he was acting under an administration that was not very friendly to him. His situation one of cruel hardship. The Government's praise of Spain had led the newspapers to promise great effects. But Moore had arrived to find his allies a heap of ruins. If he did anything wrong . . . he had no hopes of support from those who had sent him . . . With the exception of officers who happened to be connections of Ministers, he had not heard of one returned from Corunna who did not vent execrations against the authors of their disaster."[4]

At last Canning was obliged to make the statement which vindicated Moore from all his critics, as it confirmed the greater strategy that he had been following in luring Napoleon north, whilst everyone in England now wished to argue over the petty details of his achieving this end. He closed thus: "If we have been obliged to quit Spain, we have left it with fresh laurels blooming on our brows . . . Whatever may be the fruits of Buonaparte's victories in other respects, the spirit of the Spanish nation is yet unsubdued."

In this manner, by giving Moore the overall strategic victory, he exonerated him from all blame, whilst himself accepting none for his government's actions. Indeed, Napoleon himself, writing to General Savary from imprisonment, stated: "I agree that it was only Moore's action which stopped me taking Spain and Portugal, by lockjawing (sic) all of my planned movements, and I admire him for it."[5]

By now the dossier of Colonel Charmilly, containing the previously denied letters of Minister Frere, sent to Moore at Salamanca, were in the hands of Lord Liverpool, the leader of the Government party in the Lords. The final word of Lord Grenville, the First Minister, to his Cabinet after these revelations was "that he thought that Ministers were reprehensible, firstly for having allowed Mr Frere to interfere – luckily unsuccessfully – in military affairs, but above all for trying to escape from their responsibility by transferring the blame for an ill-equipped and ill-conducted expedition upon General Moore."[6]

Lord Liverpool's final statement in the Lords also vindicated Moore's grand strategy: "The French ruler had been obliged to abandon his preconcerted programme on the south of Spain, in which country considerable successes had since taken place. He would like to add that Sir John's advance, which was as a spontaneous result of his own free judgement, had saved Spain."[7]

On that same day as the final Lords debate concerning the campaign Sir Arthur Wellesley was, by coincidence, landing at Lisbon. He had Moore's value completely clear; without his diversion of the French thrust Portugal would now be in their hands and there would be no friendly, garrisoned Lisbon from which to begin his own Peninsular Campaign. He knew Charles Stewart to be now intriguing against him with Castlereagh, as he had against Moore, and, when final victory was his, acknowledged that he could not have done it without Moore's contribution in ridding Spain of Napoleon.[8]

A marble monument was ordered to be erected in St Paul's Cathedral, the only delay being on the part of the sculptor who took six years to finish the commission, but the painstaking result was worth the wait from a technical aspect. The likeness to Moore in life was said to be almost "frightening exact" by those who knew him. Whether Moore's own unpretentious tastes would have approved of the eight-foot-high buxom angels, represented as lowering him into the ground, may be open to question. Regardless, the nation had publicly been seen to honour and acclaim its hero in what had become the national shrine.

If the people of Britain were at first deceived in respect of the honour due to Moore, the inhabitants of Galicia were in no doubt. After six months of pitiless slaughter by the mountain partisans the armies of both Soult and Ney were so reduced that a total withdrawal from the region became the only option.

When General Romana rode back into Corunna he ordered Moore's remains to be removed from their shallow grave to a more prominent spot. A temporary memorial was erected and the Moore family invited to send their design for a permanent one. In 1811 the body was again disinterred and an appropriate coffin was constructed, with a grave 7ft in depth excavated to receive it a few yards away in a prominent spot overlooking the Atlantic. The result was the sturdy simple shape which stands there to this day, its contours defying the worst storms that Biscay can hurl at it.

In 1834 the Military Governor of Corunna, Francisco Mazarredo, decided that he too wished to honour the memory of the British General and had a formal garden laid out around the tomb. It was segmented by paths, which radiated out like the spokes of a wheel from the tomb to a circumferential walk. The whole was surrounded by a wall, with window-like apertures framing the panoramic views, as the visitor walked the circular path, shaded by trees. Carved into marble tablets attached to this wall is the memorial poem of the otherwise unknown Irish poet Thomas Wolfe, Curate of Ballyclog, written eleven years after the event, for the poet had been only 18 at that time. When he published it anonymously in the local newspaper he had no pretensions that it would be acclaimed as a work of genius, said

216

to be worthy of Byron, and become, until the end of Empire, an obligation of every British schoolboy to learn by heart. The historical inaccuracies contained therein are poetic license and of no importance to the sentiments raised by its reading.

Next to the work of the Irish poet, another identical plaque carries the work of the respected Galician poetess Rosalia de Castro. The lady also composed a work in her native language to honour the memory of the man who had fought beside her countrymen. Appropriately translated by request into Castilian Spanish by a retired member of the present Spanish military, it has been further translated into appropriate English blank verse by the author and follows Wolfe's words below.

The Burial of Sir John Moore
(fragment)

Not a drum was heard, nor a funeral note,
As his corpse to the rampart we hurried;
Not a soldier discharged his farewell shot
O'er the grave where our hero we buried.

We buried him darkly at dead of night,
The sods with our bayonets turning;
By the struggling moon beam's misty light
And the lantern dimly burning.

No useless coffin enclosed his breast,
Not in sheet nor in shroud we wound him;
But he lay like a warrior taking his rest,
With his martial cloak around him.

Few and short were the prayers we said,
And we spoke not a word of sorrow;
but we steadfastly gaz'd on the face of the dead,
And we bitterly thought of the morrow.

Slowly and sadly we laid him down,
from the field of his fame fresh and gory;
We carved not a line, and we raised not a stone,
But we left him alone with his glory.

Rev. Charles Wolfe.

'In the Tomb of the British General Sir John Moore.'
(fragment)

When, from afar, I sing of the dark clouds,
Of the green pines, of the boiling waves,
From your native land! . . .; from the paternal house
Under the sky of the Motherland, what fond offspring
Went to fall under the enemy blow,
Nevermore to raise himself.

More than beautiful and without equal,
Is the fortune of your mortal remains, . . .
Perhaps God found for you, noble foreigner,
A resting place not set so far apart! . . .
That there is no poet who would not have
Their spirit moved, when contemplating in the autumn
The sea of dry and yellowing leaves
That lovingly cover your mausoleum;
That early in the freshness of dawns
Of the month of May the roseate lights
That are always happy to visit you come
Who will not say: "Thus, when I die that I
Could sleep in peace in this flowered garden,
Near to the sea . . ., A far away cemetery! . . ."
When your brother comes crossing the waves
Of that sea to visit you,
Join in the tomb lovingly listening;

And if you sense a moving of your ashes,
And if you hear indefinable voices,
And if you understand that which these voices say,
Your soul will feel consoled
And to us say that in all the world
No better tomb than I have found there is nor will be
If not covered with your hereditary love.

Rosalia de Castro[9]

When the centenary was celebrated in 1909, a magnificent plaque of bronze and marble was placed on the wall of the house in which Moore died, which still stands today, its façade unchanged, whilst internally converted into a bank.

In 1931 the then Prince of Wales, who would have his own battle with British Ministers, made an expedition to Elviña. He discovered, and restored, the original stone plaque set in the ground on the slope down which the final assault was made, which led to victory. Another marble plaque was added at his initiative. Two others were recently added by local historical associations in 1997, which were unveiled by the British Ambassador.

Appendix One

Composition of troops under the command of General Sir Ralph Abercromby, assembled at Barbados, as of 26 April 1796.

— 1st Brigade under Maj. Gen. Campbell, made up of:
14th, 27th, 28th, 44th, 48th Brigades.   3,291 men

— 2nd Brigade under Maj. Gen Morshead, made up of:
27th, 38th, 42nd, 43rd, 55th, 75th Brigades   c2,700 men

— Foreign regts, under Brig Gen. Perryn.

with York Rangers and York Fusiliers.   1,269 men

— Reserve force under Lt.-Col. Macdonald:

14th, 26th, 38th, 44th, 48th, 53rd, 55th, 63rd,
   88th Brigades   No Returns

— Artillery men, engineers, and hospital corps.   c1,000 men

Negro Pioneers and Native Black Troops   3,600 men

To this number must be added Navy Marines and sailors available to fight if required as reserves. Moore states in his diary that he embarked for St Lucia with 5,000 of this assembled force, intended to subdue the whole of the West Indies, island by island, as required. Hence the differing figures given for the men sent to invade St Lucia by different authorities. Moore's own figure must, logically, be taken as definitive.

(War Office Records 1796, quoted by R.J. Devaux O.B.E.)

Appendix Two

Black troops employed by the British in the West Indies Campaign

In 1783 a Black Corps of Dragoons, Pioneers and Artificers was raised to fight in the American War of Independence. At the end of hostilities the corps was removed to the eastern Caribbean and continued, but renamed the Carolina Corps, as it was in that American state that it had been raised.

It was in Martinique that the first truly Caribbean Black Corps was raised, in 1794, by the then Captain Malcolm, and named Malcolm's Rangers. The recruitment was from the unemployed free blacks and mulattoes, to hunt down bands of armed slaves who had taken to the woods. The Rangers accompanied Moore's invasion of St Lucia to fulfill the same function there.

After a struggle between the planters' lobbying group and the British War Office, General Vaugh was finally given permission to arm and recruit both slaves and free blacks into the British Army after the revolt of the remaining Carib Indians and slaves in St Vincent and Grenada. Two regiments were initially raised in 1795, and named for their Colonels, becoming Whyte's and Myers' Foot.

The Royalist French had also formed Black Corps when they fled the revolutionary terror period, taking their loyal slaves with them, together with other slaves, free blacks and mulattoes, disillusioned with the anarchy of Republicanism. Druault's Rangers, Solter's Royal Island Regiment and O'Mearer's Rangers were all formed by individual initiative to fight the guerrilla bands. Freedom, upon surviving to retirement age, was the incentive to these slaves made soldiers, for their previous owners feared nothing more than having trained men return to their own islands and possibly begin new insurrections.

General Vaugh succeeded in raising four regiments during 1795 totalling 5,000 infantry of all ranks, with white officers, all then became collectively known as the West Indian Regiment. Slaves might be volunteered by their owners, or sold to the British Army. To fill any shortfall, the hypocritical Pitt administration, that was voting anti-slavery bills through parliament, secretly allocated funds to buy slaves in the open market to train as soldiers. In 1798 four more regiments were raised in this manner.

When slavery was abolished in the United Kingdom, in 1808, by Earl Stanhope's bill, all serving soldiers became free men and recruits were found among 'volunteers' in the West African Colonies, the idea having originated from Colonel Hislop, of the 11th West Indian Regiment in a report to the War Office as early as 1801; at the time he merely wished to cut out the middle men in the slave trade.

After the Napoleonic wars ended, the regiments continued to recruit true volunteers to defend their islands, and they also took a largely unsung part in many of Britain's wars, including the two World Wars of the twentieth century.

The above is a synthesis composed by the author from historical facts mentioned in the following works: Fortescue, Devaux, and the Diary, Letters and Life of Moore.

Notes

Chapter One

1 The term 'Whig' was devised as a derisory term after the 1689 expulsion of James II. It was drawn from an abbreviation of the term 'Whigamore', being the Scottish term for a cross border raiding party sent to steal cattle. In political terms the significance was that the Whigs were a group trying to steal the King's power for the aristocratic class.

2 The term 'Tory' was applied to the followers of James II who went with him into exile, or stayed in the country to further his cause. It was derived from the Irish Gaelic word 'Tóraighe', or pursuer, as applied to a type of highwayman who would not confront his victims, but follow them and attack them at a moment of debility. In general it came to mean the party which sided with the reigning monarch, and has nothing to do with the current usage of the name in modern party politics.

3 Moore, James Carrick, *The Life of Sir John Moore*, 1834, p.2 (hereafter abbreviated to 'Life').

4 ibid. p. 3.

5 ibid. p. 3.

6 ibid. p. 4.

7 ibid. p. 4–5

8 ibid. p. 7–8

9 Maurice . F. (Ed.), *The Diary of Sir John Moore*, 1903, p. 5. (hereafter abbreviated to 'Diary')

223

10 'Diary', p. 6.

11 Brownrigg. B. *The Life and Letters of Sir John Moore*. 1921. (hereafter abbreviated to 'Letters') p. 6–7, 11 July, 1776.

12 See illustration.

13 'Diary', p. 8.

Chapter Two.

1 'Letters', p.11.

2 'Life', p.17.

3 ibid. p.22.

4 'Diary', p.10.

5 'Life', p.22.

Chapter Three.

1 Fortescue, *History of the British Army*, 1921, (2nd Ed.) Vol.iii, p.517

Chapter Four.

1 'Diary', p.12.

2 Camps, Fernando Marti, *History of Menorca*, 1971, p.195

3 'Diary', p.14.

4 ibid. p.14.

5 ibid. pp. 14–15.

6 ibid. p.15.

Chapter Five.

1 Camps, *History of Menorca*, 1971, p.196.

2 'Life', p.51.

3 The name of the tower of Mortello became corrupted in the English usage to 'Martello' and when such towers were incorporated into the defence of the Kentish coast a decade later, the name was given incorrectly by English dictionaries as deriving from the name of a French military engineer and not the place where the British had first found, to their cost, the near invulnerability of such towers to naval bombardment,

the more so if given stone vaulted ceilings, and not inflammable wooden ones.

4   'Life', p.68.
5   Mahan, *Life of Nelson*, Vol.1, p.124.
6   'Life', p.70.
7   ibid. p.70.
8   ibid. p.71.

Chapter Six

1   'Life', p. 72.
2   ibid. p. 73.
3   ibid. p.75.
4   ibid. p.77.
5   ibid. p.79.
6   'Letters' p.32. "On the outbreak of the French Revolution, the Corsican Chieftain – Pascal Paoli – was recalled from England (where he had been living since the Corsican defeat at Ponte Nuovo in 1769) by the French National Assembly. He became Mayor of Bastia and Commander-in-Chief of the National Guard, and was appointed by Louis XIV military commandant in Corsica. After the execution of Louis XIV he appealed for help from England to drive the French out of the island."
    Author's additional note: the King attempted to defuse the situation by writing to Paoli personally, offering a pension of £1,000 p.a. if he came to retire in England. He also included a miniature of himself set with brilliants, which vanished; the Corsicans accused Sir Gilbert of "abstracting" it (Minto, ii., p.314). Paoli died in London in 1807. Sir Gilbert's career prospered regardless; he ended it as Governor–General of India, and 1st Earl of Minto.
7   Public Record Office, (hereafter referred to as P.R.O.), Corsica Correspondence, letter of 28 Feb, 1795, from King George III to Sir Gilbert Elliot declining to give him more than formal military command of the island.

8 'Diary', p.29.

9 ibid. p.137.

10 ibid. pp.160–161

11 Minto, 1st. Earl of, *The Life of Sir Gilbert Elliot*, Vol.II, p.322, 1874 (3 vols.)

12 'Diary', pp.171–3.

13 ibid. p.174.

14 ibid. p.178.

15 Later 1st Viscount Melville.

Chapter Seven

1 'Diary', p.193.

2 'Letters', p.55.

3 ibid. p.57.

4 'Diary', p.199.

5 ibid. p.199.

6 ibid. pp.202–3.

7 ibid. p.220.

Chapter Eight.

1 Fortescue, Hon. J. W., *History of the British Army*, 7 vols. 1915–20., 2nd. Ed., 1921 (hereafter 'Fortescue'). Vol.II,

2 Devaux. R.J., *They Called Us Brigands*, p.20., 1997.

3 Sloper. F.L., *Clinical Tropical Medicine*, Chap. 32, 1944.

4 'Diary', p.213.

5 ibid. p.203.

6 ibid. pp.220–1.

7 ibid. p.231.

8 ibid. p.232.

9 ibid. p.233.

10 ibid. p.235.

11 'Letters', p.62.

12 'Diary', p.235.

13 ibid. p.231.

14 ibid. p.243.

15 'Letters', pp.68–71.

16 ibid. p.72.

17 Letter, Duke of Portland, (Colonial Office ref. 253/1–2) quoted by Devaux R.J. (as above) pp.38–9.

Chapter Nine.

1 'Britannica', (1964 Ed.) see Ireland - History of.

2 'Diary', p.270.

3 ibid. p.273.

4 ibid. pp.273–4.

5 ibid. p.288.

6 'Letters', p.75.

7 'Diary', p.275.

8 ibid. p.277.

9 'Letters', p.76.

10 'Diary', p.292.

11 'Life', p.189.

12 'Diary', p.299.

13 'Life', p.200.

14 'Diary', p.309.

15 'Letters', p.81–2.

16 ibid. pp.82–4.

17 'Letters', p.84.

18 'Life', p.207.

19 ibid. p.222.

20 'Diary', p.326.

21 see ref. 10, chap. 1

Chapter Ten.

1 'Diary', p.340.

2 'Life', p.234.

3 'Letters', pp.93–4.

4 'Diary', p.353.

5 'Life', p.242.
6 'Letters', pp.95–6.
7 'Diary', p.343.
8 'Letters', pp.99–100.
9 'Diary', p.356.
10 'Life,' p.249.
11 'Letters', p.102.
12 'Diary', p.358.

Chapter Eleven.
1 'Diary', p.367.
2 'Letters', pp.109–10.
3 'Diary', V.II, p.54.
4 'Letters', p.113.
5 ibid. p.113.
6 'Diary', p.387.
7 'Letters', p.116.
8 'Diary', V.II. p.9.
9 ibid. p.14.
10 ibid. p.19

Chapter Twelve.
1 'Diary', V.II. p.21.
2 'Diary', p.386.
3 Bunbury,G, *Campaign in Egypt*, 1836, pp.127–8.
4 Wartenburg, Count von, *Napoleon as a General*, Ed.1856, pp.136–7.

Chapter Thirteen.
1 'Diary', V.II, p.112.
2 'Letters', p.164.
3 'Diary', V.II. p.150.
4 'Letters', p.170.
5 Napier, Sir William, *Life of Charles Napier*, 1857, Vol.I, p.39.

6   Agapeyeff, A. D., *Codes and Cyphers*, 1960, p.43–4.

Note. The loose document was finally decoded in 1893 by M. Bazieries. It was found to be the order committing one Vivien Labbe, Siegneur de Bulunde, Lieut. Commander of the Royal Forces, to life imprisonment by Louis XIV for his miserable raising of the seige of the fortress of Coni without a realistic assault. He was required to wear an iron mask when exercising on the battlements to inescapably hide his face, for the King feared a rescue attempt, were it known he had not been executed, as given out. Otherwise he was to be treated as a nobleman by his guards and allowed fine clothes, also to eat and drink of the best, for he had been Grand Master of the orders of St Lazare and Carmel of Jerusalem. Also, a Knight of St Louis. His prison was principally the Citadel of Pignerole.

Example of Chiffre code. Both Letters and syllables were interchangeable for numbers. (ie.) A=15, ar=25, al=39 etc. The Grande Chiffre was used between Napoleon and his General Staff, whilst a less complex Petite Chiffre was utilised when the army communicated from the field to the General Staff. During the retreat from Moscow the only master cipher books were lost, and all was from then on in plain language, greatly leading to the French defeat. Whilst Lady Napier had opened the codes to the British, they remained a mystery to the French until Bazieries work in the 1890s, and pathetically inferior substitutes replaced them. The British kept the key as their secret weapon, were more wars to be fought with the French.

Chapter Fourteen.

1   'Letters', p.175–6.
2   ibid. p.176.
3   'Diary', Vol.II., pp. 205–21.
4   'Letters', p.183.

Chapter Fifteen.

1   This chapter is a synopsis by the author of material given in 'Britannica' under the refs. Napoleonic Wars, Spain, and Napoleon. (1964 Ed.) Also included are points made in the Spanish language works covering the period in the Madrid Military Archives: *Diccionario Bibliografico de la Guerra de la Independancia Española*, Servicio Historica Militar, 1944–54., Gomez de Arteche, J. *Guerra de la Independancia – 1808–14, pub. 1868–1907 14 Vols., Tomo 1., & Gonzalez Lopez, E.* El Aguila gala y el Buho gallego, 1975, pp. 59–71.

Chapter Sixteen.

1   Oman, C., *A History of the Peninsular War*, 1902, Vol.I, p.85.
2   In addition to the material contained in the refs, cited as used in 'Britannica' for Chap 15, the author's synopsis contains concepts contained in Napier, W, *The War in the Peninsular* and *Ensign Aitchison, The Letters of*, Ed. by Thompson,W.

Chapter Seventeen.

1   Day, R.W., *Decline to Glory*, 1997, p.95.
2   'Letters', p.92.
3   Foreman, Amanda, 'Spirits of the Age', Express T.V. Magazine Dec., 1998.
4   ibid. p.p.112–13 & p. 203.
5   'Diary', Vol.II, p.265–6.
6   ibid. p.203.
7   Castlereagh Letters, 2nd., series, 454, Public Records Office W/O.1/189.

Chapter Eighteen.

1   'Diary', Vol.II.,p.273.
2   ibid. p.270
3   ibid. pp. 135–46
4   'Fortescue', Vol.VI.,p.366.

5   'Diary', Vol.II., p.135–46.

6   ibid. p.279.

7   ibid. p.274.

8   ibid. p.313.

9   'Letters', p.214.

10 'Diary', Vol.II., p.281

11 Napier. Gen. W., *Peninsular War*, Vol.I, appx. p.79.

12 Robertson, Father James, *Narrative of a Secret Mission to the Danish Islands in 1808*, pub. 1863 (Quoted in Oman, C., nt., p.673).

13 'Letters', p.217–19.

14 Stanhope, 5th. Earl of, 'Stanhope Miscellany', 2nd series, p.51–4.

15 'Life', p.171.

16 'Letters', p.225–6.

17 ibid. p.224.

18 'Life', p.166–7.

Chapter Nineteen.

1   P.R.O. ref., W.O./1/236.209.

2   'Diary', Vol.II, p.363.

3   'Letters', pp.233–4.

4   ibid. pp.235–6.

5   Harris, Rifleman, 52nd. regt, (M.S.) *The Recollections of*, Ed. Curling. H., 1848. (Hereafter, 'Harris')

6   'Letters', p.233–4.

7   'Diary', Vol.II, p.286.

8   'Letters', pp.241–5.

9   Letters referred to exist in the P.R.O. in full as refs. W.O/1/236, p.201–8; W.O./1/232, p.50–6, p. 151–77, p.199 & 1/233 p.73–100, p.161; & F.O. 72/60/32 (qtd. Oman C.)

10 Original Journal M.S. notebook 9, p.161. Note: Twelve blank pages are left at the end, which Moore would have filled

with notes scribbled on loose paper in the field, had he survived to do so. (qtd. Oman. C.)

Chapter Twenty.
1 'Diary', Vol.II, Maurice's commentary quotes Captain Sterling. M.S. p.74 (hereafter 'Sterling').
2 'Sterling', p.77.
3 'Life', pp. 204–5 & Wellington to Castlereagh, 17 June, 1809, 'Despatches' 2nd series, Vol.III, pp.88–9.
4 'Sterling', pp.90–4.
5 Later the Marquess of Anglesey.
6 P.R.O. ref. W.O./236 p.213, & 'Letters' p.189.
7 'Letters', pp.247–8 (only these troops are mentioned in Moore's letters to Castlereagh as taking part in the action, Paget's cavalry arrived afterwards to hold the river bank.
8 'Life', p.192.
9 Balagny, Commandant *Campagne de L'Empereur Napoleon en Espagne, 1906, Vol.IV, pp.48–58.*
10 *'Fortescue', Vol.VI, pp. 286–90.*
   Lanfrey, P., Histoire de Napoleon 1er, 1867–75, Vol.III, p.171.
   'Diary', Vol.II, Maurice's commentary, pp.290–8.
11 'Life', p.197.
12 'Fortescue', Vol.VI, pp.362–5.
13 Napier, W., *Peninsular War*, Vol.I, p.477–8.
14 'Letters', p.249.
15 Napier, W., *Peninsular War*, Vol.I, pp.480–88.
16 'Life', pp.207–8.
17 ibid. p.254.

Chapter Twenty One.
1 'Fortescue', Vol.VI, pp.369–73.
2 'Letters', p.260.
3 ibid. p.260. (org. doc. P.R.O. ref. W.O. 1/236, pp.265–77)

4   *Daily Telegraph*, Centenary Commemorative Ed. 20 Jan., 1909.
5   The word then referred to any part of a command delegated to subordinates, and not to a specific number of men as today.
6   Napier, W., *Life of Charles Napier*, V.,I, pp.94–96.
7   Note: Soult decorated the drummer boy with the Legion d'Honneur. When Napier's mother became very ill, Soult and Ney had him sent home to show he was alive, on a year's parole; they did so without allowing Napoleon to know of it.
8   Wilkinson-Latham, R., *British Artillery 1790 to 1820*, 1973. The impact-exploding tubular shell filled with grape was invented in 1784 by Lieut. Henry Shrapnel and introduced to service in 1802. It was first used in battle at Rolica and Vimiero, where it decimated the French.
9   'Life', p.224.
10 ibid. p.224.
11 Synopsis of material contained in: 'Letters', p.267; Gen. Hope's final despatch, P.R.O. W.O. 1/236, pp.511–24; Napier, W., 'Peninsular War', V., I, pp.493–7; 'Fortescue' V., VI, pp.382–5.
12 The translation from the Latin original was first rendered into Spanish by the Sta. Maria Institute representative of the Spanish Soc. for Classical Studies. The translation into convenient English verse of Horace's odes was then made by the author; with apologies to Horace for liberties taken.

Epilogue.

1   Cleveland, Duchess of, *The Life of Lady Hester Stanhope*, 1914, pp. 83–4.
2   ibid. pp.78–80.
3   Hansard, 24 April, 1809.
4   ibid. 21 April, 1809.
5   Napier, W. *Peninsular War*, Vol.I, Appx. p.ii.
6   'Letters', p.275.

7 Hansard.

8 'Letters', pp.75–6.

9 Translated from an engraving supplied by the Association of the Friends of Sir John Moore, Corunna, giving copies of the inscriptions from the tomb and the walls of its garden. Translation from Gallego to Castilian (Standard Spanish) made by D. Xesus Constenia Mosquera, a retired member of the Spanish Military. Rendered from Castilian into English blank verse by the author.

Bibliography

Agapeyeff, A., *Codes and Cyphers*, 1960.

Aitchinson, Ensign, (Thompson, Ed.) *The Letters of*, 1891.

Balagny, D., *Campagne de l'Empereur Napoleon en Espagne 1808–9*, 5 Vols, 1902.

Brownrigg, B., *Life and Letters of Sir John Moore*, 1923.

Bunbury, G., *Campaign in Egypt*, 1836.

Camps, Fernando, M., *History of Menorca*, 1971.

Castlereagh Letters, 2nd series, Public Records Office.

Charmilly, Col. Venault de, *Narrative of his Transactions in Spain with the Rt. Hon. Hookham Frere, 1810.*

Cleveland, Duchess of, The Life and Letters of Lady Hester Stanhope, 1914.

'Corunna', The Bulletin of the Association of Collectionists of The Royal Green Jackets, #O,1997 & #3, 1998.

Day, R., *Decline to Glory – A Reassessment of the Life of Lady Hester Stanhope*, 1997.

Devaux, R., *They Called Us Brigands*, 1997.

Fortescue, The Hon. J., *History of the British Army*, 2nd Ed, Vols V & VI, 1921.

Hansard, Vols for 1809–10.

Harris, Rifleman, 52nd Regiment, (MS) *The Recollections of*, Ed Curling, H., 1848.

Lanfrey, P, *Histoire de Napoleon 1er 1867–75*, Vol. III.

Lopez, I, & Hernandez, X., *La Guerra de la Independancia*, 1990.

Mahan, A.T., *Life of Nelson*, Vol. I, 1896.

Maurice, Maj. Gen. Sir J., Ed. *The Diary of Sir John Moore*, Vols I & II, 1904.

Minto, 1st. Earl of, *The Life of Sir Gilbert Elliot*, Vol. II.

Moore, J., *The Life of Lt. General Sir John Moore*, Vols I & II., 1834.

Napier, Sir W., *History of the War in the Peninsular etc*, Vol. I, 1857.

Oman, C., *Sir John Moore*, 1953.

Oman, Sir C., *A History of the Peninsular War*, Vol.I, 1902.

Paget, Sir A., *The Paget Papers*, Vols I & II, 1896.

Robertson, Rev. Father James, *Narrative of a Secret Mission to the Danish Islands in 1808*, 1863.

Sloper, F., *Clinical Tropical Medicine*, 1944.

Stirling, Capt. J., *Memoirs of the Campaign in 1808 in Spain*

Surtees, W., *Twenty-five Years in the Rifle Brigade*, 1833.

The Daily Telegraph, newspaper archives.

Wartenburg, Count von, *Napoleon as a General*, English edition, 1856.

Wilkinson-Latham, R., *British Artillery 1790–1820*, 1973.

Index

240

244